The Contested Castle

D1104122

The Contested Castle

GOTHIC NOVELS AND
THE SUBVERSION OF
DOMESTIC IDEOLOGY

Kate Ferguson Ellis

UNIVERSITY OF ILLINOIS PRESS

URBANA & CHICAGO

Publication of this work was supported in part by a grant from the Andrew W. Mellon Foundation.

© 1989 by the Board of Trustees of the University of Illinois
Manufactured in the United States of America
1 2 3 4 5 C P 5 4 3 2 1

This book is printed on acid-free paper.

Library of Congress Cataloging-in-Publication Data

Ellis, Kate Ferguson, 1938–
    The contested castle: Gothic novels and the subversion of
    domestic ideology/Kate Ferguson Ellis.
        p.   cm.
        Includes bibliographies and index.
    ISBN 0-252-01594-0 (cloth : alk. paper), ISBN 0-252-06048-2
    (paper : alk. paper)
    1. Horror tales, English—History and criticism. 2. Gothic
    revival (Literature) 3. Home in literature. 4. Sex role
    literature. 5. Domestic fiction, English—History and criticism.
    6. Women—Books and reading. 7. Feminism and literature.
    I. Title.
    PR830.T3E53 1989
    823'.0872—dc19   88-27887
                                                                CIP

CONTENTS

ACKNOWLEDGMENTS

Any author of a book that has taken this much time to write has a long list of people whose comments and support along the way are a pleasure to acknowledge. First chronologically comes Louise Bernikow, who suggested to me that scholarship and feminist activism could enhance each other, from which came the work on *Frankenstein* that generated the rest of the book. Then, continuing in alphabetical order, I want to express my gratitude to Ann Alter, Carolyn Burke, George Chauncey, Anna Clark, Jackie DiSalvo, Tom Edwards, Barbara Ehrenreich, Dierdre English, Susan Fernandez, Leslie Fiedler, Keitha Fine, Cora Kaplan, Uli Knoepflmacher, Bill Leach, George Levine, David Leverenz, Alicia Ostriker, Barry Qualls, Elaine Showalter, Ann Snitow, Julia Sokoloff, Catharine Stimpson, Martha Vicinus, Judy Walkowitz, the residents of Paradox House in San Francisco, and the New York University seminar on sex, gender, and consumer culture. Gene Brown's careful editing of an earlier version of the manuscript provided encouragement when it was needed, and at crucial moments Michael Kimmel defined the project for me in a way that enabled me to take it to the next level. Mary Poovey and Lillian Robinson gave me the benefit of their critical wisdom, Pat Hollahan contributed her knowledge of Milton's biblical borrowings as well as her editing skills, and Edward Tayler offered up his insights on Milton to uses he could not have foreseen. I hope my debt to other scholars is evident in my notes. Finally, I want to thank the members of my department at Rutgers whose support allowed this project to come to completion, my Illinois editor, Ann Lowry Weir, for her wonderful combination of enthusiasm and patience, and my son, Philip, who survived adolescence with a mother who wrote, and made his own dinners all too often.

INTRODUCTION

The theme of this book can be summed up by a comment made to me as an undergraduate by an elderly French professor into whose class I had brought a copy of *Paradise Lost*. "Ah, the *Paradise Lost* of Milton," she said in her dreamy, Gallic voice. And then, turning to the rest of the class, she added: "And then he got married and wrote *Paradise Regained*." She may have been joking, but her remark points up the extent to which the opinion of our culture about home and family is still summarized by Cowper's lines from "The Task": "Domestic happiness, thou only bliss / Of Paradise that has survived the fall." This typological conception of "domestic happiness" emerged toward the end of the eighteenth century, as the middle-class home, distanced in ideology and increasingly in fact from the place where money was made, became a "separate sphere" from the "fallen" world of work.

Alongside this preoccupation with the ideal home, a distinct subcategory of the English novel, the Gothic, began to make its appearance on publishers' lists and on the shelves of circulating libraries. Focusing on crumbling castles as sites of terror, and on homeless protagonists who wander the face of the earth, the Gothic, too, is preoccupied with the home. But it is the failed home that appears on its pages, the place from which some (usually "fallen" men) are locked out, and others (usually "innocent" women) are locked in. The theme of "paradise lost" links the paired strands of literary Gothicism that critics have variously identified as Radcliffian and Lewisite, "feminine" and "masculine," "terror Gothic" and "horror Gothic."[1] Either the home has lost its prelapsarian purity and is in need of rectification, or else the wandering protagonist has been driven from the home in a grotesque reenactment of God's punishment of Satan, Adam, and Eve.

This book investigates the relationship between these two epi-phenomena of middle-class culture: the idealization of the home and the popularity of the Gothic. The point of connection between them is the woman novel reader, whose newly created leisure allowed her to make use of the circulating library and whose "placement" in the home made her a reader eagerly courted by publishers. Judging from the success of the Minerva Press and other houses that followed the lead of its publisher, William Lane, these readers were a major market not simply for novels but for novels about haunted houses and their haunters. Why did these books become so popular just at the time when women were becoming a significant part of the reading public? What in the culture created the demand for such fare, and what were its messages to readers? Finally, did these messages offer to their readers possibilities subversive of those available elsewhere in the culture?

Initially, I had intended to write about the literary use of the home as a place of security and concord, but found myself writing instead about the home as a place of danger and imprisonment. Any enclosed space seemed to me to present this paradox, which links the "safe" sphere of home inseparably to its dark opposite, the Gothic castle. I therefore decided to look at the ways in which the female reading public was made possible by the separation of spheres that released women, at least ideally, from physical work. The debate about the nature and purpose of female education that proliferated in print during the second half of the eighteenth century made it clear that women's reading was a matter of public concern, not just of private choice.[2] Thus the mass-produced novel was both a product of the construction of separate spheres for men and women and, insofar as it gave women examples to follow, a medium through which that construction of gender relations could be elaborated. But it could also subvert that construction, and I will argue that the Gothic novel does this, creating, in a segment of culture directed toward women, a resistance to an ideology that imprisons them even as it posits a sphere of safety for them.

For if the violence, danger, and breakdown of community ties that accompanied the development of eighteenth-century capitalism provided a justification for the separation of spheres, it also threatened the sense of superiority on which the middle-class claim to moral leadership rested. A well-regulated home, as Leonore Davidoff and Catherine Hall have argued, was an outward sign of male competence and trustworthiness, a valuable economic asset in a situation where traditional markers of reliability were inappropriate, inadequate, or breaking down.[3] It distinguished the middle class from the potentially dangerous lower orders, who could not afford it, and also provided a rallying point for middle-class hostility toward an aristocracy that had lost its capacity for moral leadership. Yet in a period of revolution abroad and class realignment at home, keeping the domestic sphere impregnable in the face of so much political agitation and social unrest required immense vigilance. So reading, for which the middle-class woman now had the education and the time, was potentially a stand-in for the absent male intent on maintaining control over his "castle."

The importance in the middle-class worldview of the home as a safe refuge suggests some anxiety about the safety of the surrounding space, particularly for women, and there is plenty of evidence to support a picture of eighteenth-century social life, both in the countryside and in the growing urban centers, that is filled with uncertainty and violence. The emergence of a waged labor force, which drew working women increasingly out of the home, made those women particularly vulnerable to assault and rape. At the other end of the social scale, in 1753 Parliament was so concerned with the rape of rich heiresses as a way of forcing them into marriage (and thus gaining control over their fortunes and family connections) that it debated and finally passed a law, the Hardwicke Act, "for the better preventing of clandestine marriages." But whether the woman's fortune was the object of her assailant, or whether he was simply confirming a bottom line of male power in a culture where new class lines were being drawn, she was a still a possible outlet for male frustration from which "the home" could not adequately protect her.[4]

Thus the middle-class idealization of the home, though it theoretically protected a woman in it from arbitrary male control, gave her little real protection against male anger. Rather, it was her endangered position that was so ideologically useful, allowing her to stand for the class itself, beset on all sides by aristocratic license and lower-class violence. The Gothic novel of the eighteenth century foregrounded the home as fortress, while at the same time exposing its contradictions. Displacing their stories into an imaginary past, its early practitioners appealed to their readers not by providing "escape" but by encoding, in the language of aristocratic villains, haunted castles, and beleaguered heroines, a struggle to purge the home of license and lust and to establish it as a type of heaven on earth. To this end, they created a landscape in which a heroine could take initiative in shaping her own history. By allowing the heroine to purge the infected home and to establish a true one, by having her reenact the disobedience of Eve and bring out of that a new Eden "happier far," these novels provided a mediation between women's experience of vulnerability and the ideological uses to which that experience was put.

What I hope to demonstrate is that popular literature can be a site of resistance to ideological positions as well as a means of propagating them. In the eighteenth century, discussions of prose fiction began to distinguish between the novel and the romance, with romance usually being the devalued term of the pair, "an heroic fable, which treats of fabulous persons and things" as opposed to "a picture of real life and manners, and of the time in which it was written."[5] Walpole claimed, in his preface to the second edition of *The Castle of Otranto*, to be blending "the two kinds of romance, the ancient and the modern," but this comment would seem to be in the spirit of mockery in which he wrote his first preface, claiming to have found the work "in the library of an ancient Catholic family in the north of England." By deliberately choosing to work in the domain of romance, Walpole's heirs created a genre in which they could critique the premises about women and the home to which realistic writers of the later eighteenth century felt obligated to adhere.

My discussion of the Gothic novel begins inevitably with Walpole, and with the use to which the earliest Gothicists, who in fact were women, put material they had inherited not only from him but from a much more formidable predecessor: Milton. As a feminist critic, I am interested in ways in which writers, both male and female, have neither combated nor "swerved"[6] from the male tradition but have used it to their own ends. In *The Castle of Otranto*, we can see elements that would later separate out into the "feminine" or Radcliffian and the "masculine" or Lewisite Gothic. Both focus on the home, represented by the (often-usurped) Gothic castle. In the feminine Gothic the heroine exposes the villain's usurpation and thus reclaims an enclosed space that should have been a refuge from evil but has become the very opposite, a prison. The masculine Gothic gives the perspective of an exile from the refuge of home, now the special province of women. It works to subvert the idealization of the home, and by implication the ideology of "separate spheres" on which that idealization depends.

In contributing to the development of the bourgeois myth of its own origins and triumph, the Gothic novel expanded the female sphere to the point where women could challenge the basis of their own "elevation." Two writers, Mary Wollstonecraft and Charlotte Smith, consciously used Gothic conventions to expose the evils of autocratic power, especially that exercised by men over women. But even their contemporary, Ann Radcliffe, who came closest to making the Gothic novel respectable, undermines the hierarchy of "home" and "world" by allowing her heroines as well as her heroes both unassailable virtue and space to move beyond the restrictions of "the proprieties" set by critics and others interested in the reformation of morals. Too much innocence is hazardous, Radcliffe concludes, to a heroine's health. She needs knowledge, not protection from the truth.

M. G. Lewis was inspired by Radcliffe's *The Mysteries of Udolpho* to write a novel that both exploited and exploded the conventions of the feminine Gothic that Radcliffe made the most popular genre of her day. One plot of *The Monk* follows the rather gruesome story of Lorenzo and Agnes along the paths of the Radcliffian Gothic, with its strong, initiative-taking heroine. In the other plot, murderous lust takes control of Ambrosio, a Capuchin abbot from whom all knowledge of the flesh was kept throughout his youth. In the innocent Antonia he meets his counterpart, his victim, and, as it turns out, his sister. With all its sensational details, Lewis's novel is an attack on the "cloistered virtue" of monks, but also of women brought up in circumstances created to protect them from contact with evil.

The reconceptualization of womanhood that was being argued out in the culture called forth a parallel discourse about men. If the home is closer to heaven than the world in which he operates, what kind of virtue is appropriate for a man? The solution of the Romantic is to elevate his alienation from the world. This alienation is then viewed as the true shape of the human condition, rather than as a solution to the crisis of masculinity posed by the redefinition of woman as the repository of "innocence." Of course the male artist is alienated also from "the world" that is supposed to be the province of men. Yet it is a double alienation, from the world *and* from the home, that we see in the work of Godwin and Maturin, with their "fallen wanderer" protagonists whose distance from the domestic ideal only serves to reinforce its value. Mary Shelley's *Frankenstein*, building on the work of both of her parents, delivers one of the sharpest critiques of the ideology of "separate spheres" to be found in fiction.

Both the Radcliffian villain and the Lewisite protagonist act out a counterscript in which men rebel against the feminization of the home. But unlike the male heroes of American literature, who go off into the wilderness together to escape the constraints of the female sphere, the English Gothic villains either usurp the castle or try to destroy it from the outside. They then try to reinstate there the "shame culture" of an earlier era, when the home was not women's sphere.[7] A shame culture stresses the public expiation of wrongdoing, the maintaining or regaining (by men) of honor defined as a public perception of the individual. Its quintessential ritual is what Foucault calls "the spectacle of the scaffold."[8] In contrast, women's honor, and the loss of it, are private matters associated with the body, with violations that cannot be undone. Guilt cannot be eradicated by manipulations of public perception. Therefore the Gothic villain wants to return to a shame culture where conscience— embodied in the woman as mother and helpmeet—cannot follow. In his castle, his monastery, or his lab, he attempts to establish a base from which he can attack the home, where guilt is produced under the rule of women.

Guilt, of course, is the debased term of a pair of which innocence is its valorized opposite. In *The Monk*, the protagonist is brought up under conditions that are supposed to produce innocence— seclusion from "the world." In *Caleb Williams*, the protagonist pro- tests continually that he is innocent, and presents himself as a simple youth inexperienced in the ways of "the world" in which his antagonist has so much power. In *Melmoth the Wanderer*, Alonso de Moncada is the "innocent victim" of his mother's "frailty." Having been conceived out of wedlock, he is an affront to a thoroughly Protestant, eighteenth-century system of morality that condemns his mother's impulsive act. The masculine Gothic asks, can a man be "innocent" in a world that makes seclusion from "the world" a prerequisite for that state? Necessarily the answer is no, and from this answer issues a radical deconstruction of the pairing of guilt and innocence upon which the separation of spheres, with its attendant guilt culture, rests.

If we look at the Gothic novel as an increasingly insistent critique of the ideology of separate spheres, it is clear that the male exile is no more empowered, ultimately, by the division than the female prisoner. Mary Shelley's vision of the alienated-male-turned-monster has entered our mythology so completely that it is a driven Adam, rather than a wanton Eve, who is imaged as bringing "Death into the World, and all our woe." When the woman, figuring the triumph of middle-class culture as the victory of virtue over entrenched aristocratic power, is positioned simultaneously closer to nature and closer to God, the fall takes the form of an attempt to usurp her place. Eve, then, becomes the *agent* of redemption, reappropriating the garden, or at least calling forth a countermove in which the usurper is dropped from the highest mountain or otherwise returned to the primordial realm of "chaos and old night."

Though the concerns of this book are primarily feminist, it rests also upon the postulates of Marxism. It is Marxist in that it treats Gothic novels as barely diluted ideology, inventing, as Fredric Jameson has put it, imaginary or formal "solutions" to the unresolvable social contradictions raised by placing men and women in separate spheres.[9] It is feminist in that it takes a position on this gender-based division. That is to say, it welcomes subversive fictional strategies that expose the privileging of "the home" over "the world" and make clear where real power in a patriarchal society lies. Eighteenth-century proponents of separate spheres for women and men may have been concerned for women's interests as they saw them, but modern feminism may be said to begin when Mary Wollstonecraft and her contemporaries began using the bourgeois idea of "the rights of man" to point out the harm done to women in the name of protecting them from the world.

This book deals with male as well as female Gothic writers, but it treats the masculine Gothic as a reaction to the feminine. The marginal feminine Gothic is thus placed at the center of my model for the development of the genre. Having placed it there, I propose to show how a popular form which claims to support a typological reading of home, the only place where "the bliss of Paradise . . . has survived the fall," in fact undermines and subverts that claim. The safety of the home is *not* a given, nor can it ever be considered permanently achieved. At best it must be restored by women's *activity*, not only within its walls but outside in the world as well. And even this may not always be possible. When we move away from the pure Radcliffian Gothic, as I do in the second half of this book, even the desirability of such a protected space is questioned.

The displacement of the central by the marginal takes place throughout the book. For in the same way that Derrida takes apart such paired oppositions as reason and madness, by showing, in this case, that reason is always menaced by a madness anterior to it, so the home as type of heaven is always menaced by an anterior, but historically specific, world.[10] Of course this privileging was put forward, and is still being put forward, as a utopian vision of harmony between the sexes, with the home the highest expression of that harmony. The unequal power relations that this vison conceals have been a focus of feminist concern since the late eighteenth century, when Mary Wollstonecraft and her contemporaries began to attack it. That a genre of popular fiction written, in the main, by women and for women, should be a site of resistance to this concealment therefore adds a historical and cultural dimension to an issue that is still far from resolved.

NOTES

1. The distinction between the two modes derives from an opposition in eighteenth-century aesthetics between "terror," which Burke treated as an opening to "the sublime," and "horror." Radcliffe used Burke as the theoretical base for her work, as Malcolm Ware shows in *Sublimity in the*

Novels of Ann Radcliffe: A Study of the Influence upon Her Craft of Edmund Burke's "Enquiry into the Origin of Our Ideas of the Sublime and Beautiful," Essays and Studies on English Language and Literature, no. 25, English Institut, Uppsala University, 1963. Her preference for terror over horror is expressed in the following often-quoted distinction: "Terror and horror are so far opposite, that the first expands the soul, and awakens the faculties to a higher degree of life, the other contracts, freezes, and nearly annihilates them" (*New Monthly Magazine* [1826], 149). Even before the twentieth century, not all critics found her use of terror elevating: see for instance Sir Walter Scott, "Mrs. Ann Radcliffe," *Lives of the Novelists*, 2 vols. (London: H. C. Carey, 1825), vol. 1, 187–241. Montague Summers, *The Gothic Quest: A History of the Gothic* ([1938; New York: Russell and Russell, 1964] 28–31), employs three categories: terror-Gothic, historic-Gothic, and sentimental-Gothic, but does not treat the third. Leslie Fiedler in *Love and Death in the American Novel* (rev. ed. [New York: Stein and Day, 1966]) and Judith Wilt in *Ghosts of the Gothic: Austen, Eliot, and Lawrence* (Princeton: Princeton University Press, 1980) discuss Gothicism as a flight from community and especially from the domestic sphere ruled by women. Robert D. Hume regards "sentimental" and "historical" Gothic as "misnomers," while "horror-Gothic" novels are "at the same time more serious and more profound" ("Gothic versus Romantic: A Revaluation of the Gothic Novel," *PMLA* 84 [1969], 282–90).

2. A chronological sample of this debate for the eighteenth century would include James Fordyce, *Sermons to Young Women* (1765); Hester Chapone, *Letters on the Improvement of the Mind Addressed to a Young Lady* (1772); John Gregory, *A Father's Legacy to His Daughters* (1774); Mary Wollstonecraft, *Thoughts On the Education of Daughters* (1786); *A Vindication of the Rights of Woman* (1792); Clara Reeve, *Plans of Education; With Remarks on the Systems of Other Writers* (1792); Maria Edgeworth, *Letters for Literary Ladies* (1795); Thomas Gisborne, *An Enquiry into the Duties of the Female Sex* (1796); Mary Hays, *An Appeal to the Men of Great Britain on Behalf of Women* (1898); Priscilla Wakefield, *Reflections on the Condition of Female Education With Suggestions For Its Improvement* (1798); and Hannah More, *Strictures on the Modern System of Female Education* (1799).

3. Leonore Davidoff and Catherine Hall, *Family Fortunes: Men and Women of the English Middle Class, 1780–1850* (Chicago: University of Chicago Press, 1987). See also Mary Poovey, *The Proper Lady and the Woman Writer: Ideology as Style in the Writings of Mary Wollstonecraft, Mary Shelley and Jane Austen* (Chicago: University of Chicago Press, 1984), 1–94.

4. See Anna Clark, *Women's Silence, Men's Violence: Sexual Assault in England 1770–1840* (London: Pandora Press, 1987), esp. 21–58.

5. Clara Reeve, *The Progress of Romance* (1785), ed. Esther McGill (New York: Facsimile Text Society, 1930), 111.

6. Cf. Virginia Woolf, *A Room of One's Own* (New York: Harcourt Brace Jovanovich, 1929), referring to Charlotte Brontë: "Her imagination swerved from indignation, and we feel it swerve" (76).

7. These terms are borrowed from the anthropologist Ruth Benedict, *The Chrysanthemum and the Stone* (Boston: Houghton Mifflin, 1946).

8. See Michel Foucault, *Discipline and Punish: The Birth of the Prison*, trans. Alan Sheridan (New York: Vintage, 1979), 32–67. The privatization of criminality, on the one hand, and insanity, on the other, are part of a wider social practice that is manifest in the creation of the prison and the asylum as well as the "sphere" of home. See Michel Foucault, *Madness and Civilization*, trans. Richard Howard (New York: Vintage, 1973); Jacques Donzelot, *The Policing of Families* (New York: Pantheon, 1980).

9. Fredric Jameson, *The Political Unconscious: Narrative as a Socially Symbolic Act* (Ithaca: Cornell University Press, 1981), 77 and passim.

10. See Jacques Derrida, "Cogito and the History of Madness," *Writing and Difference*, trans. Alan Bass (Chicago: University of Chicago Press, 1978), 31–63.

PART I

The Myth of the Fall
and the Rise of
the Heroine

Neighbours in Jane Austen are not the people actually living nearby; they are the people living a little less than nearby who, in social recognition, can be visited. What she sees across the land is a network of propertied houses and families, and through the holes of this tightly drawn mesh most actual people are simply not seen. To be face-to-face in this world is already to belong to a class.

RAYMOND WILLIAMS,
The Country and the City

CHAPTER I

The Language of Domestic Violence

THE STRAND of popular culture we call the Gothic novel can be distinguished by the presence of houses in which people are locked in and locked out. They are concerned with violence done to familial bonds that is frequently directed against women. Given these boundaries, which restrict our subject more narrowly than David Punter's Marxist and Freudian history of the genre, we can begin by asking what fears and expectations the audience for Gothics might have brought to its reading, and what problems the writers of Gothic were facing, which, for both groups, the haunted house could metonymically represent.[1] Domestic violence as a literary theme was not invented in the mid-eighteenth century, and the question of how much of it might pass unnoticed, as a "normal" part of family life, is still under negotiation. It is when the home becomes a "separate sphere," a refuge from violence, that a popular genre comes into being that assumes some violation of this cultural ideal.

Feminism and a concern with domestic violence emerge in the context of the Enlightenment, with its faith in the power of masculine reason to correct and check social abuses.[2] Henry Tilney in Jane Austen's *Northanger Abbey* is a spokesman for an enlightened England when he admonishes Catherine Morland for imagining that his father murdered his mother in the style of a Gothic villain. "Does our education prepare us for such atrocities?" he asks. "Do our laws connive at them? Could they be perpetrated without being known, in a country like this, where social and literary intercourse are on such a footing; where every man is surrounded by a neighbourhood of voluntary spies, and where roads and newspapers lay everything open?"[3] He has even provoked a humiliated Catherine to conclude that "in the central part of England there was surely some security for the existence of a wife not beloved, in the laws of the land and the manners of the age."

But is the power of surveillance sufficient to keep evil out of the central part of England, where eyes and the written word go everywhere? Is Henry's faith in a benevolent patriarchal order, discoverable by reason and supported by custom and law, the point of view that Catherine comes to share, a mark of the success of her education? It is true that Henry is quite aware of his father's private vices: his views on marriage and money, for instance. What he learns from the general's treatment of Catherine is that private vices can have public consequences, and may even sometimes require more of him than a knowing glance exchanged with his sister. Had General Tilney been an amiable man like Mr. Morland or Mr. Allen, Catherine might not have felt the need to create a story to fill in the gap between her own discomfort in the general's presence and his children's embarrassed acquiescence to his arbitrary commands, his nocturnal pacing, his "incessant attentions" to his young guest.

It is in fact because it is not safe for a woman, even "in the central part of England," to travel seventy miles alone that the general's precipitous and unexplained expulsion of Catherine relieves Henry of the duty of filial obedience and allows him to play a role that has, as we will see, the stamp of the Gothic on it: the child who rebels against a parent and whose rebellion is vindicated. The rebellion of Gothic children is confined to the matter of marriage choice, and *Northanger Abbey* is a Gothic novel as well as a parody of the genre. But the event that forces Henry to alter his view of his father means that he is not a Mr. Knightley, not an older, experienced father-lover who always knows best. Rather, he is an Austen male with a blind spot, one who needs to step back from his unexamined relationship to male privilege, embodied in his father, just as Catherine needs to step back from her unexamined Gothic imagination.

Had Catherine's carriage been stopped on the road, her reputation would not have been protected by "a neighbourhood of voluntary spies," that is, by a community that takes care of its members and prevents abuses of power. Henry speaks of this community as the product of modern enlightenment, coming into being with better roads and the rise of newspapers. Yet anyone who has looked at the history of the English Poor Laws between the reigns of Elizabeth and Victoria is aware of a decline in the sense of community responsibility for the weaker members of parishes, as reflected in laws designed to keep the poor rolls down and to punish those who could not find work to support themselves.[4] The general's wife might not have been the mother of an illegitimate child, or an applicant for poor relief, but her isolation from neighbors, servants, and other potential "voluntary spies" was supported by an ideology of domestic privacy that was being consolidated in the enlightened England toward which Henry is so partial.

In fact there are no voluntary spies in the novel, no articulators of restraints upon men in their homes by which the general might have been enjoined from sending a young girl on a long journey home by coach simply because she did not have the fortune he thought she possessed. Nor would the presence of prying neighbours necessarily make for a safer community for women. Anne Brontë, in *The Tenant of Wildfell Hall*, shows the effects of such vigilance on a woman whose heart is pure though her behavior might be called unconventional by the standards of her "community." As long as those standards encode a patriarchal view of women as "the weaker sex," unable to resist "temptation" when they are not themselves instigators of it, women will not be safe from abuses of male power. As long as their power is unequal to that of men, their behavior can be controlled by the threat of violence even when it is not carried out.

Catherine's only preparation for the general's reckless endangerment of her person comes from the pages of Radcliffe, which she can put into perspective only when she has had some experience of the kind of evil represented, in displaced and exaggerated form, in the novels she has devoured. In moving beyond the protective coverings of her benignly patriarchal upbringing, sent alone into the midst of dangers from which that upbringing was supposed to protect her, she travels the same path that the Radcliffian heroine does, from innocence (Milton's "fugitive and cloistered virtue"), through imagined terrors that are later "explained," to a level of experience of good and evil ("as two twins cleaving together") which allows her "to feel that, in suspecting General Tilney of either murdering or shutting up his wife, she had scarcely sinned against his character, or magnified his cruelty."

A less-fortunate outcome for Catherine's seventy-mile journey from Northanger Abbey to her home in Wiltshire is present only as an excluded possibility. Like the fate of Lydia Bennett had a determined Darcy not intervened and forced her irresponsible suitor, Wickham, to marry her, this reminder of women's vulnerability, in a world where they had no legal protection, remains at the edge of the page. It is at this outer edge that "voluntary spying" turns into that other enemy of women's freedom to follow their consciences so often mentioned in Austen's witty asides, gossiping. Secret activity and unstated violence are recurring motifs for the general, with oblique references to his late-night writing of pamphlets and to the "improving hand" that tears down cottages on his son's estate.[5] But direct violence within the home, from Henry's point of view, is inconceivable, and it is Henry's forgiveness that Catherine must merit. It therefore cannot be spoken about in public, nor even thought about privately without shame.

Thus in Austen's highly selective world, "social and literary intercourse" does not, as Raymond Williams points out, "lay everything open."

> Neighbours in Jane Austen are not the people actually living nearby; they are the people living a little less than nearby who, in social recognition, can be visited. What she sees across the land is a network of propertied houses and families, and through the holes of this tightly drawn mesh most actual people are simply not seen. To be face-to-face in this world is already to belong to a class. No other community, in physical presence or in social reality, is by any means knowable. And it is not only the people who have disappeared, in a stylized convention as precise as Ben Jonson's. It is also most of the country, which becomes real only as it relates to the houses which are the real nodes; for the rest of the country is weather or a place for a walk.[6]

But the space between Fullerton, her parental home, and the residence of her future father-in-law is neither weather nor a place for a walk. It is a place where things can happen to women about which they may not speak. Catherine's ignorance of violence in the real world is mocked when she puts an end to Henry's "short disquisition on the state of the nation" with the comment, "I have heard that something very shocking indeed will soon come out of London," and Henry chides his sister for thinking their friend is referring to an actual political upheaval. Even if for middle-class women in the late eighteenth century "from politics it was an easy step to silence," it is this enforced stupidity on which Austen has been ironically commenting that is the real object of her mockery.

Reading Gothic novels, for Catherine Morland and for the middle-class woman reader for whom she stands in, is not an "escape" from everyday experience. Rather, their authors develop another set of conventions to draw up a world that an Austen character does not "know." The relationship between these two sets of conventions is not that of an observed world to a fantasized one. Rather it is one of the manifest and the secret, the center and the margin: what exists from Henry's optimistic male vantage point and what, as he sees it, lies outside the female sphere, if indeed it exists at all. The Gothic in fiction, then, is a set of conventions to represent what is not supposed to exist. The Gothic castle in the eighteenth century is a site upon which this contradiction is explored and given an imaginary resolution, one that became popular precisely because it could take in areas of social reality about which middle-class women were supposed to have no knowledge. It is these subjects about which it takes considerable courage to speak, and it is because courage is required that novelists must "not desert one another."

The conventions of the Gothic novel, then, speak of what in the polite world of middle-class culture cannot be spoken. Silence around the issue of violence against women is still problematic, and it is difficult to sort out, even now, whether a shift in consciousness about it indicates an actual increase in incidents of violence or not. By a shift in consciousness I mean a perception that what was thought to be inevitable is not necessarily so. The redefinition of "home" and woman's place in it that began in the middle of the eighteenth century addressed the issue of violence and danger in a new way. The world is a dangerous, violent place, but it is possible to exclude those elements from the home, and to keep women "innocent" of them. Moreover, women themselves have some power in the matter. By acting like Pamela, they can purify the fallen aristocratic castle and make it into a home worthy of the name. This is the premise that the Gothic novel takes up.

For readers of this genre, the ideological reframing of violence, and of women's relationship to it, occurred in a context of industrialization and urban expansion. When the conditions that govern daily life appear to be created by man rather than by God, there is a need to redefine what is natural. Conversely, certain occurrences once thought to be outside of human control are now perceived as manageable. I am suggesting that danger to women, coming from a man-made world of agricultural and industrial improvements, came to be perceived in the latter part of the eighteenth century as controllable by the human operation of setting apart the home as a "haven" from "all that." The vision of home as a heaven created by human endeavour, which could draw out the benevolent aspects of technology to serve as a protection from the harmful effects of the same technology, is an essential precondition for Gothic fiction.

A world without community is beyond the edges of Jane Austen's map, but eighteenth-century readers of Gothics, and of novels in general, are likely to have had at least some experience of its urban version. This is because the highest concentration of readers was in urban areas. Literacy in London was as much as six times that found in the remote countryside.[7] A steady migration into the city led to a rising population despite the fact that the death rate in London remained higher than the birth rate until the end of the century.[8] Wrigley estimates that, in order to sustain an average rise in population of 2,700 per year, the net immigration into London must have been about 8,000 per year.[9] Ian Watt speculates that "it is probably from them that the most substantial additions to the book-buying public were drawn, rather than from the impoverished majority of the population."[10]

At the upper end of the scale of city residents were "that class of leisured and predominantly urban families who, by their manner of life, were commonly regarded as gentry, though they were not supported by a landed estate," middle-class families involved in what has been called "competitive ostentation."[11] If they bought novels, or sent their servants to the circulating library, it is probable that the servants themselves would at least investigate the books, even if they never read a whole one. Would General Tilney's wife have been able to assume protection by such "voluntary spies," at least some of whom might well be as enraptured by Gothic novels, either from reading or hearing about them, as Catherine was? Nor might reading "horrid novels" be the only aspect of eighteenth-century servant life that might work to contravene from below the kind of community of interest that could serve as a basis for action of the sort Henry is talking about?

So strong was the pull to London on men and women from the countryside that Patrick Colquehoun made the claim, in 1800, that there were as many as 10,000 servants of both sexes "out of a place," that is, unemployed, in London. This was the same year that he estimated the servant population of London to be as high as one in four.[12] Surrounded by unfamiliar neighbors and underpaid servants, and with the home increasingly viewed as a private place where people could do as they wished without interference, the middle-class woman was not necessarily safe from male anger, and with her resources legally belonging to her husband she was not in a strong bargaining position. Under these conditions, it is easy to see how the image of benevolent paternalism that underlies the concept of the "true home" with its "good" master, "good" mistress, and faithful servants might break down and give way to "voluntary" spying far more hostile than anything dreamed of in Catherine Morland's innocent philosophy, or in Henry's more experienced one.

The swelling market in London servants is part of a larger economic upheaval: the enclosure movement, the substitution of wages for the traditional exchange of land for goods and services, changes in the Poor Laws, the establishment of workhouses and other manifestations of the slow transition from feudalism to capitalism in the English countryside. Ivy Pinchbeck's study of women workers from 1750 to 1850 makes the point that when wages were introduced into agriculture the status of the landowner's wife became more privatized. The practice of boarding laborers went out of use as the supply of day laborers increased due to enclosure and the throwing together of small farms. This meant that the landowner was no longer responsible for feeding his laborers, a task whose supervision had fallen to his wife. Even when tenant farmers were replaced by servants the task of supervision still fell to the wife, but now her education was directed toward leisure accomplishments rather than skilled household management.[13]

The same conditions that created the female servant created also her mistress, whose leisure to read was obtained by the enlargement of the servant class as one index of increasing middle-class wealth. Because urban life was so impersonal, so lacking in the integrated social network that Henry Tilney is talking about, visible indicators of social status were given greater weight in the city than in the country. Servants were one such indicator. Wives who did no work and daughters who went to boarding schools to learn subjects and "accomplishments" that had nothing to do with economic activity also served that function, and this emerging group became the audience for numerous writers aiming at a market needing, as they saw it, guidance, direction, and a new set of gender distinctions appropriate to its new social and economic function.

The sheer density of a city population gave practical force to the idea of protecting women from the rough world outside the home. In actuality, the transportation necessary to separate work and home was available only to the wealthiest merchants, and "protection" was not extended to a woman who worked outside the home, or to one who traveled without a man whose property she could be presumed to be.[14] It seems to me, therefore, that the kind of safe "community" that Henry Tilney assumes did not exist in either the city or the country, the working class or the middle class. Raymond Williams makes the point that the breakdown of "community" in the eighteenth century, which many contemporary writers blamed on the city, was observed by others to be taking place in the country at the same time, brought on by some larger cause that embraced both terms of the pair. Even in Austen's regulated world, midway between the two, spies were as likely to gossip about a heroine as to protect her.

With the wealthy corrupted by "luxury" made possible by increased productivity, both in agriculture and in manufacturing, and the poor corrupted by cheap spirits and overcrowded living conditions, the very future of England seemed to some commentators to be in danger. The appeal of the concept of "separate spheres" was that it gave women a role in creating a bulwark against this danger, a revolution in "manners" whose aim was, paradoxically, to keep them ignorant of corruption, immorality, and violence. In effect, women were being told to reverse the events of the fall, to give up knowledge in return for safety. Part of this bargain entailed giving up knowledge of sexuality, embracing an ideal that Nancy Cott has called "passionlessness," with the result that "a tradition-ally dominant Anglo-American definition of women as *especially* sexual . . . was reversed and transformed between the seventeenth and the nineteenth centuries into the view that women (although still primarily identified by their female gender) were *less* carnal and lustful than men."[15]

One anxiety behind this new construction of the female was that, with men gone during working hours, women no longer spent their days under the tacit supervision of their husbands or fathers. If women were, as tradition would have it, the source of temptation, and too lustful and weak to resist it when it came from without, the whole structure of patriarchy would collapse under these new social arrangements. A redefinition of womanhood is thus called forth: a "true woman" who sees, hears, and therefore does no evil. Women could thus be a symbol for the stability that the middle class saw itself bringing to a society whose aristocrats (all the way up to the royal family) had lost the capacity for moral leadership and whose lower orders might at any moment become a Jacobin mob. In some respects the ideology of passionlessness gave women greater control over their bodies and their lives. Nevertheless this new female ideal created contradictions within the patriarchal context in which it came into being.

The campaign to reform English morals was a protest against the religious laxity of the Church of England on the one hand, and against the sexual laxity of the aristocracy on the other. The publica-tion of Richardson's *Pamela* is an important milestone in this cam-paign, many of whose leaders were affiliated with the Evangelical movement, and in particular with its activist core, the Clapham Sect. William Wilberforce, Hannah More, Thomas Gisborne, and James Stephen (Virginia Woolf's grandfather) were the most prominent members of this group, which saw the redefinition of woman-hood in the context of their mission to abolish the slave trade and to redefine what it meant to lead a Christian life. Thus when More and Gisborne wrote about the nature and duties of the sexes they spoke for a group of men and women who saw themselves as the conscience of their nation.

Gisborne's *An Enquiry into the Duties of the Female Sex,* published in 1796 as a companion volume to *An Enquiry into the Duties of Men in the Higher and Middle Classes of Society in Great Britain Resulting from Their Respective Situations, Positions, and Employments* sums up the grounds upon which the male and female spheres were to be divided. God in His wisdom has given to men "the science of legislation, of jurisprudence, of political economy; the conduct of government in all its executive functions; the abstruse reaches of erudition, the inexhaustible depths of philosophy; the knowledge indispensable in the wide field of commercial enterprise; the arts of defence and of attack . . ." These activities "demand the effort of a mind endued with close and comprehensive reasoning, and of intense and continued application, in a degree which they are not requisite for discharge of the customary office of female duty." The special virtues of women, on the other hand, were manifest in the following ways:

> First, in contributing daily and hourly to the comfort of husbands, of parents, of brothers and sisters, and of other relations, connections, and friends, in the intercourse of domestic life, under every vicissitude of sickness and health, of joy and affliction.
>
> Secondly, in forming and improving the general manners, disposition, and conduct of the other sex, by society and example.
>
> Thirdly, in modelling the human mind during the early stages of its growth, and fixing, while it is yet ductile, its growing principles of action.[16]

Gisborne, and other writers who contributed to this developing ideology of womanhood, resolved a contradiction that arose for a class whose claim to superiority rested on its rigorous marshaling of time, its abhorrence of idleness. If women focus all their attention on ameliorating the lot of those with whom they are in contact, if their sole interest in themselves takes the form of a desire for improvement of themselves in order to benefit those near them, then the dangerous consequences of their freedom from physical or gainful labor will not appear.

From a contemporary point of view, these duties appear to deny the woman an existence in her own right, so concerned is she with others. Alice Clark has argued that the dependent status of the eighteenth-century middle-class woman was not only a new development but one that put women in a worse position vis-à-vis men than the mutual dependence they had enjoyed as economic partners in agriculture or small businesses, where the labor of each was equally necessary to the survival of the economic enterprise and the family unit.[17] But Clark minimizes the inequality of women and men within the family economy, and the misogyny that viewed women of all classes as given to insubordination and unable to control their sexual demands. In reconstructing womanhood in accordance with the needs of their class, reformers like the Evangelical Thomas Gisborne were also reacting against the denigration of women that found expression in the loose morality of the Restoration.[18]

Gisborne claims that women have benefited from being placed outside the nexus of the household economy in which their labor was economically necessary. "In the last age," he comments, "she who was completely versed in the sciences of pickling and preserving, and in the mysteries of cross stitch and embroidery; she who was thoroughly mistress of the family receipt-book and her needle, was deemed, in point of solid attainments, to have reached the measure of female perfection." To this he contrasts a brighter present in which "it has been universally acknowledged that the intellectual powers of women are not restricted to the arts of the housekeeper and the sempstress. Genius, taste, and even learning have appeared in the number of female endowments and acquisitions." Moreover, the home is not necessarily inferior to the wider sphere of male endeavors as a setting for the drama of human salvation. "Fortitude is not to be sought merely on the rampart, on the deck, on the field of battle. Its place is no less in the chamber of sickness and pain, in the retirement of anxiety, grief and disappointment."[19]

Both radical and conservative writers on the subject of middle-class women argued passionately for a reformation of the image of womanhood that had emanated, in an earlier period, from the aristocracy. They deplored the emphasis on debility and female frailty, the dependence on physical charm they found in the age preceding their own, and held up a new ideal emphasizing strength and a sense of the public value of motherhood. Both were stirred by the events of the French Revolution. It was rational motherhood that would either save England from a similar fate or hasten a similar triumph on English soil. The idea that child-rearing would become woman's primary contribution to public life was at the center of the ideology of the eighteenth-century "new woman." It solved, at the same time, the problem of a woman's idleness and her detachment from the sphere in which men exercised their God-given superiority.[20]

Of course the mind (and heart) of a woman charged with the duties Gisborne describes cannot be allowed to absorb, either from reading or from observation, scenes that might draw her away from her duties. The moralists of the period had therefore to contend with the emergence of women as a reading public. As John Tinnon Taylor has shown, much of the early opposition to the novel was expressed in terms of the harm it did to women, or to "young persons." The whole issue of reading for women was extremely conflictual in a period that was coming to view innocence as the defining quality of womanhood. Dr. John Gregory, author of the popular *A Father's Legacy to His Daughters* (1774), confesses:

> I am at the greatest loss what to advise you in regard to books.
> . . . If I was sure that nature had given you such strong principles of taste and sentiment, as would remain with you, and influence your future conduct, with the utmost pleasure would I endeavour to direct your reading, in such a way as might form that taste to the utmost perfection of truth and elegance. But when I reflect how easy it is to warm a girl's imagination, and how difficult deeply and permanently to affect her heart—how readily she enters into every refinement of sentiment, and how easily she can sacrifice them to an injury by artificially creating a taste, which, if nature never gave it you, would only serve to embarrass your future conduct.[21]

What could this taste, the product of a "warmed" imagination, be for? And why did "nature" give woman such weak defenses against it that reading poses a danger to her future conduct? Reading was not generally viewed as a danger to men's future conduct. But innocence that is an ignorance of evil, however defined, was by its very definition defenseless against what it did not know. Gregory seems to connect evil with sexuality: the expression of warm feelings toward the opposite sex. If his daughters were innocent in these matters, as he certainly felt they ought to be, they would not know what they were doing. Thus the danger of novel reading that would stimulate such behavior.

But there is another problem. Protected from "the world" so that they might not lose their innocence, women were thrown, perhaps even more than the active male who busied himself with "real" matters, upon their imaginations. A doctor quoted in the *Monthly Review* for 1773 laments that

> a young girl, instead of running about and playing, *reads*, perpetually reads, and at twenty becomes full of vapours, instead of becoming qualified for the duties of a good wife, or nurse. . . . I have known persons of both sexes, whose constitutions would have been robust, weakened by the too strong impressions of impassioned writings. The most tender romances hinder marriages instead of promoting them. A woman, while her heart is warmed by the languors of love, does not seek a husband; a HERO must lay his laurels at her feet.[22]

The argument is a circular one: women are taken in by what they read because they are kept away from the kind of experience that might offer points of comparison. Mrs. Barbauld, the editor of a fifty-volume series of British novelists, might defend the reading of novels on the grounds that it made female innocence more secure, since "it is safer to meet with a bad character in the pages of a fictitious story, than in the polluted walks of life."[23]

But the problem went beyond good and bad characters to a cultural difference between men and women that the subject matter of novels reflected. "For the usual strain of these compositions," remarked the *Critical Review* in 1765, "one would be apt to conclude, that love is not only the principal, but almost the sole passion that actuates the human heart." By reading novels, "the youth of both sexes" fill their minds with "the grossest of illusions," only to find out (perhaps too late) that "though love has a strong influence over the actions of men, yet it is frequently overpowered by avarice, ambition, vanity, and a thousand other passions."[24] It was inconceivable that middle-class daughters could entertain any of these passions. So their very lack of experience made it all the more necessary that they be shielded from encountering such passions, whether "in the pages of a fictitious story" or "in the polluted walks of life."

There is, of course, real danger behind these warnings, and more than a grain of truth in the assumption that, in our culture at least, women are more susceptible than men to illusions about the power of love. It is a tactic they are supposed to use, in fact, "in forming and improving the general manners, dispositions, and conduct of the other sex." Mary Wollstonecraft, herself no stranger to the damaging effects of romantic illusions, spoke out against them in her reviews as well as in her feminist writings. She was critical, for instance, of Charlotte Smith's *Emmeline, the Orphan of the Castle* on the grounds that "the false expectations these wild scenes excite, tend to debauch the mind, and throw an insipid kind of uniformity over the moderate and rational prospects of life, consequently adventures are sought for and created, when duties are neglected and content despised."[25]

Yet this line of argument is used against women more often than it is invoked on their behalf. When Robert Southey told Charlotte Brontë that "literature cannot be the business of a woman's life, and ought not to be," adding that "the more she is engaged in her proper duties, the less leisure she will have for it, even as an accomplishment and a recreation,"[26] we can see clearly that it is not Charlotte's interests that are being served by the suppression of the female imagination for the sake of a proper performance of female duties. Protecting women against mental improprieties means locking the door of the mind from both sides. That Charlotte was well aware of the cost of this double bolting is clear from her anguished letters to Ellen Nussey, in which she makes statements like: "If you knew my thoughts, the dreams that absorb me, and the fiery imagination that at times eats me up, and makes me feel society as it is, wretchedly insipid, you would pity and I dare say despise me."[27]

Naturally this concern with female innocence and the correlative fear of the female imagination had an impact on the development of the novel. The early history of the genre is that of a disparaged form, and part of the mechanism of this disparagement was to associate it with women. The *Monthly* and the *Critical Review* complained regularly that the field was being overrun with women writers, and even in novels themselves, as Austen complains in her defense of the genre in *Northanger Abbey*, novel reading is portrayed as a form of recreation to which only a woman would stoop. Women writers sometimes joined in the condemnation of the genre that was making it possible for them to reach an audience. "Perhaps were it possible," bemoans Fanny Burney in her preface to *Evelina*, "to effect the total extirpation of novels, our young ladies in general, and boarding school damsels in particular, might profit from their annihilation." Denying that she is seeking any sort of recognition for herself, Burney suggests that her novel "may be read, if not with advantage, at least without injury."

These are narrow constraints indeed for a writer to accept. But given the prevailing definition of "female duties," which certainly left no time for writing, women had little choice, if they wanted to avoid condemnation by male critics, but to deny any wish to cause a stir through what they wrote. Moreover, as the standard of female virtue became increasingly "angelic" in the course of the eighteenth century, constraints on virtuous female behavior in novels increased as well. But by displacing its action backwards in time, the writers of Gothics enlarged the space within which a virtuous heroine could act. They thus resolved in fiction a contradiction between the demand of an increasingly self-conscious bourgeois class for a pure female ideal to contrast with the dissolute behavior of those above and below it and the need of writers to engage their readers by providing action that would leave them awaiting the next volume eagerly.

NOTES

1. David Punter, *The Literature of Terror: A History of Gothic Fictions from 1765 to the Present Day* (London: Longman, 1980), ascribes the continuing

popularity of the Gothic to unresolved class conflict, which the "mystery" at the center of the plot both figures and conceals.

2. Anna Clark, *Women's Silence, Men's Violence: Sexual Assault in England 1770–1845* (London: Pandora Press, 1987), esp. 1–45.

3. Jane Austen, *Northanger Abbey*, ed. Ann Henry Ehrenpreis (Harmondsworth: Penguin Books, 1972), 199.

4. The classic study is Sidney Webb and Beatrice Webb, *English Local Government: English Poor Law History*, pt. 1, *The Old Poor Law* (1927). For the effect of these laws on women and children, see Ivy Pinchbeck and Margaret Hewett, *Children in English Society*, vol. 1, *From Tudor Times to the Eighteenth Century* (London: Routledge and Kegan Paul, 1963).

5. See Robert Hopkins, "General Tilney and the Affairs of State: The Political Gothic of *Northanger Abbey*," *Philological Quarterly* 57 (1978), 213–24.

6. Raymond Williams, *The Country and the City* (New York: Oxford University Press, 1973), 166.

7. Lawrence Stone, "Literacy and Education in England 1640–1900," *Past and Present* no. 42 (Feb. 1969), 125.

8. M. Dorothy George, *London Life in the Eighteenth Century* (New York: Alfred A. Knopf, 1925), 21–61.

9. E. A. Wrigley, "London's Importance 1650–1750," *Past and Present* no. 37 (July 1967), 46.

10. Ian Watt, *The Rise of the Novel* (Berkeley: University of California Press, 1964), 40.

11. Wrigley, "London's Importance," 54; see also Lawrence Stone, "Social Mobility in England, 1500–1700," *Past and Present* no. 33 (Apr. 1966), 16–55; Alan Everitt, "Social Mobility in Early Modern England," *Past and Present* no. 33 (Apr. 1966), 56–73. For the role of servants in "competitive ostentation," see Jean Hecht, *The Domestic Servant Class in Eighteenth Century England* (London: Routledge and Kegan Paul, 1956), 2–8.

12. George, *London Life*, 112.

13. Ivy Pinchbeck, *Women Workers and the Industrial Revolution* (London: Frank Cass and Co., 1969), esp. 33–43.

14. See Lewis Mumford, *The City in History* (Harmondsworth: Penguin Books, 1961), 437ff.

15. Nancy F. Cott, "Passionlessness: An Interpretation of Victorian Sexual Ideology, 1790–1850," in *A Heritage of Her Own*, ed. Nancy F. Cott and Elizabeth H. Pleck (New York: Simon and Schuster, 1979), 162–81. See also Gordon Rattray Taylor, *The Angel Makers: Psychological Origins of Historical Change* (London: Heinemann, 1958).

16. Thomas Gisborne, *An Enquiry into the Duties of the Female Sex* (London, 1797), 12–13.

17. Alice Clark, *The Working Life of Women in the Seventeenth Century* (1919; rpt., London: Routledge and Kegan Paul, 1982) esp. 290–308.

18. For the role of the Evangelical movement in the formation of the ideology of separate spheres, see Catherine Hall, "The Early Formation of Domestic Ideology," in *Fit Work for Women*, ed. Sandra Burman (London: Croom Helm, 1979), 15–32.

19. Gisborne, *Enquiry*, 20–22.

20. John Tinnon Taylor, *Early Opposition to the English Novel: The Popular Reaction from 1760 to 1830* (New York: Columbia University Press, 1943), esp. ch. 3, 53–86.

21. John Gregory, *A Father's Legacy to His Daughters* (Philadelphia, 1818), 62.

22. *Monthly Review*, Series 1, 47 (July 1773); rpt. in *Novel and Romance, 1700–1800: A Documentary Record*, ed. Ioan Williams (London: Routledge and Kegan Paul, 1970), 279.

23. Anna Laetitia Barbauld, "On the Origin and Progress of Novel-Writing," preface to *The British Novelists*, 50 vols. (London, 1810), vol. 1, 50.

24. *Critical Review* 20 (Oct. 1765), 173.

25. *Analytical Review* 1 (May-Aug. 1788), 333. Ralph M. Wardle identifies the author of this anonymous review as Wollstonecraft in "Mary Wollstonecraft, *Analytical* Reviewer," *PMLA* 62 (1947), 1000–1009.

26. Quoted in Elizabeth Gaskell, *The Life of Charlotte Brontë* (Harmondsworth: Penguin, 1975) 175.

27. Ibid., 161.

CHAPTER II

Guarding the Gates
to the Female Mind

𝕴 WANT NOW to look at the development of the popular eighteenth-century novel, and the discourse on gender that runs through it, in relation to the major shift in the representation of relationships between the sexes discussed in the previous chapter. Representational practices in Western Europe have drawn on the Genesis creation myth to embody and justify ideas about the distribution of power between the sexes, and contesting discourses have been advanced as differing interpretations of that myth. The premise which is the background to my discussion of Haywood is that the triad put forward in the story of the fall, one male, one female, and one tempter, is recast, most dramatically in Richardson's *Pamela*, in a form that is more congruent with the ideology of separate spheres. As passionlessness becomes the defining attribute of the new Eve, as hearth, home, and motherhood become her particular responsibilities, she achieves superiority to Adam inasmuch as she not only is able to resist the tempting serpent but is required to do so.

I am making *Pamela* a line of demarcation in the development of gender ideology in order to privilege a shift in the representation of temptation itself. Roughly speaking, before 1740 sexual temptation was a force that heroines were either unwilling or unable to resist. Accidents and coincidences might come to their aid, but the imagined alternatives to ruin were limited to renouncing men entirely or becoming a controlling vampire, a stranger to virtue. With the publication and popularity of *Pamela*, the possibility of resistance is called forth and participates as a necessary component in the new discourse on female virtue. Heroines gain in power by this move, but their hearts must now select their future spouse on the basis of feelings that are disconnected from sexuality, or what Lawrence Stone calls "affect" as a motive for marriage, and also from "interest" in her hero's wealth, title, or social position.[1] She can marry for love, but only if love is divorced from what we might call a material base.

No author better illustrates the pre-Richardsonian phase of this cultural revolution than Eliza Haywood, whose career as a writer began with the publication of *Love in Excess* in 1719, continued through ninety-four authored or attributed works, and ended with her death in 1756. The focus of her attention in the early phase of her career was, as she wrote in 1723, to "remind the unthinking Part of the World, how dangerous it is to give way to Passion."[2] Since the men in these novels find it enjoyable rather than dangerous to give way to passion, it would seem that "the unthinking Part of the World" is inhabited by women only. Explicitly, then, she has a female audience in mind, and she felt the need to defend her work in terms of its beneficial effect on this group. This included countering an accusation of writing to entertain rather than to edify, a critique raised by opponents of the novel throughout the eighteenth century, particularly those who opposed novel-reading for women.[3] Haywood, in this same preface of 1723, denied the charge and hoped her readers would "excuse the too great Warmth, which may perhaps appear in some particular pages; for without the Expression being invigorated in some measure proportionate to the Subject, 'twould be impossible for a Reader to be sensible how far it touches him, or how probable it is that he is falling into those Inadvertencies, which the examples I relate would caution him to avoid." Male pronouns notwithstanding, it is women who need these warnings.

As a woman writing to warn women, then, Haywood was also aware that women writers were not supposed to overreach themselves, but rather to confine themselves to what they knew. Yet she had no doubt but that passion was a subject about which women were supposed to know something. In her dedication to *The Fatal Secret*, published in 1724, she points out that she, being "a Woman, and consequently depriv'd of those Advantages of Education which the other Sex enjoy," has declined "to Soar to any Subject higher than that which Nature is not negligent to teach us." On the other hand, "Love is a Topick," she insists, "which I believe few are ignorant of; there requires no Aids of Learning, no general Conversation, no Application; a shady Grove and purling Stream are all Things that's necessary to give us an Idea of the Tender Passion. This is a theme, therefore, which, while I make choice to write of, frees me from the Imputation of [being] vain or self-sufficient." Passion, in other words, is a particularly appropriate subject for a woman writer.

Haywood's early novels depict vividly what they warn against. In *Love in Excess*, she demonstrates what will be her forte in her early career: an ability to incorporate a good deal of explicit sexuality within a didactic frame. Sharing with Swift's *Gulliver's Travels* and Defoe's *Robinson Crusoe* "the distinction of being the most popular English fiction of the eighteenth century before *Pamela*,"[4] this novel tells the story of the reformation of a rake, D'Elmont, at the hands of Melloria, after he has "ruined" one innocent member of "the unthinking part of the world" and married a shrew as his punishment. Like many of Haywood's early heroines, Amena, D'Elmont's victim, has been taught right from wrong, and is at one point locked up by her strict father to keep her out of harm's way. Yet these heroines are powerless against temptation.

They are innocent in the sense of being inexperienced, which means they have only the weapon of unquestioned obedience to authority with which to exert control over their suddenly awakened sexual feelings. "What now could poor Amena do," asked Haywood, "surrounded with so many Powers, attack'd by such a charming force without, betrayed by tenderness within: . . ." Haywood's answer is unequivocal—nothing. "Vertue and Pride, the Guardians of her Honour, fled from her Breast, and left her to her Foe, only a modest bashfulness remain'd, which for a time made some defence, but with such weakness as a Lover less impatient than D'Elmont would have little regard."[5] Men are, in Haywood's world, all-powerful and thus irresistible. Moreover, we are given to understand that the ability to control the feelings to which Amena gives way would diminish the quality that makes a Haywood heroine superior to more calculating women, and even superior to the rake who pursues her: she is "natural" rather than "artful." What causes her "fall" is that she wants what her tempter is offering. "She had only a thin silk Night gown on, which flying open as he caught her in his Arms, he found her panting Heart beat measures of consent, her heaving Breast swelled to be pressed by his, and every Pulse confess'd a wish to yield; her Spirits all dissolv'd, sunk in a lethargy of Love, her snowy Arms unknowingly grasped his Neck, her Lips met his half way, and trembled at the touch, in fine there was but a moment betwixt her and Ruine" (28–29). The key word here is "unknowingly." Amena ruined is sent to a convent, but her wish to yield is only halfheartedly condemned. We can say this because Melloria, who is not ruined, also wishes to yield. She nourishes, as Amena did, a passion equal to, though perhaps different in kind from, that of D'Elmont, "whom she knew it was a crime to love, yet cou'd not help loving," to the point where "the more she Thought, the more she grew distracted, and the less able to resolve any Thing; a thousand times she called on Death to give her ease" (63).

It is in sleep, however, when the barriers of consciousness are in abeyance, that she "unknowingly" experiences the imaginary fulfillment of her desires, "embracing him yet closer" and crying out in the privacy of her bedroom, "O too, too lovely Count, Extatick Ruiner!" (104) The count has, of course, been watching her, and makes use of the access she gives him "unknowingly" to the "true self" she cannot knowingly reveal.[6] Immediately "he tore open his Waistcoat, and joyn'd his panting Breast to hers, with such a Tumultuous Eagerness! Seized her with a rapidity of Transported hope Crown'd Passion, as immediately waked her from an imaginary Felicity, to the Approaches of a Solid one." Had another member of the household not entered Melloria's bedroom at this time, she might have gone the way of Amena. "Virtue and Pride," for Melloria too, are quick to flee in the presence of a desired man, and she is saved not by her own strength but from without.

Yet when the count later pleads with her to deliver him from the agonies of frustrated passion, she acknowledges to him that she feels them too. "No more, no more (said she letting her Head fall gently on his Breast) too easily I guess thy sufferings from my own." And then: "do I not bear, at least, an equal share in all your Agonies?" (115). D'Elmont's "agonies" have their source in the fact that he is married to a scheming, controlling woman, Alovisa, who constitutes D'Elmont's punishment for ruining the innocent Amena and many others like her. Of the three main characters, this woman is the unredeemably villanous one because she lacks a susceptibility to the power of love. Amena suffers for her "errors" and ends her days in a convent. But Alovisa dies violently, the more "fallen" of the two.[7]

Seen in contrast to these exchanges, Pamela constitutes a turning point in the development of the heroine. Her sexuality is certainly not extinguished, but it is held below the surface. However, this act of suppression is counterbalanced by an elevation in her power to form and improve "the general manners, dispositions, and conduct of the other sex, by society and example." Haywood's Melloria finally reforms her promiscuous count, but her system of belief involves a notion of innocent, artless passion that is quite alien to Richardson.

> Ambition, Envy, Hate, Fear, or Anger, every other Passion, that finds entrance into the Soul, Art and Discretion may disguise; but Love, tho' it may be feign'd, can never be conceal'd; not only the Eyes (those true and most perfect Intelligencers of the Heart) but every Feature, every Faculty betrays it! It fills the whole air of the person possess'd of it; It wanders round the Mouth! plays in the Voice! trembles in the Accent! and shows itself in a thousand different ways! even Melloria's care to hide it, made it more apparent. (80–81)

The love that Melloria feels (with its lustful component) is a virtuous emotion because she cannot resist or control it. Virtue requires no policy, no split between inner and other self, because ruin, or its opposite, is not finally in a woman's power. There is therefore no need for a virtuous heroine to conceal her feelings from herself or from others, as Pamela does. The very different message of *Pamela* is that women can win. They need not be "betrayed by tenderness within."

Yet there was concern, among some critics of the novel, that the didactic message in Richardson's novels was not clear enough. The criticism focused not on the heroines, but on the possible effect that a "mixed" character like Lovelace, Clarissa's "ruiner," might have on the unsophisticated reader with an imagination ready to be enflamed. Writing in defense of Richardson in 1750, Johnson criticizes other authors who, "for the sake of following nature, so mingle good and bad qualities in their principal personages, that they are both equally conspicuous; and as we accompany them through their adventures with delight, and are led by degrees to interest ourselves in their favour, we lose the abhorrence of their faults, because they do not hinder our pleasure, or, perhaps, regard them with some kindness for being united with so much merit."[8] Were novels written for, and read by, intelligent people, such precautions might not, in Johnson's view, be necessary. But since "these books are chiefly written to the young, the ignorant, and the idle, to whom they serve as lectures of conduct, and introductions into life . . . it is therefore not a sufficient vindication of a character," Johnson insists, "that it be drawn as it appears, for many characters ought never to be drawn."

Johnson did not put Lovelace in this category, yet others did find him too mixed. James Beattie, writing in 1783, did not rule out some mixture of good and bad traits in a male character, since "the history of a person, so very worthless as to have not one good quality, would give disgust or horror, instead of pleasure." Nevertheless, "when a character like Richardson's Lovelace, whom the reader ought to abominate for his crimes, is adorned with youth, beauty, eloquence, wit, and every other intellectual and bodily accomplishment, it is to be feared, that thoughtless young men may be tempted to imitate, even while they disapprove, him. Nor is it sufficient apology to say, that he is punished in the end."[9] Certainly Lovelace is more deeply evil than the exuberantly one-track-minded D'Elmont. It is hard to imagine D'Elmont enjoying an unconscious Amena, for instance, since his pleasure came not from the assertion of his power merely, but also from the fact that her every pulse confessed, as Clarissa's cannot, a wish to yield. Nevertheless his final punishment might not deter a female reader from imagining herself a little more flexible than Clarissa and winning, not only in the next world but in this one as well, the battle of the sexes that Richardson delineates in such detail. It might even be possible for her to agree with him that a reformed rake does not make the best husband and still feel that such a man would make a better husband than the one her parents had chosen for her.

The line of development set forth by Richardson continues in the sentimental novel, whose heroes and heroines are increasingly restricted by narrowing definitions of female virtue, but whose compliance with these restrictions is rarely rewarded in the fallen world in which they live. The prototypical sentimental novel in England, appearing thirty years after *Pamela*, was Henry Mackenzie's *Man of Feeling*, the perusal of which, J. M. S. Tompkins suggests, "was often undertaken as a sort of drill to keep the sensible heart in training."[10] The story consists of a series of heartrending scenes of human suffering to which the hero responds with what was later considered the prerogative of women, unrestrained tears. It is clear that anything as aggressive as sexuality would undo such a delicate creature, and he dies at the end with his grieving fiancée at his bedside.

This celebration of male tears is hard to understand unless we take see it as an index of a general cultural anxiety about a reorganization of gender boundaries which places feeling on the female side, while at the same time purifying it of "masculine" elements too coarse for a virtuous female to acknowledge. But if virtue, male as well as female, is incompatible with the expression of intense feelings such as sexuality or anger, how can heroes and heroines be made interesting? Even Henry Pye found it necessary that heroes have a few vices, though not enough to make them attractive villains. The sentimental novel attempts to solve the problem of the attractive villain by having no villains, only victims. In Mackenzie's *Julia de Roubigné*, the heroine, unlike Clarissa, does not suffer because she yields to temptation, for there is no one to tempt her. Nor is her family bent on financial gain, as Richardson's Harlowes are. Rather, her father has been ruined by a lawsuit, and to save him from jail Julia marries the wealthy and well-meaning Count de Montauban, though her heart belongs to the impoverished Savillon. Unaware of Julia's marriage, Savillon sets to work and succeeds in overcoming the financial obstacles to their union, only to discover that his success has come too late. Making a clandestine, though technically virtuous, visit to his beloved, he is discovered by the count, who refuses to believe in Julia's innocence. She has, in fact, kept a picture of Savillon in her drawer to weep over and is punished for thoughts rather than actions. Her husband, that is to say, in a fit of jealous rage, poisons himself and his wife.

But despite this impulsive act, it would be a mistake to view Montauban as a villain. His vengefulness arises more from the discovery that his wife had never loved him than from the possibility that he had been robbed of her virtue. He is fond of Julia and her family, and succumbs to jealousy only at the end of the novel. The castle to which he takes her is gloomy, but more in the manner of George Eliot's Lowick than of Ann Radcliffe's Udolpho. It is thus not disobedience, nor any other human failing, that is the source of Julia's woe. She did the right things, but, through no fault of her own, her heart was not in them and her virtue in so acting did not prevent her from coming to an unhappy end. Like Shakespeare's Desdemona, she is a victim of a male lack of faith in female innocence that is as much a cultural phenomenon as it is an individual flaw. But she is also the victim of tightening moral standards, expressed as restrictions not only on what women could do but on what they could feel and know, that were part and parcel of the creation of the middle-class female ideal.

On the surface, it might seem that Julia is the victim of a culture in which incriminating appearances count for everything and the true state of the heart means nothing. But in fact she is punished for what she secretly wanted to do, even though she did not act on her wishes. Given such stringent requirements for innocence, the possibility of virtue that can be rewarded in a happy ending dwindles almost out of sight. Of course if the intensity of suffering has replaced, for readers of these novels, the more dangerous forms of passion that enflamed the imagination, and if anxiety, anguish, pity, and tears are the only intense emotional states to which a "good" character can give way without endangering that goodness, a happy ending would rob these characters of a major opportunity to indulge in the activity that is the hallmark of their virtue. Moreover, if vice is excluded or explained away, thus avoiding the risk of making it too attractive, there is nothing for virtue to triumph over, hence no real basis for a happy ending. Finally, if the imagination of readers was to be steered away from "wild scenes" and toward the sufferings of those less lucky than themselves, unrewarded virtue would accomplish this as well as or better than virtue rewarded.

Nevertheless, raising what Mrs. Barbauld called "the softer passions" turned out to involve as many rules as avoiding the more dangerous ones. In her "Enquiry into those Kinds of Distress Which Excite Agreeable Sensations," published in 1773, Mrs. Barbauld warns would-be novelists that "the misfortunes which excite pity must not be too horrid or overwhelming." Thus "a judicious author will never attempt to raise pity by any thing mean or disgusting." One who tries to do so will fail, since "there must be a degree of complacence mixed with our sorrows to produce an agreeable sympathy; nothing, therefore, must be admitted which destroys the grace and dignity of such suffering; the imagination must have an amiable figure to dwell on."[11] Mrs. Barbauld is not suggesting that a novelist hold a mirror up to life. The response she is describing is "the reflex of self-approbation attending virtuous sympathy, . . . which makes us again desirous of being again witness to such scenes, instead of flying from them with disgust and horror." Yet she is well aware of the limitations of such a response. "Nothing is more dangerous than to let virtuous impressions of any kind pass through the mind without producing their proper effect. The wakening of remorse, virtuous shame and indignation, the glow of moral approbation, grow less and less vivid every time they recur, till at length the mind grows absolutely callous."[12] To avoid the epithet of "mere entertainment," it is not enough that a novel give the reader a momentary bath of emotion, no matter how commendable that emotion may be.

The emphasis on receptivity on the part of the reader standing in for the major character makes the novel of sensibility, from Mrs. Barbauld's point of view, more dangerous even than the representation of bad characters. In exchange for an extraordinary capacity to suffer and endure, heroes and heroines who specialize in sensibility are deprived of the possibility of extricating themselves from the situations that are causing them pain. The plots of novels influenced by Richardson, and the social customs inscribed within them, make it impossible for a heroine to act in her own behalf, with the occasional exception of such action in self defense. Nevertheless the heroine of a sentimental novel has a moral superiority in her suffering that was not available to Mrs. Haywood's early heroines, for whom men were all-powerful and innocent women were helpless to fight against that power. The "conduct of the other sex" can sometimes be improved "by society and example," and men, too, can be portrayed as victims aspiring, at least, to virtue. The key difference is that the ideal of womanhood has become so spiritualized that female powerlessness has become not a source of a woman's "ruine" but an inextricable part of her virtue.

This new attitude toward female power comes up for discussion in a scene in *Evelina* (1778) that takes place during a performance of Congreve's *Love for Love* (1695), which Burney uses to exemplify the old, unpurified moral code of the Restoration and to contrast it to attitudes that had taken hold by the time her novel was published. In *Love for Love,* none of the male characters is particularly competent or virtuous. Nevertheless the heroine, Angelica, manipulates them in such a way as to end up with the one she wants. A display of feminine helplessness or forbearance in this situation would clearly have benefited no one. Men have fouled things up, but to exhibit suffering resulting from this fact is not the point of the play. Instead Angelica uses her power over men, particularly over the father of her lover Valentine, and by the time she has carried out her scheme, all parties have received their just deserts.

In the scene in *Evelina*, the impeccable Lord Orville suggests that "the only female in the play worthy of being mentioned to these ladies is Angelica," to which Mrs. Mirvan, Evelina's companion, replies: "Yet in a trial so long, there seems rather too much consciousness of her power." This gives Lord Orville an opportunity not only to agree with her but to deliver a short lecture on the new female ideal, which concludes as follows: "Generosity without delicacy, like wit without judgement, generally gives as much pain as pleasure. The uncertainty with which she keeps Valentine, and her manner of trifling with his temper, gives no very favorable idea of her own."[13] Evelina is thus warned that Lord Orville disapproves of women who employ power of any sort to get what they want from men. Since she is an innocent girl from the country, who is constantly acted upon and worried that she will appear to Lord Orville to have placed herself in a given compromising situation on her own initiative, she is in absolutely no danger of violating his

implicit injunction. Burney captures the anxieties of female adolescence better, perhaps, than any novelist has done since. But power
is so threatening to a Burney heroine that she never really grows
up.[14] So little consciousness of her own power does Evelina have
that when Lord Orville does make his inevitable proposal, her
reaction is to faint, to lose consciousness entirely.

The initial popularity of the Gothic novel at the end of the
eighteenth century thus comes at a point in the history of the novel
at which the sphere of virtuous action has narrowed to a very thin
line. Confined to passivity, a woman cannot determine her own
actions, or even influence in any active way what other people think
about her. Most serious of all, as a comment on the lives of women
imprisoned by these strictures, she cannot even protect herself from
poverty. Burney's last novel, *The Wanderer* (1814), is a vivid portrait
of socially enjoined helplessness in conflict with the need to make
a living. The sentimental novel is thus a vehicle for protesting "the
wrongs of woman," and surely owes much of its popularity with
women readers to this fact. But its heroines cannot even imagine,
much less act upon, liberatory alternatives.

The sentimental novel is, as Katherine Rogers has pointed out,
on the side of women as they struggle against the limitations within
which they must live if they do not want to forfeit respectability. It
does this "by appealing to the emotions, but without shocking."[15]
Yet emotional release devoid of action, as Mrs. Barbauld observes,
is not an agent of change. Behind the sentimental novel, perhaps
as an explanation for its popular success, is the belief that a rectification of "the wrongs of woman" can take place without challenging
its structure. Yet if the debate around woman's sphere had not fed
into a wider current of radical ideas, including challenges to the
division of the human race into two nonoverlapping halves, the
sympathetic depictions of women as victims that we find in women
writers from Mrs. Haywood on would have had little impact on the
position of women. De-emphasizing female agency, the sentimen-
talists used the novel to place the femine sphere at the center of
their plots, and to reveal it as the power vacuum it was. Conscious
of their largely female audience, but also of their critics, they opened
a door for their readers but did not urge them to walk through it.

If we look for a line of development between *Clarissa, Julia de Roubigné*, and the Gothic, the feminine Gothic plays not a marginal but a central role in opening up new possibilities for the novel. The common theme that links these three is framed by Julia as follows: "In every one's own case, there is a rule of judging which is not the less powerful that [*sic*] one cannot express it. I insist not on the memory of Savillon; I can forget him, I think. . . . But should I wed any man, be his worth what it may, if I feel not that lively preference for him, that waits not on reasoning to persuade its consent?"[16] For Julia's "lively preference" to be a valid basis for marriage, to be given primacy over parental wishes, class allegiance, and other expressions of public opinion, it must spring from a place where those structures set up after the fall to protect man from his own sinful nature are not the final authority. The extension of this Protestant impulse into the secular domain of home and family involves nothing less than a modification of the myth of the fall itself.

NOTES

1. Lawrence Stone, *Family, Sex and Marriage in England 1500–1800* (New York: Harper and Row, 1977), 282, 284.

2. Eliza Haywood, "Preface" to *Lasselia, or The Self-Abandoned* (London, 1723) in *Novel and Romance 1700–1800: A Documentary Record*, ed. Ioan Williams (London: Routledge and Kegan Paul, 1970), 79.

3. See John Tinnon Taylor, *Early Opposition to the English Novel: The Popular Reaction from 1760 to 1830* (New York: Columbia University Press, 1943), esp. ch. III, "Women and Fiction," 52–86.

4. W. H. McBurney, "Mrs. Penelope Aubin and the Early Early Eighteenth-Century English Novel," *Huntington Library Quarterly* 20 (May 1957), 250.

5. Eliza Haywood, *Love in excess, or, The Fatal Inquiry*, (1719), 5th ed. (London, 1724), 28. Future references will be to this edition and cited in the text.

6. For an elaboration of this point from a different angle see Margaret Doody, "Deserts, Ruins and Troubled Waters: Female Dreams in Fiction

and the Development of the Gothic Novel," *Genre* 10 (Winter 1977), 529–99.

7. For a discussion of this type of heroine in the work of Eliza Haywood, see Mary Ann Schofield, *Quiet Rebellion: The Fictional Heroines of Eliza Fowler Haywood* (Washington: University Press of America, 1982), 49–65.

8. Samuel Johnson, *Rambler*, no. 4 (Mar. 31, 1750).

9. James Beattie, "On Fable and Romance," in *Dissertations Moral and Critical* (London, 1783), 569.

10. J. M. S. Tompkins, *The Popular Novel in England 1770–1800* (London: Constable, 1932), 105.

11. John Aiken and A. L. [Barbauld] Aiken, "An Enquiry into those Kinds of Distress which Excite Agreeable Sensations," in *Miscellaneous Pieces in Prose* (London, 1773), 200.

12. Ibid., 211–12.

13. Fanny Burney, *Evelina or A Young Lady's Entrance into the World* (1778; New York: W. W. Norton, 1965), 70–71. For a discussion of power in *Evelina* see Judith Lowder Newton, *Power and Subversion: Social Strategies in British Fiction 1778–1860* (Athens: University of Georgia Press, 1981), 23–54.

14. Patricia Meyer Spacks, *The Female Imagination* (New York: Knopf, 1975), esp. "The Adolescent as Heroine," 113–58.

15. Katherine Rogers, *Feminism in Eighteenth-Century England* (Urbana: University of Illinois Press, 1982), 149.

16. Henry Mackenzie, *Julia de Roubigné*, in *The British Novelists*, ed. A. L. Barbauld (London, 1810), vol. 29, 254.

CHAPTER III

Milton's Progeny

THE TRANSFORMATION of "history" into "nature" through myth is as much a part of the revolutionary process as are changes in the mode of production.[1] For Milton, history was part of God's creation, participating, along with nature, in a providential design. When he wanted to "justify the ways of God to men," including the Restoration and the defeat of Cromwell, he drew upon the myth of the fall, which incorporates into God's redemptive scheme domination and hierarchy, suffering and the need for obedience. But if all forms of rebellion are both blasphemous and treasonous, the myth that has been interpreted to make this point can be reconciled only with difficulty to the needs of a revolutionary class. Hence the importance of the triumph of the weak and virtuous over the strong and corrupt in both the Old and New Testaments. It is when this motif gets read through the new gender politics that we get a new version of the myth of the fall, with a new Adam and, most importantly, a new Eve.

Throughout Christian history, interpretations and revisions of the Genesis story have occupied a central place in its discourse on gender. For the early Christian communities, inwardly divided and outwardly persecuted by the militarily superior Romans, gender relations were seen in the light of a need to prepare for the imminent collapse of earthly power relations as they were then constituted. As Elaine Pagels has shown, a diversity of opinion on the role of women was held in these communities, and even inscribed into the texts that became canonical as the New Testament.[2] But after the conversion of the emperor Constantine in 313, "the politics of paradise," as Pagels calls it, underwent a radical shift as it found itself confronted with new problems stemming from a new set of power relations. The enemy within replaced the enemy without, and woman became, in the Augustinian vision that prevailed from the fourth century on, Satan's principal ally in setting into motion that inner enemy.

The "new Eve" who replaced this vision of woman can be seen as the central figure in a similar, and similarly dramatic, revision of the biblical creation story. Her first fully developed, mass-produced representation is Richardson's *Pamela*, a novel whose humble origins are the conduct book, written not for the wise and discerning but for an audience unsure of its footing in a shifting class alignment. Conduct books rank low in the hierarchy of genres, but their function is similar to that of myths: to speak with authority about a particular culture, to ground behavior that is time-bound and adaptive in a system of transcendent truth. Given the aims of its author, *Pamela* becomes an easy object for what Northrop Frye calls "kidnapping," that is, "the absorbing of it into the ideology of an ascendant class."[3] So the new Eve, whom Jesus addresses in *Paradise Lost* as the mother of his mother, Mary, (XI, 183; cf. V, 385 and Genesis 3:20), becomes superior to Adam when motherhood is redefined.

In exploring the ways in which the ideology of separate spheres reshapes that myth, and the role of the Gothic in subverting that project, I use Milton's version of this myth as my point of departure, in part because Milton was so widely known by literary figures and the literate public during the period under investigation in this book. James Thorpe points out that there were over a hundred editions of *Paradise Lost* during the eighteenth century, and it might be argued that "a majority of eighteenth-century verse can be said to have been modelled on, imitative of, or influenced by Milton."[4] Moreover, unlike poets of previous generations, his influence extended beyond the literary few, not only in periodicals but also through John Wesley's edition, intended for his followers at the lower end of the social ladder. "It would be difficult to imagine," Thorpe concludes, "a more exalted poetic reputation, and the attitude of the eighteenth century toward Milton will probably never be duplicated toward any writer."

But over and above the matter of its wide readership, Milton's treatment of the fall, as Diane McColley has argued, is the first to present the unfallen world, and Eve within it, as "an image of the goodness that can be found and practiced even in the fallen world by regenerate persons whose actions can help restore it, or parts of it, to something nearer its primitive brightness."[5] Writing before the separation of spheres, he did not designate, as clearly as was later done, which parts might be thus restored. Rather, he points up the contradictions that follow from connecting regeneration to an ideal of innocence too narrowly defined, and takes on directly the issue of subordination and the problems it creates in the "heavenly family." Gothic writers take up these arguments and use them to make a case for disobedience itself, under certain conditions, on the part of a child against a parent, while at the same time showing that female innocence, protected behind walls, is ineffectual in the fight against evil, and may even unwittingly promote it.

In using Milton in this way I am entering an argument with a body of criticism that construes generational relationships between writers as an Oedipal battle, with each new generation aiming to kill off the previous one in order to create a space for its own vision. Harold Bloom's compelling model has been taken up by Sandra Gilbert and Susan Gubar, who argue that women writers, unable to kill their fathers in direct combat, devise "cover stories" and other subversive strategies for displacing them indirectly.[6] I do not wish to deny that antagonism and displacement may be a necessary part of the creative process. But I am suggesting that for the Gothic novelists discussed in these pages Milton may have been a source rather than a "bogey." Displacement is one strategy for dealing with a dominant culture, or a literary figure who embodies that culture, but appropriation is an equally revolutionary one. Throughout this book, I will be arguing that Gothic writers used Miltonic material for ends far different from Milton's, and that the early successors of Walpole did the same with that male predecessor.

Milton's rhetorical strategy in *Paradise Lost*, as Stanley Fish has pointed out, was "to recreate in the mind of the reader . . . the drama of the Fall, to make him [*sic*] fall exactly as Adam did, and with Adam's clarity, that is to say, 'not deceiv'd.' "[7] Readers of both sexes identified with Adam, who is more spiritually developed than Eve, and the carrier of the meaning of Christian consciousness. But the historical shift in the social position of women that we have seen in the previous chapter was not made "natural" by a myth that attributed the entrance of "Death into the World, and all our woe," to the disobedience of a woman. As "the duties of the female sex" fanned out from simple obedience to "contributing daily and hourly" to the comfort of family members, the new discourse engendered an alteration of the myth that made natural the new relations between the sexes.

With its relatively open form and its popularity with women readers, the novel readily absorbed and gave shape to the proliferating cultural scripts that constituted woman's new relationship to the fall as represented in Genesis. Using the same materials out of which Milton fashioned his poem "doctrinal and exemplary to a nation," novelists of the eighteenth century set forth a new myth which accounted for the ascendancy of the bourgeois class and its values, while at the same time removing that social regrouping from the domain of historical contingency. And the figure that bodied forth the triumphant conclusion of this drama was not a hero but a heroine, not Adam "not deceiv'd," but Eve rewarded for her virtue.

She is very much at the center of the emerging myth of home as a type of Paradise Regained here on earth. David Daiches has remarked that for Richardson, Eden "is no garden but an estate, and Adam is a landlord with tenants, Eve a lady with social duties and dangers, and the serpent a neighbouring squire who violates the rules of the game by combining the genuine attractiveness of rank with an immoral character."[8] The lady who resists the serpent is required to exercise surveillance: she sees evil coming and keeps it at bay. For Hannah More, the proper exercise of this power was the whole point of female education, something akin to a divine calling. "Christianity, driven out from the rest of the world, has still, blessed be to God, a 'strong hold' in this country; and though it be the special duty of the appointed 'watchman, now that he seeth the sword come upon the land, to blow the trumpet . . .'; yet in this sacred garrison, *impregnable but by neglect,* YOU, too, have an awful post,—that of arming the minds of the rising race with the 'shield of faith, whereby they shall be able to quench the fiery darts of the wicked.' "[9] This image of a militant "true wife" is reiterated, sixty-six years later, in Ruskin's *Sesame and Lilies:*

The man, in his rough work in the open world, must encounter all peril and trial; to him, therefore, must be the failure, the offence, the inevitable error; often he must be wounded or subdued; often misled; and *always* hardened. But he guards the woman from all this; within his house, as ruled by her, unless she herself has sought it, need enter no danger, no cause of error or offence. This is the true nature of home—it is the place of Peace; the shelter, not only from all injury, but from all terror, doubt, and division. So far as it is not this, it is not home; . . . it is then only part of that outer world which you have roofed over, and lighted a fire in. But so far as it is a sacred place . . . and roof and fire are only types of a nobler shade and light, . . . so far it vindicates the name, and fulfills the praise, of Home.[10]

In such a paradise, and with such an Eve, the fall might never have taken place.

Almost midway between *Paradise Lost* and "Of Queens' Gardens" Walpole's *The Castle of Otranto* made its appearance. Its publication in 1764 is followed, though not immediately, by a spate of novels, primarily by women, which feature haunted castles owned by usurping aristocrats, heroines who are persecuted but not "ruined" by these false owners, and young men of the sentimental-hero type who marry the heroines in the end. What does it mean for the castle to be haunted? It means that the owner of the castle is trying to conceal a secret upon which his continued ownership depends. In consequence, the castle becomes a space where the next generation cannot be produced, or more generally, where the domestic activities over which women are beginning to "rule" cannot be carried on. The exposure of the secret, then, sometimes accompanied by the destruction of the castle, frees the female protagonist to reassert the primacy of "home" and its values by marrying the man of her choice, not as an innocent "young lady" but as a heroine who has encountered evil, learned from it, and triumphed over it.

This heroine is not the new Eve of the Evangelical vision of home as a type of heaven, nor is the castle "the shelter, not only from all injury, but from all terror, doubt, and division." In fact, it is because women are restricted by an ideal of unconditional obedience that they are powerless to rid the home of the always already present danger of unchecked male power. Departing from this model of female virtue, the Gothic heroine transgresses the boundaries that divide the spheres in order to carry out the mission her culture has assigned to her. Often she must actively challenge the prejudice against female inheritance in order to gain what is rightly hers. She invariably disobeys a parent and chooses knowledge over innocence, without being banished from the garden of wedded bliss. In presenting such transgressions, the creators of the Gothic drew upon Miltonic materials, though not necessarily to Ruskinian ends.

In justifying his vision of God's ways, Milton used the method of his angel Raphael, who tells Adam about events in heaven by "lik'ning spiritual to corporeal forms," and thus portraying an invisible world in terms of a visible one. The corporeal form that underlies the relationships between various personages in *Paradise Lost* is the family, the father of which is not the tyrannical patriarch that William Empson perceived, yet one who nevertheless insists that what he wills is fate.[11] All the other personages are brothers except Eve, who is Adam's sister who becomes his wife. Male bonding, and the jealously that undermines it, are at the heart of Milton's view of the drama of salvation.

But this underlying structure of "blood" relationships exists inside a cosmogony that was not available *as truth* to eighteenth century Gothicists, nor to the Gothic revivalists who succeeded them in the nineteenth century.[12] At the heart of this system is the Great Chain of Being, where

> one Almighty is, from whom
> All things proceed, and up to him return,
> If not deprav'd from good, created all
> Such to perfection, one first matter all,
> Indu'd with various forms, various degrees
> Of substance, and in things that live, of life;
> But more refin'd, more spiritous, and pure,
> As nearer to him plac'd, or nearer tending

> Each in thir several active Spheres assign'd,
> Till body up to spirit work, in bounds
> Proportioned to each kind.
>
> (V, 469–79)

Here we have the ground on which the home as type of heaven might be justified. Raphael speculates to Adam and Eve that, just as angels can move down the scale of nature and eat real food, so

> Your bodies may at last turn all to spirit,
> Improv'd by tract of time, and wing'd ascend
> Ethereal, as wee, or may at choice
> Here or in Heav'nly Paradises dwell;
>
> (V, 497–500)

Because this was still the unfallen world, one could roof over any part of it, and light a fire therein.

Not so in industrial England. Even in Milton's time the "old science" that united ethics with the natural world was being discredited as an adequate description of the latter, and God and nature would never again "bid the same" in the way Milton envisions in *Paradise Lost*. Nevertheless, the problems in human conduct for which his cosmogony provides an analogue in natural law were, if anything, more pressing in the world of early capitalism. Milton's Raphael suggested that human beings could make earth "the shadow of Heav'n," but they needed to work "in bounds," ascending one note on the scale at a time. Eating the apple entailed a refusal to do this, a leap. Yet early capitalism entailed a revolution against the limits set by "nature" thus envisioned, a rejection of the distinctions that underlay Dante's condemnation of usury, for instance, and that bound the workday to "natural" demands of seedtime and harvest, daylight and darkness. Blake called the mills of his day Satanic, yet they were the basis of the very bourgeois prosperity that made possible the separation of spheres.

Limits, boundaries, and circumscription are traces of divine perfection in *Paradise Lost*, and Milton's God is an encloser of spaces. Heaven is surrounded by a crystal wall, which only Christ can open up to expel the defeated rebels (VI, 860–66). Moving down the scale, we have paradise, above whose "verdurous wall" stood "a circling row / Of goodliest Trees" (IV, 143–47), whose "Insuperable hight" makes the garden difficult, but not impossible, to penetrate. Finally there is hell, with its ostensibly impassable "thrice three-fold" gates (II, 644–48). But since these gates are guarded by Sin and Death, Satan's consort and only son, he has little difficulty persuading them to let him out. God is thus making a joke at the expense of Satan: *he* thinks escaping from an enclosed space will make him free, whereas in fact Hell is not the most but the least enclosed space in God's universe.

The virtue of Milton's God is expressed in his first act, in which he, originally "uncircumscrib'd," *retires* into the boundaries of a figure which expresses his perfection, a circle. But in the world of the Restoration, "enclosure" was coming to mean something very different. In the first place, it refers to a land policy that accelerated in the eighteenth century.[13] But it also refers, as Foucault has shown us, to a solution to a problem in part caused by dislocation of people and spearheaded by parliamentary acts of enclosure. Confining the poor and compelling them to work, a practice begun in the late seventeenth century, led to discriminations among those requiring confinement—the merely idle poor, the criminal, and the mad. The modern prison and the asylum, Foucault observes, arise from a reforming mentality, a desire to substitute humane supervision, regulation, and recovery for what was deemed essentially irresponsible behavior.[14] In a postfeudal society that defines freedom as the right to move around at will, walled-in spaces represent the abrogation of that right.

At the time Milton was writing, and into the early eighteenth century, the practice of concentrating inherited wealth in the hands of the eldest son was becoming increasingly common among both landed and mercantile families, the former aiming to regain the control of the economy that they had lost during the Civil War, the latter wishing to enter the aristocracy through marriage. This "increasing subordination of marriage to the increase of landed wealth, at the expense of other motives for marriage" required the obedience of both daughters and sons.[15] Primogeniture fits into this emphasis on economic control by parents, at the same time that it is increasingly criticized, along with the sibling rivalry it generates, as incompatible with an individualistic family ideology.

One French treatise, written in 1661, decries the situation of younger children in Catholic countries:

> People are afraid that if they share their property equally among all their children, they will not be able to add to the glory and luster of the family as much as they would wish. The eldest son will not be able to hold and keep the posts and offices which they are trying to obtain for him, if his brothers and sisters enjoy the same advantages as he. They must therefore be rendered incapable of challenging this right of his. They must be sent into monasteries against their will and sacrificed early in life to the interests of the one who is destined for the world and its vanity.[16]

The forcing of younger brothers and sisters into a cloistered existence, a recurring motif in the Gothic novel, had not been an option for English parents since the dissolution of the monasteries in 1542. But given that criticisms were beginning to be raised against fathers "who do not love their sons equally, but introduce distinctions where Nature put none," it is significant that the mythic apparatus by which Milton justified "distinctions" of hierarchy, the Great Chain of Being with its long history, was being challenged politically even before scientific discoveries in the eighteenth century invalidated it as a cosmology.

Yet this contradiction-ridden institution is the principal corporeal form that Milton used to explain the entrance of evil into God's creation. In *Paradise Lost* God appears to initiate this rivalry by elevating one of his "sons" above the others with this rather extreme declaration:

> This day have I begot whom I declare
> My only Son, and on this holy Hill
> Him have anointed, whom ye now behold
> At my right hand; your head I him appoint;
> And by my Self have sworn to him shall bow
> All knees in Heav'n, and shall confess him Lord:
>
> (V, 603–8)

The use of the word "begot" almost asks us to interpret this decree in a Satanic manner. Even if Christ was not born "on this day," but merely "exalted," such a political act could certainly give Satan grounds for concluding that it was God who first injected discord into the happy family of father and angels by showing favoritism to one son after creating them all equal. Like the prohibition of the fruit, the demand for a symbolic social gesture (that "all knees in Heav'n" shall bow) is an arbitrary one. Even granted that it was not uncommon for aristocratic children to kneel in the presence of their parents, just as subjects were expected to kneel before their king, it still sounds like the *idée fixe* of a parent intent on instituting deferential rather than affective relationships in the heavenly home.[17]

This interpretation of the passage is complicated by the fact that, as Milton's readers would certainly have recognized, God's text is Paul's Epistle to the Hebrews (I:6–7), which was also, in the Anglican liturgy, the Epistle for Christmas Day. This language, and its association with the historical moment in which this son entered the sphere of human time, introduces into God's message to the angels a sequence of future possibilities for his anointed "favorite" that Satan cannot pick up. Much more shall be required of this "favorite" than of his younger "siblings." God is speaking a secret language which the initiated reader can understand, but to which the perennial ingrate, Satan, is deaf. "Holy hermeneutics," to adapt a felicitous phrase of Andrew Marvell, is here, as it is throughout *Paradise Lost*, both a sign of the condition of salvation and the way to it.

Yet even at this level of conjectured reader response the scene cuts two ways. An expectation of absolute obedience to a parent based on the child's ignorance, an ignorance, moreover, that is fostered by withholding on the part of the parent through the use of a secret language the child cannot understand, goes against the grain of the close-knit "affective nuclear family" that was coming into favor at the time Milton was writing. Advocates of the use of reason and explanation with children must acknowledge that children's powers of reasoning are initially very limited. To the preverbal infant, the language of the parents is wholly secret, and the possessor of that secret is, like Milton's God, omnipotent within the domain of events controlled by the possession of language. To a child with sufficient verbal skill to apprehend this signifier of unevenly distributed power, it might well appear unjust, especially if the possesion of language is backed up by other forms of power expressed, as God does in his speech to his angels, with a threat of punishment.

Thus hierarchy in the heavenly family, backed up by force, is perceived as "natural" if the members of a family are part of a chain that extends downward from the father to the youngest child. Yet Satan's case for equality among children envisions as "natural" a different sort of family bonds that are closer to the bourgeois "affective nuclear" model. Heavenly and Satanic speech are both present in the poem, representing different interpretive matrices and combining as Bakhtinian heteroglossia. By juxtaposing two systems of signification, the "old science" and the new discourse on the family, Milton's poem incorporates into its structure a critique of his own "justification." For critics such as Blake and Shelley, that critique becomes the primary text of the poem.

Paradise Lost thus dramatizes a rupture in patriarchal ideology that Gothic novelists take up. The Gothic villain twists the unfairness of primogeniture to his own purposes, just as Satan did.[18] But it is through this rupture that disobedience to a parent can emerge as sometimes virtuous. The villain cannot be rewarded for his rebellion, but the heroine, defending her purity, can escape from the castle in which she is confined, redeem Eve's act of disobedience, and subvert the myth that placed her below her husband. And she demonstrates her moral superiority not simply by passivity and refusal of seduction, but by actively pursuing her own marital object.

The Gothic villain is usually a second son and thus a victim of primogeniture and the practices linked to it, such as involuntary detention in a monastery. But his discontent presents itself as a discontent with all limits, in particular those imposed by the purportedly limitless commodity, capital.[19] Extravagance without industry is an unforgivable failing in an economic system where patrimony can be increased or destroyed with a suddenness unknown to precapitalist exchange economies. Rather than using industry and perspicacity, qualities that were being presented in the post-Restoration pulpit as signs of divine favor, to surpass by means of merit the unfairly acquired fortune of his elder brother, the villain goes into debt and even demands that his brother pay his creditors.[20] He resorts to vice and crime, both economic and sexual, to take what he cannot acquire by merit and hard work.

But it is when this Satanic "sibling," driven by a discontent that knows no limits, becomes a father and thus a person with power over his own dependents, that rebellion in the Gothic world finds an appropriate target—a parent who demands blind obedience and who will sacrifice his own child to his will to power and his need for money. In *Paradise Lost*, obedience was never "blind," but simply a way of delimiting the scale of nature. In the absence of this touchstone for wrongdoing, the Gothicists substitute the bourgeois one of merit. Just as Satan refused to accept an unequal distribution of this asset among the angels, so the Gothic villain refuses to accept the fact that the deity of the bourgeoisie may prefer an Abel over a Cain. Not only prosperity but even being honored by one's children cannot be demanded unconditionally. When the criterion of merit is brought into the domain of family politics, the Fifth Commandment is being stretched considerably.

Insofar as the Gothic father asserts his power by confining others, he is an inversion of the Miltonic deity who cast Satan out of heaven but did not, in all seriousness, imprison him. Milton's Satan forces Adam and Eve out of an enclosed space, but since enclosure is good, he cannot take possession of it. The Gothic fall leaves Satan in control of a walled Eden, where he can stay as long as its walls conceal the crime that allows him to be there. The fall in the Gothic world, then, in line with the tradition of the spotless regainer of paradise set in motion by Richardson, happens to a virginal place, not to a virginal person. The Gothic landscape is in this respect very much like the world through whose manifold dangers Pamela and Evelina make their way: only a heroine who does not fall can emerge from her trial-filled journey to make herself a home. By having the villain violate the Garden rather than the heroine, we can have an "angel" for the "house" in the process of reconstitution, and at the same time provide her with some real evil over which to triumph.

The foregrounding of women as subjects through which the experience of salvation is conveyed raises contradictions about the enclosed space she "rules." A space where "terror, doubt, and division" cannot enter is a place where innocence cannot be undermined by the "rough world" outside it. But walls that cannot be penetrated become a prison. A castle turned into a prison and reconverted into a home (or destroyed so that its prisoners can establish a home elsewhere) is the underlying structure of the feminine Gothic. But not all enclosed spaces can become homes. Walls can confine and conceal as well as protect, and evil can flourish in a climate of privacy no less easily than good. Where the home is destroyed utterly and the destroyer continues to wander upon the face of the earth, we have the Lewisite or masculine Gothic. Both types focus on domestic space, but see it from different points of view.

The Gothic landscape is filled with enclosed but negative spaces which, like hell, extend and augment the fallen castle, now haunted by the ghost of its concealed past but capable, perhaps, of restoration. These are institutions whose antipathy to the true nature of domestic life is perceived as intrinsic: monasteries, most obviously, but also the prisons and insane asylums whose modern form emerged in the eighteenth century. In the Gothic novels of this period, these institutions are set up as foils to the domestic sphere, an opposition that covers over the commonality of their "humane" procedures—in particular their shift from spectacle and brute force to a cultivation of guilt, remorse, and a sense of responsibility on the part of their inmates—with the methods of child-rearing being advocated for the mother-centered home.[21]

Institutions of enforced confinement thus called up a particular historically based cluster of associations for eighteenth-century readers, even as the power they represented was undergoing a transformation, one that brought them more in line with the aims of the well-run home. But in the Gothic world their overtly horror-producing attributes are compounded by the villainy of the husband or relatives who force their victim into them, or by the looming presence of the Inquisition. The opposition between these "fallen" institutions and the home is especially sharp when the home is defined as a place where coercion, on the one hand, and hypocrisy, on the other, are experiences that belong to the outer world only. As we know, violence did not disappear from the home, but its purported absence created new possibilities for conflicts and tensions.

A prison may be connected to the Inquisition, and thus to the Church. Or it may be located underneath a castle, concealing the secret that haunts the castle as well as providing a repository of coercive power for its villain-owner. If the villain has a daughter, niece, or ward, these Satanic impulses appear in force when she comes of marriageable age. Then, to make sure she will never enjoy "pleasure not for him ordain'd," he insists that she marry a seemingly wealthy and well-connected aristocrat with a personality similar to, or capable of being dominated by, his own. When he hears her inevitable refusal, he may then do more than turn the refuge of her youth into a prison: he may confine her to an unseen part of it, from which rescue seems impossible. Under the villain's control, the home becomes not a sanctuary from terror but a source of it. In contrast, the home that is the end of her journey toward a happy ending is very much hers.

One of the real achievements of the Gothic tradition is that it conjures up, in its undefined representation of heroinely terror, an omnipresent sense of impending rape without ever mentioning the word. A young girl pure enough to be a heroine cannot have the forbidden knowledge that would lead her to suspect the presence of ideas of *that* nature in the minds of men. Given the constraints on female virtue, terror becomes, in the hands of Gothic practitioners, *the* intense emotion (more intense, certainly, than the tears of the sentimental heroine) that a "good" female character in a novel can have without threatening her innocence with respect to male lust. Pamela's terror came from knowing what her pursuer was after, but the terror of the Gothic heroine is simply that of being confined and then abandoned, and beyond that, of being, in an unspecified yet absolute way, completely surrounded by superior male power.

The villain, in turn, is not provoked by lust so much as by a wish to make his victim suffer for imposing limits on his male will. The substitution of economic interests for sexual ones (or the absence of that substitution in the case of Lewis) suggests a divergence of purpose between the Radcliffian Gothic, which expands the female sphere while stripping its villains of Lovelace's dangerous charms, and Lewis's outright attack on the ideal of "passionlessness." Thus the Radcliffian villain, rather than violating the heroine over whom he has absolute power, turns her innocent, Edenic life into an imprisoned one. He seals her off in a space he thinks impenetrable, and proceeds to try to break her will, assuming that before her beauty fades he can transform her body into the capital he needs in order to continue his life of dissipation.

As an alternative to turning his castle into a prison, the villain may force her into a convent if she does not marry the man of his choice, giving her the alternatives of virtual rape, in the form of sex with a man she despises, or celibacy. Since in England monastic lands and buildings had no actual social function, other than providing wealth for those to whom they had been distributed, they were available as vehicles for other concerns.[22] Like the asylum, the prison, and the "fallen" castle controlled by the villain, the monastery inverts the companionate ideal of domestic life for which Milton made Eden a type. Its members as they appear in the thoroughly Protestant Gothic novel simulate familial bonds by calling each other "father," "mother," and "sister," while denying the true basis of family life, chaste sexuality. At the same time, they use seductive wiles to lure innocent men and women into their clutches.

In the real Middle Ages, the convent may have been for some women an authentic "haven in a heartless world." But the landscape of the English Gothic novel, in its early stages, is hardly complete without at least one monastery with a wife or child forcibly held within its walls. The fact that this means of disposing of younger sons and undowried daughters had not been open to English parents for over two centuries allowed Gothic writers to use these spaces in an almost purely symbolic way, though traces of England's Catholic past were still visible to readers, some of whom were living on land that had once belonged to the Church, some even in buildings with names like Nun Appleton and Northanger Abbey. These "fallen" buildings had, of course, been claimed long ago for domestic life, and the horrors of life in them were probably no worse than the lot of a woman whose marriage had been arranged. Nevertheless it is easy to see how they might be regarded, by generations removed from those who had profited from the demise of Catholicism, as haunted.

The Church of Rome, because it is not part of the real landscape of England, can be used in the Gothic to point up abuses existing in real institutions such as the family, with whose worst elements, in plot after Gothic plot, the Church aligns itself. What is being made "natural" is not the displacement of Catholicism by Protestantism, which had been thoroughly absorbed into popular consciousness, but the shift away from the absolute power of the father over his wife and children. The role of the daughter in this myth-making process is to embody Protestant individualism, as castle, convent, and prison work together to thwart the "natural" desire of young people to be sexual within marriage. With its network of closed spaces hostile to the "lively preference" of the daughter, the imaginary medieval landscape of the Gothic novel becomes an analogue for the corrupt, male-dominated world against which Mrs. Haywood's heroines were powerless to prevail.

A map of the Gothic cosmos, then, would consist of a central ghost-ridden interior space that may be augmented with ancillary structures, spaces that were never capable of enclosing pure, unfallen domestic life but which, with the castle, form an interconnected "world" from which escape is a necessary condition for salvation. Besides confining virtue, these secondary spaces can serve as launching places for an attack on the castle that turns it into a fallen enclosure, just as Satan's Pandemonium, built to parody heaven, serves as a launching place for his attack on Eden. Mary Shelley uses Frankenstein's laboratory in this way, carrying the Gothic convention of the monastery one step further. Here we have a space that is hostile to domesticity, one from which women are excluded while the female function of giving birth is replicated without them. Abandoned there, the monster must escape from its confines if he is to survive. Yet it is not until he enters the circle of the Frankenstein household and kills his first victim that an irrevocable "fall" takes place. For it is only at this point that the idyllic paradise where Victor grew up comes under the control of one who, denied companionship by *his* creator, sets out on a path of revenge that both imitates and comments on the ways of Satan and his maker.

Sometimes the castle can be purged of the villain's influence and repossessed as a place where family life is able to flourish. This element of the Gothic happy ending brings to an end the "dark ages" of universal Catholicism and feudalism, and connects the coming into being of the new pair with the advent of a class brought to the fore by the same divine Providence that has rid the castle of its usurper and brought its true heir to it. The bourgeoisie was then able to read, in Gothic fiction, the creation myth of its own coming into being: of how it "repaired the ruins" of its medieval past as part of God's scheme of providential history. But the very terms in which this victory is represented raise questions about innocence itself, about the validity of the division between "home" and "world" that the new myth presents as part of nature, about the capacity of any enclosed space to keep evil out permanently, if the innocent person enclosed therein is unable to detect it. Again, we can see the dramatization of this contradiction in Milton, where Uriel, unable to detect the true purpose of Satan, directs him toward the garden he is seeking. Milton explains:

> For neither Man nor Angel can discern
> Hypocrisy, the only evil that walks
> Invisible, except to God alone,
> By his permissive will, through Heav'n and Earth:
> And oft though wisdom wake, suspicion sleeps
> At wisdom's Gate, while goodness thinks no ill
> Where no ill seems:
>
> (III, 682–89)

In the fallen Gothic world, enclosure cannot prevent the fall of the house. Thus, what the heroine needs is not the protection of men against the unfamiliarity of the world, nor a role that limits her relationship to evil to one of inexperienced surveillance, as More and Ruskin would have it, but a capacity to take the initiative, to face danger and follow her convictions no matter how slim the possibility of success appears. Her lack of power is precisely what fuels her determination to win against a network of oppressive relations that from her unfallen vantage point are totally corrupt. Women in Milton's scheme are inferior because they are literally the weaker sex. The Gothic heroine is superior to her Satanic father or father surrogate, for the very same reason.

In moving Eve to the center of the drama of middle-class salvation, the Gothicists took a radical position on the contradictions between patriarchal authority and the weaker but purer sex that are part of the ideology by which the bourgeoisie justified its moral and economic supremacy. Support for the rights of the young in matters of marriage was growing, at least in print, along with a revaluation of childhood as a period of innocence over which vigilant protection was necessary. But, as we have just seen, the notion of a walled Eden guarded by those who are innocent of the experience of evil is intrinsically problematic. What is radical in the Gothic solution is that the terms "home" and "world" are inverted: evil is thus enclosed in the home and freedom lies in the world beyond it, however dangerous. It is the fact that the evil is concealed that gives it the power to "haunt" over time. Once it is let out, the house becomes pure. Therefore the purification of the house is accomplished not by locking the gates of Eden but by leaving them open.

What they are left open *for* is the freedom of the heroine to choose her husband in defiance of her father. As with the issue of primogeniture, which devolves into an issue of "children's rights," the contradiction between the power of the father to make all major decisions, which is reinforced by the ideology of separate spheres, and the purity of the daughter, which is also reinforced by that ideology, is in the Gothic novel resolved in the daughter's favor. That this fictional resolution becomes popular at the time when pressures to marry for motives other than love are on the increase, as one historian of eighteenth-century marriage settlements has observed, suggests that "separate spheres" increased, rather than diminished, the power of the father in the family, especially around issues of marriage choice.

This balance of power, too, was being argued out at the level of the law, especially in the parliamentary debates on the Hardwicke Act. Prior to 1753, a valid marriage required only a verbal exchange of vows in front of witnesses followed by consummation. Verbal consent of both parties was essential, while parental consent, though important, was not.[23] A struggle in the early eighteenth century between the civil courts and the ecclesiastical courts created considerable chaos, in which women had in fact much less protection than men. The Hardwicke Act made a church wedding, entered in a parish register and signed by both parties after banns had been read on three consecutive Sundays in the parish where one of the parties lived, the only legally binding contract.

The point of this law was not to protect women as such but to protect parents from having a valuable piece of their property "carried off by a man of low birth, or perhaps by an infamous sharper."[24] It forbade marriages without parental consent to persons under the age of twenty-ne, and stressed prudence over passion as a motive for marrying. Opponents of the bill saw it as an aristocratic plot to prevent marriages across class lines and argued against making it more difficult for a young commoner to marry up. "The highest bloom of a woman's beauty," observed one of this number, "is from sixteen to twenty-one; it is then that a woman of no fortune has the best chance for disposing of herself to advantage in marriage; shall we make it impossible for her to do so [he asks] without the consent of an indigent and mercenary father?" The reality of a mercenary father is one that can be recognized in the Gothic novel, even, we should note, by Henry Tilney.

The subversive nature of this Gothic secret may best be understood, I think, if we see in it a way of resolving, in fiction, problems and tensions in the world of the reader arising from the polarization of work and home, where "home" is a sanctuary guarded by an angel whose education may have rendered her sufficient to stand, but who is also, theoretically at least, "free to fall." In the Gothic, the fall need not be anticipated with anxiety: it has been removed in time to a past whose negative features call forth popular conceptions of "the Middle Ages," the locus of the novel's present time, but are also sufficiently visible in the present time of its readers to elicit their recognition. A Gothic author allows evil into the house, not as a lapse on the part of a "true wife" but as a residue from a more primitive, unenlightened era. The castle walls then cease to represent protection, but instead mark off an area to be purified from the demands of absolute obedience levied in the name of a contaminated religion and a contaminated domestic ideology.

Success in this endeavor is accompanied, with amazing frequency, by the heroine's coming into an inheritance that makes her financially independent in just the way Virginia Woolf would have approved. This is because the invisible hand that guides the finances in the Gothic world is not Adam Smith's metaphor for the law of supply and demand, but the hand of God himself, the same that guides the heroine through the castle corridors and gloomy forests, sometimes with her hero-consort and sometimes alone, sometimes in breathless haste and sometimes "with wandering steps and slow," to the Eden that she, through her courage, has brought into being. This view of the route to salvation is highly gynocentric, so it will come as no surprise that the pioneers of the Gothic genre were primarily women. That is to say, although Horace Walpole is the father of the Gothic, it was women writers in the late eighteenth century who took up his literary curiosity and transformed it into a vehicle capable of didacticism as well as entertainment.

NOTES

1. See Roland Barthes, "Myth Today," *Mythologies* (New York: Hill and Wang, 1983), 109–59. The statement that myths reconcile antagonisms, or "contraries," is sweeping but, I would argue, useful. Whether it be Demeter's rage over the abduction of her daughter that gives us the seasons or the Black colonial subject saluting the French flag on the cover of *Paris Match* to whom Barthes assigns mythic status, the outcome of a myth takes us, if not into the domain of the "marvellous" as commonly understood, at least outside of the domain of what can be explained by reason. Characterizing the agents of myth and romance as more than human comes from Northrop Frye, *An Anatomy of Criticism* (Princeton: Princeton University Press, 1957), 33 and passim.

2. Elaine Pagels, *Adam, Eve, and the Serpent* (New York: Random House, 1988).

3. Northrop Frye, *The Secular Scripture: A Study of the Structure of Romance* (Cambridge: Harvard University Press, 1976), 57.

4. James Thorpe, "Introduction" to *Milton Criticism: Selections from Four Centuries* (New York: Holt, Rinehart and Winston, 1950), 8. For a discussion of the merits of Wesley's emendation, see Oscar Sherwin, "Milton for the Masses: John Wesley's Edition of *Paradise Lost*," *PMLA* 12 (1951), 267–85.

5. Diane McColley, *Milton's Eve* (Urbana: University of Illinois Press, 1983), 10.

6. Harold Bloom, *The Anxiety of Influence* (New York: Oxford University Press, 1973); Sandra Gilbert and Susan Gubar, *The Madwoman in the Attic: The Woman Writer and the Nineteenth-Century Literary Imagination* (New Ha-

ven: Yale University Press, 1979), esp. "Milton's Bogey: Patriarchal Poetry and Women Readers," 187–212.

7. Stanley Fish, *Surprised by Sin: The Reader in "Paradise Lost"* (New York: Macmillan, 1967), 1.

8. David Daiches, "Samuel Richardson," in *Twentieth-Century Interpretations of "Pamela,"* ed. Rosemary Cowler (Englewood Cliffs: Prentice Hall, 1969), 15.

9. Hannah More, *Strictures on Female Education*, "On the Effects of Influence," in *The Works of Hannah More*, 11 vols. (London: T. Cadell, 1830), vol. 5, 41.

10. John Ruskin, "Of Queens' Gardens," *Sesame and Lilies*, in *The Works of John Ruskin*, ed. E. T. Cook and Alexander Wedderburn (London: George Allen, 1912), vol. 18, 122.

11. William Empson, *Milton's God* (London: Chatto and Windus, 1961).

12. See A. O. Lovejoy, *The Great Chain of Being* (Cambridge: Harvard University Press, 1936); Walter Clyde Curry, *Milton's Ontology, Cosmology and Physics* (Lexington: University of Kentucky Press, 1957).

13. See Raymond Williams, *The Country and the City* (New York: Oxford University Press, 1973), esp. 96–107.

14. Michel Foucault, *Madness and Civilization* (1964), trans. Richard Howard (New York: Vintage, 1973) and *Discipline and Punish: The Birth of the Prison*, trans. Alan Sheridan (New York: Vintage, 1979).

15. H. J. Habbakuk, "Marriage Settlements in the Eighteenth Century," *Transactions of the Royal Historical Society*, 4th Series, 32 (1950), 24. See also G. E. Mingay, *English Landed Society in the Eighteenth Century* (London: Routledge, 1963), and Christopher Hill, "Clarissa Harlowe and Her Times," in *Samuel Richardson: A Collection of Critical Essays*, ed. John Carroll (Englewood Cliffs: Prentice Hall, 1969), 102–23.

16. Varet, *De l'éducation des enfants* (1661), quoted in Philippe Ariès, *Centuries of Childhood* (New York: Vintage, 1962), 372.

17. See Lawrence Stone, *The Family, Sex and Marriage in England 1500–1800* (New York: Harper and Row, 1977), 412–14.

18. Since Milton's Christ was present at the creation of everything but himself (V, 837), he functions less like a brother than like the second (male) parent of the angels. As such, he can be seen, in a creation myth that has scrupulously eliminated all women, as an analogue of the consort of the Great Mother goddess with whom she created all other living creatures. For Milton's use of bourgeois family ideology in *Paradise Lost*, see Jackie DiSalvo, "Blake Encountering Milton: Politics and the Family in *Paradise Lost* and *The Four Zoas*" in *Milton and the Line of Vision*, ed. Joseph Anthony Wittreich (Madison: University of Wisconsin Press, 1975), 143–84.

19. The idea that capital was not a fixed entity, that its growth was limited only by the growth of the market, was first presented in a systematic fashion by Adam Smith in *The Wealth of Nations*, first published in 1776.

20. See my dissertation, "Rhetoric and Ideology: A Study of Changing Forms in Seventeenth Century Prose Style" (Columbia University, 1972), 192–230. For the economics of the dissolution of the monasteries, see Christopher Hill, *Economic Problems of the Church from Whitgift to the Long Parliament* (Oxford: Clarendon Press, 1963).

21. See Isaac Kramnick, "Children's Literature and Bourgeois Ideology: Observations on Culture and Industrial Capitalism in the Later Eighteenth Century," *Studies in Eighteenth-Century Culture* 12 (1983), 11–44.

22. Max Byrd makes an argument similar to mine in "The Madhouse, the Whorehouse, and the Convent," *Partisan Review* 44 (1977), 268–78.

23. See Alan Macfarlane, *Marriage and Love in England: Modes of Reproduction 1300–1840* (Oxford: Basil Blackwell, 1986), esp. "Who Controls the Marriage Decision?" 119–47.

24. Quoted in Christopher Lasch, "The Suppression of Clandestine Marriage in England: The Marriage Act of 1753," *Salmagundi* 26 (Spring 1974), 98, 100.

PART II

Insider Narratives

The high wall, no longer the wall that surrounds and protects, no longer the wall that stands for power and wealth, but the mysteriously sealed wall, uncrossable in either direction, closed in upon the now mysterious work of punishment, will become . . . the monotonous figure, at once material and symbolic, of the power to punish.

MICHEL FOUCAULT
Discipline and Punish

CHAPTER IV

Otranto Feminized:
Horace Walpole, Clara Reeve,
Sophia Lee

𝔐ICHAEL SADLEIR, in an essay on the "horrid" novels in *North-anger Abbey*, makes a gendered distinction between two types of Gothicism. One is an inside view: "In mentality essentially English, despite their taste for foreign garb; romantic, but in a friendly, bourgeois fashion, the Radcliffians are like persons who sit about a blazing fire of a stormy night. Their sensitiveness to the beauty of the terrific depends less on the actual quality of terror than on the shuddersome but agreeable contrast between the dangers of abroad and the cosy security of home." In contrast to this essentially interior perspective on "the world," the Lewisite Gothicist gives an outsid-er's view of the same domestic enclave: "Into the firelit refuge of the Radcliffian novelist the follower of Lewis would fain intrude, haggard and with water streaming from his lank hair, shrieking perhaps, as would befit a demon of the storm; then, when he had struck the company to silent fear, he would wish to vanish again into the howling darkness."[1] I use the terms "insider" and "out-sider" Gothic interchangeably with these to emphasize the narrative point of view in relation to an idealized, imaginary, recovered Eden where domestic life could flourish.

The Castle of Otranto introduced English readers to the conventions we have identified as components of the Gothic revision of the myth of the fall: the subversion of primogeniture expressed in the theme of usurpation, the inadequacy of innocence as a defense against evil, and the validity of female rebellion against an autocratic father.

The haunted castle has been usurped, not by a second son but by a servant, a member of a class that was barred by birth from the ranks of castle-owners. His grandson now owns the castle, and so willing is he to sacrifice domestic ties to his unlawful gain that when his son is mysteriously killed by the statue of the castle's true owner, he proposes to divorce his wife so that he can marry his son's potentially fertile fiancée in order to gain the male heir he needs to keep the castle. His plans are foiled by supernatural forces, but female initiative moves the plot along as Isabella, the object of his pursuit, refuses to comply and escapes from the castle that has become her prison.

Manfred's wife, Hippolita, so epitomizes wifely submission that when the equally irreproachable Father Jerome wants to speak to her and her husband and Manfred objects to her presence, she echoes Milton's Eve when she tells him, "You must speak as your duty prescribes—but it is my duty to hear nothing that it pleases not my lord that I should hear." She is quite willing to acquiesce to her husband's plan to divorce her in order to marry Isabella, saying, "It is not ours to make election for ourselves: heaven, our fathers, and our husbands, must decide for us" (87). Yet like the innocent Uriel in *Paradise Lost,* it is her inability to perceive evil, coupled with Father Jerome's comparable "innocence," that propels Manfred forward in his determination "never to submit or yield." Of course they cannot really abet evil any more than Uriel can. The "fall" they help to precipitate is a fortunate one, a part of a larger plan to deprive Manfred of his ill-gotten castle.

Nevertheless their poor judgment keeps them from being agents of good in the plot. It is Hippolita who suggests to Manfred that, in the wake of Isabella's refusal, disaster might be staved off if their daughter, Matilda, should marry Isabella's father, a descendant of the castle's true owner. When she announces this to Matilda and Isabella, both of whom are in love with a "noble peasant" named Theodore, Isabella cries out: "What has thou done! what ruin has thy *inadvertent goodness* been preparing for thyself, for me, and for Matilda!" (86, my italics). Similarly Father Jerome, "ignorant of what had become of [Theodore] and not sufficiently reflecting on the impetuosity of Manfred's temper," thinks it might be useful to plant in Manfred's mind the idea that there is something between

Theodore and Isabella. Later it is this jealousy that propels Manfred to kill his daughter, assuming that she is Isabella involved in a prearranged meeting with his young rival. Clearly the purification of the castle cannot be left in the hands of well-intentioned innocents like Hippolita and Father Jerome, whose goodness, for all their fine sentiments or religious training, is "inadvertent."

And finally, if the Gothic heroine is distinguished from others of the same period by her determination to follow her own vision, then Isabella's initiative is surpassed by that of the villain's own daughter. Matilda has fallen in love with Theodore, a "noble peasant" of unknown (but finally aristocratic) origins. On learning that her father, in a characteristic fit of paranoia, has imprisoned this man, she makes the declaration that Jane Austen was to parody in *Love and Freindship:* "Though filial duty and womanly modesty condemn the step I am taking, yet holy charity, surmounting all other ties, justifies this act. Fly, the doors of thy prison are open." This gesture begins an interview at the end of which "the hearts of both had drunk so deeply of a passion, which both now tasted for the first time."[2] Earlier in the novel, and again on her deathbed, she is a picture of obedience, declaring that "a child ought to have no ears or eyes, but as a parent directs," and finally, seizing the hand of the father who has murdered her and that of her all-too-submissive mother, she "locked them in her own, and then clasped them to her heart."

At the end of the novel vice is punished and virtue is rewarded, but not with particular vigor. Manfred is trundled off to the local convent after his confession: "In the morning Manfred signed his abdication of his principality, with the approbation of Hippolita, and each took on them the habit of religion, in neighbouring convents." We see here Walpole's vision of the infinite capacity of the medieval Catholic Church to absorb evil and even to provide to a villain willing to confess a reasonably pleasant old age. But the same fate is meted out to the saintly Hippolita, who has on several occasions expressed a wish to quit the castle and live a monastic life rather than interfere with her husband's bigamous plans. Nor is the marriage of the two virtuous characters who remain alive after Manfred has killed his daughter a particularly festive occasion: "Theodore's grief was too fresh to admit the thoughts of another love, and it was not until after frequent discourses with Isabella of his dear Matilda, that he was persuaded he could know no happiness but in the society of one, with whom he could for ever indulge in the melancholy that had taken possession of his soul." The ability to feel melancholy, a defining characteristic of the sentimental hero, is both put foward and undermined with a characteristically Gothic ambivalence toward the "reform of manners" that underlies the separation of spheres.

Walpole could flout the conventions of sentimental realism, introducing supernatural retributions and undermining happy endings, because he had the resources to be his own patron and publisher.[3] Following three privately printed editions, which sold rapidly, a commercially printed fourth edition did not appear until eighteen years later, five years after the publication of a work that gained wide approval because its author aimed to bring Walpole's story "within the utmost verge of probability."[4] This was Clara Reeve's *The Old English Baron*, a novel which leaves no supernatural event unexplained and ends on a note of joyous marriage and an explicitly Christian moral lesson. Readers might look in vain for a heroine who stood on her own two feet, and Walpole was scornful of Reeve's efforts, but the critics and the reading public loved them. Looking back in 1793, a reviewer for the *British Critic* wrote of the novel's popularity: "When 'The Old English Baron' made its appearance, every mouth was opened in its praise: every line carried fascination along with it. The younger branch of readers found their attention absolutely riveted to the story; and at its conclusion, they have been actually seen to weep, in the spirit of Alexander, because they had not another volume to peruse."[5]

For the elements she cut out, Reeve substituted a domestic drama that focused on the "usurpation" of a father's affection by a "noble peasant" named Edmund, who has been virtually adopted by a well-meaning "innocent," Baron Fitz-Owen. The baron holds the bourgeois view that merit, not birth, should be the grounds on which privilege is meted out. He therefore "seeks out merit in obscurity, he distinguishes and rewards it" (16). And in the aristocratic skills of archery and hunting, not to mention sheer good looks, Edmund surpasses the baron's own two sons and his two nephews. One strand of the plot, then, involves the efforts of the nephews and one of the brothers to get their rival killed.

The other strand is concerned with the discovery that the castle where the baron lives has been usurped by Sir William Lovell, brother of the baron's now-dead wife. This discovery is begun when the baron tests Edmund by making him spend the night in the reputedly haunted east wing of the castle. Edmund hears a groan beneath the floor, discovers there a body, and learns from a faithful servant that it belongs to the real owner, a younger son who had died at the hands of his greedy brother. Edmund then goes to visit his peasant mother and learns from her that his real mother died in a field in childbirth while fleeing her husband's murderer. Putting two and two together, Edmund realizes that he is the true heir of Lovell castle. He finds a champion in an old friend of his father's, Sir Philip Harclay. A duel is arranged between Sir Philip and Sir William, the villain confesses and dies, and the remaining characters are rewarded or punished as evidence, in Reeve's concluding words, of "the over-ruling hand of Providence, and the certainty of RETRIBUTION."

The castle, the "noble peasant," and the theme of usurpation are in both Walpole's story and Reeve's. But whereas Walpole sees medieval domestic life in consciously Shakespearean terms, Reeve's novel looks forward to a cozier, nineteenth-century vision of home. In other words, she domesticated Walpole's curious structure, and this required modification of some of its deliberate irregularities. In the first place, she adds a frame narrative, though not of the sort that distances the enlightened English reader from the barbarous events of the story. Rather, the frame introduces Sir Philip Harclay, returned from abroad to seek out his old friend, Sir Arthur Lovell. Informed by a local peasant that his friend is dead, he enters the circle of the unwitting usurpers, the Fitz-Owens. When he meets Edmund, he wants to adopt him also, and does so when Baron Fitz-Owen yields to the pressure of his sons and nephews to send Edmund away. Sir Philip is no distancer, then, but the sort of figure Emily Brontë created in Lockwood: a loner who arrives at the beginning of the story, leaves at the end, and provides a normative English point of view on events that eighteenth-century readers would find neither normative nor English.

Another structural modification that Reeve makes is to separate the father and the villain. By having Sir Walter Lovell move, after murdering his brother and concealing the body, to an unhaunted castle in Northumberland, Reeve can fill the haunted castle with the "innocent" Fitz-Owens, so that domestic problems such as sibling rivalry can be at the center of her story. In fact, the greater part of Reeve's narrative is focused not on the villain at all (thus avoiding the possibility that he may engage our sympathies) but rather on the feeble but well-intentioned attempts of Baron Fitz-Owen to maintain order in his family without becoming an authoritarian father. Reeve saw herself as a didactic novelist writing, as she claimed in the preface to her third novel, "to support the cause of morality, to reprove vice, and to promote all the social and domestic virtues."[6] In writing about a family whose peace is disturbed not only by a ghost from the past but also by an internal conflict between fairness and order, she was directing her lesson toward parents in her own society.

Here again we have a figure whose ignorance of evil makes him an inadequate guardian of Eden, and whose efforts to rule by a universalized meritocratic standard of justice in disregard of "natural" bonds and hierarchies creates conflict rather than dissipating it. The rivalry among the males in the baron's family is a mini-war in heaven where the slighted family members gang up on the father's favorite. The fact that the baron's preference is based on Edmund's superior "merit" makes it as reasonable as God's elevation of Christ, and Reeve goes to great lengths to show that everyone in the neighborhood of the castle shared in his estimation of Edmund. Yet, if anything, the rationality of the baron's partiality increases, rather than diffuses, the anger of the siblings. Moreover, the issue at stake is not even between the legalistic "old order" in which inheritance and marriage were decided on purely economic grounds and the newer notions of parent-child relations in which rights were more equally distributed. Edmund does ultimately inherit the castle, but it is love, not wealth, that is being fought over.

From the baron's point of view, the issue in question is how to reconcile his duties as a father with his larger vision of social justice. Like Emily Brontë's equally unwitting Mr. Earnshaw, the baron would like to extend the advantages of a privileged upbringing to deserving (or appealing) underlings without creating disharmony among the members of his acknowledged family, who enjoy their privileges by right of birth. Of course the shadow of bastardy hangs over such transactions, and given the number of "noble peasants" and other unparented heroes and heroines who turn out to be the true heirs of sizeable fortunes, the brothers have, perhaps, some reason to be nervous. This fantasy solution to the perceived arbitrariness of a class system based on birth appears in many Gothic novels and links the mythmaking discussed in the previous chapter, in which the bourgeois class brings forth the myth of its own creation and triumph, with popular traditions of folklore and fairy tales.

In *The Old English Baron*, the desire to extend the boundaries of aristocratic privilege is a sign of virtue. When Sir Philip hears about the baron's partiality for Edmund, he respects him, before even meeting him, as one who "seeks out merit in obscurity." This propensity strikes a responsive chord in Sir Philip, who is characterized as one who "looked round his neighborhood for objects of charity; when he saw merit in distress, it was his delight to raise and support it" (22). Sir Philip is expressing the bourgeois attitude toward poverty that manifested itself in the creation of workhouses and the passage of laws against vagrancy, begging, and other signs of "idleness" among the poor. That is to say, he rewards not those who had given up hope but only those who had found opportunities to exhibit "merit," who did not prey upon others for their sustenance but worked hard and spent their leisure time in and around the home. Independence, deference, and domestic tranquility are defining characteristics of the virtuous poor in the world of the Gothic novel.

We see this harmony in *The Old English Baron* in a scene where Sir Philip, on his way to the castle, meets one of the neighboring peasants, whose response to an aristocrat seeking lodging in a strange place is typical of Gothic peasant behavior. "I am but a poor man," he says, "and cannot entertain your Honour as you are used to; but if you will enter my poor cottage, that, and everything in it, are at your service." Later he voluntarily gives his best bed to Sir Philip while he and his sons sleep on straw. But in the meantime "they conversed together on common subjects, like fellow creatures of the same natural form and endowments, though different kinds of education had given a conscious superiority to the one, and conscious inferiority to the other; and the due respect was paid by the latter, without being exacted by the former" (10–11). This meritocratic spirit, which characterizes all the "good" male characters in *The Old English Baron,* and which views social inequality as a function of education rather than a reflection of a hierarchical natural order, is hardly a medieval attitude, or even an eighteenth-century one. It is rather the imaginary utopian resolution to a real contradiction of which Fredric Jameson has written in *The Political Unconscious.* Similarly, Baron Fitz-Owen speaks from an imagined social order ruled by nothing but merit when he vacillates and finally gives way to the demands of his sons in the matter of Edmund because he cannot demand blind obedience from them simply on the grounds that he is their father and thus their "natural" superior. Finally, there is one son who does like Edmund. In so doing, he demonstrates that affection for him is drawn forth by merit and is not limited by class distinctions. He can therefore defect from the class into which he was arbitrarily placed by birth, and join, along with his father, Sir Philip, and Edmund, the new "natural" order their triumph brings into being.

For Reeve, this radical vision stops, however, at the institution of marriage. Emma is the baron's beautiful daughter and the only female character in the novel except for Edmund's peasant mother. She and Edmund discover their mutual attraction well before Edmund discovers his aristocratic birth, but it is unthinkable for either of them to acknowledge their feelings until the class problem is straightened out. Unlike Walpole's Matilda, Emma does not even have a garrulous female servant to confide in, let alone the kind of friendship that develops between Matilda and Isabella when they resolve the issue of being in love with the same man. She is as isolated from other women as Eve is in *Paradise Lost,* which may account for her complete passivity as well as her silence. In "domesticating" Walpole's plot Reeve toned down both sides of the conflict between a murderous father and his assertive daughter.

With the revelation of Edmund's true identity, not at the end but in the middle of the novel, the one supernatural element that Reeve has allowed, the groaning corpse under the floor of the east wing, disappears from the story without even the kind of clumsy explanation that Scott found anticlimactic in the work of Ann Radcliffe.[7] From that point on, the obstacles to denouement are social. In *The Castle of Otranto*, the "noble peasant" reclaimed his lost patrimony by expelling its usurping owner. But in the Lovell castle, bourgeois family life has been taking place, albeit marred by inter- and intragenerational conflict. The baron, moreover, is not a Satanic figure but one of the "good guys." He knew nothing of his brother-in-law's murder, and has tried to be a good patriarch. He therefore deserves a better fate than dispossession. One problem, then, is to find homes for each of the members of the Fitz-Owen family who have been living, without knowing it, in a usurped castle that is now needed by Edmund, Emma, and their descendants.

At the same time, the baron's view of social class must be reconciled with his role as the head of his family. This is accomplished in several stages. First, the two nephews of the baron who conspired to kill Edmund are not punished but simply sent home, literally with notes to their mothers. This leaves, as a candidate for rehabilitation, one Fitz-Owen son, Robert, who joined with the two nephews in attempting to do away with his father's favorite. If a happy ending involves the recovery of the harmony that preceded the "war" in the Fitz-Owen household, this cannot be accomplished until Robert returns voluntarily to the patriarchal fold, that is, until his view of Edmund is brought into line with that of his father. This happens in a way that eighteenth-century writers on women would have approved. He becomes engaged to the daughter of a friend of Sir Philip Harclay, and his conduct and manners are immediately formed and improved along domesticated lines.

We then see how fortunate it was that Sir Walter, the murderer, abandoned his haunted paternal home to the Fitz-Owen family. For with his defeat at the hands of Sir Philip, followed by his deathbed confession, his castle in Northumberland becomes vacant, and Robert, now that he has taken the first step toward establishing a family of his own, can move in with his bride. The first Lovell castle remains in the family, since Emma will be living there with her new husband. This then leaves only the baron and William, the son who was loyal to Edmund, with no place to go. But second sons in the early Gothic novel have only two paths open to them: that of the rebellious angels and that of the obedient ones. William opts for the latter and asks for no further reward. As for the baron, it turns out that he has another castle to which he plans to retire with his loyal son, saying: "I will visit my children and be visited by them; I will enjoy their happiness and by that means increase my own; whether I look backwards or forwards I will have nothing to do but rejoice, and be thankful to Heaven that has given me so many blessings" (139). This is Reeve's spokesman for the values of a life at whose center are domestic ties.

The Old English Baron contains two parallel instances of rivalry/ jealousy. The first is located in the past and causes the castle to "fall." Sir Walter describes his relationship with his older brother in the following terms: "My kinsman excelled me in every kind of merit, in the graces of person and mind, in all his exercises, and in every accomplishment. I was totally eclipsed by him, and I hated to be in his company; but what finished my aversion, was his addressing the lady upon whom I had fixed my affections: I strove to rival him there, but she gave him the preference that, indeed, was only his due, but I could not bear to see, or acknowledge it" (104). Here again Reeve emphasizes merit: it is Sir Arthur's superiority "in every kind" of it, rather than his economically advantageous position in the birth order, that arouses his brother's enmity. Even love, which arouses further jealousy, is a response to merit rather than to other, more irrational or interested factors. The parallel situation in the present is that of Wenlock, who "had a growing passion for the Lady Emma, . . . and, as love is eagle-eyed, he saw, or fancied he saw, her cast an eye of preference on Edmund." Emma is too virtuous to acknowledge these feelings, even to herself. But Wenlock knows they are there, and so does the reader.

The parallel highlighting of merit in these two instances of jealousy is at the core of Reeve's moral lesson. It is the just and rational basis on which parental and sexual love are distributed: in both cases the issue is not material goods but emotions. Family harmony will prevail if all its members recognize that love is not a right of birth but a privilege to be earned. The tasks of "forming and improving the general manners, dispositions, and conduct of the other sex," and of "modelling the human mind during the early stages of its growth" will be better accomplished if love is seen as a response to merit rather than as some doting fondness bestowed according to no rational principle. In the case of both Edmund and his father, Sir Arthur Lovell, merit consists in natural gifts rather than in "works," and natural gifts are distributed unequally among family members. But if children can accept this inequality (about which they can, in fact, do nothing) and accept also the "natural" preferences that arise from it, then sibling rivalry, that destroyer of domestic peace, will not occur. Furthermore, an upbringing in such a meritocratic family will prepare children for life in a world where bourgeois values are triumphant, since the rules that govern the two do indeed "bid the same."

What Reeve has done in emending Walpole is to insert into his medieval setting an eighteenth-century family struggling to reconcile a more narrowly patriarchal ideal with a newer, more egalitarian one. The strategy of augmenting the world of the "haunted castle" with other plots in which "normal" domestic values can be contrasted to those of the villain was taken up by later Radcliffians, especially Mrs. Radcliffe herself. The substitution of natural for supernatural means of restoring the castle to its rightful owner was adopted by later Gothicists as well. In *The Castle of Otranto*, Manfred's expulsion from the castle is effected entirely by supernatural forces, in accordance with Walpole's intention, set forth in the signed preface to his second edition, to break through the restrictions imposed by "realism" and to leave "the powers of fancy at liberty to expiate through the boundless realms of invention." Yet in his unsigned first preface, in which he claims to have found the manuscript, he wishes his author "had grounded his plan on a more useful moral than this: that 'the sins of the fathers are visited on their children unto the third and fourth generations.' "

Clara Reeve found just such a moral: it is essentially the lesson of *Paradise Lost*, in which God brings good not only out of evil but also out of ineptitude. The baron did wrong in creating antagonism between his blood kin, but he did it on the basis of a principle the reader is supposed to approve, just as the loyalty of Adam to Eve is portrayed by Milton as admirable even as it leads him into the first knowing sin, or as the innocence of Uriel makes him blameless even as he abets Satan in his plan to avenge himself on God. Though the unexplained supernatural is the essential center of Christian teaching, it was clear to the early writers of didactic romances that such violations of believability, when found in a novel, did not necessarily strengthen a reader's belief in "the over-ruling hand of Providence, and the certainty of RETRIBUTION," which is why the feminine Gothic, starting with Reeve, introduces it minimally or leaves it out altogether.

Finally, she fills the haunted castle with a wealth of domestic transactions and concerns that eighteenth-century readers could recognize as familiar. For instance, the baron responds enthusiastically to Edmund's offer to sleep in the east wing to see if it is really haunted, not because he is interested in supernatural phenomena but because, if he can renovate the east wing rather than building an entire new one, "it will spare him some expence [*sic*], and answer his purpose as well or better" (40). The transactions entailed in the transfer of property to Edmund, the settlements made on behalf of each of the Fitz-Owen children, and the compensation paid to the baron for his expenses in educating his adopted favorite, are presented with the exactitude of detail that readers relish in Jane Austen. It was probably the sense of familiarity produced by these referents, rather than the novelty of their "medieval" context or the underplayed elements of the supernatural, that caused Reeve's readers "to weep, in the spirit of Alexander, because they had not another volume to peruse."

By ending her novel on an unequivocally happy note, Reeve transformed Walpole's Gothic experiment into a vehicle for domestic optimism. Most of the writers who continued along this path were women. But the pessimistic Gothic, which offers a much more radical critique of the idealization of home than even a heroine who defies her father can provide, also had its female practitioners. Sophia Lee's *The Recess*, which came out between 1783 and 1785 and is thus one of the earliest Gothics, draws on the pessimism of the sentimental novel, in which virtue is powerless, and works this theme through the landscape of imprisoning spaces that characterizes the Gothic terrain. The idea that confinement is the lot of fallen creatures and that escape can lead only to a more intense confinement goes back to *Clarissa*, and beyond that to Milton's Satan. But at each turn of the theme, captivity is unhooked, first from the natural order of *Paradise Lost* and then from the social order of Richardson's Harlowe family, in which women are the captured and men their captors. Under these conditions, enclosure becomes not a restraint upon evil but a sign of it.

This is precisely the point in Lee's novel. Imprisonment is a way of life for her two heroines, Matilda and Ellinor, and concealment, in a world ruled by evil, is a precondition for happiness. Indeed the very survival of the two heroines depends on their remaining "underground," since they are the daughters of Mary Queen of Scots, the imprisoned enemy of the antidomestic Queen Elizabeth. Not only does Lee assume sympathy for Mary in a period that saw the Gordon riots, she unabashedly recasts history in such a way as to make passion its motivating force. Major political events like the failure of Essex's campaign in Ireland and his defection, rebellion, and execution, are brought about entirely through love on the part of himself and his fellow court favorite Leicester for the two heroines. Nor are these two even illegitimate daughters. Mary, the author insists, was married in secret to a fourth husband who fathered the girls. This practice of marrying secretly, against which the Hardwicke Act was directed, upheld passion over rational control as a motive for marrying. *The Recess* insists that secrecy is necessary only when there is repression.

Ellinor, the more violent and daring of the two, is duped into marrying Lord Arlington, Queen Elizabeth's choice for her. She escapes and pursues her lover, Essex, to Ireland dressed as a man, only to meet him when it is too late to save her from madness. Matilda's clandestine spouse is Lord Leicester, who in actuality was Elizabeth's age. An uncle of the girls murders Leicester, then forces Matilda to go with him to the West Indies, where he almost perpetrates a forced marriage. She escapes and returns to England with her daughter, Mary. They are imprisoned on trumped-up charges and Mary is ultimately poisoned, leaving her mother to moan the vanity of all things and the powerlessness of innocence. Clearly this is not a story of how paradise was regained. Rather it is an account of two virtuous girls who live in happy seclusion until the advent of sexuality, expressed initially as curiosity about the hitherto-forbidden knowledge of their real parentage.

The knowledge that their mother is Queen Elizabeth's prisoner brings with it the inevitable realization that they too are her prisoners. And once they know that the Recess is not a voluntarily chosen haven, they want to enjoy forbidden pleasures, though not in the sense that that phrase is usually understood. What is denied to them is the normally "bidden" pleasure of wedded love. They share this bitter lesson with their guardians, Father Anthony and Mrs. Marlow, who were once on the brink of marrying when they discovered they were children of the same impetuous mother, who herself had responded to her autocratic, imprisoning parents by bearing both her children out of wedlock. The virtuous rebel, but virtue itself is crushed. The hold of the old, absolutist patriarchy cannot be broken, even when (or perhaps especially when) the patriarch is a woman, when it is the phallic mother, rather than the more distant symbolic father, who controls access to love.

This negative method of valorizing home, and the familial bonds it stands in for, links *The Recess* with the sentimental novel on the one hand, and with what I call the "outsider" Gothic on the other. The sentimental novel moves toward a stance of patience and *contemptus mundi* that is enunciated at crucial points by both heroines in *The Recess*. This is the obviously intended message, just as it was in the novels of Eliza Haywood and her contemporaries, whose narrators and heroines spoke of "the danger of giving way to passion," while at the same time positing the act of yielding as a mark of artless virtue. But in *The Recess* being "inside" means being dominated, a condition the two heroines reject. They are thus cast out not because they are "betray'd by tenderness within," nor because their lovers are Gothic villains hostile to the values of companionate marriage. "Tenderness within" and the courage that accompanies it are signs of virtue in this novel. It is Elizabeth, unable to appreciate virtue, who stands in their way, a controlling parent who wants her "sons" for herself and who is bent on denying to other women what her own pride will not allow her to enjoy. Never was the personal more political.

The Recess thus encodes, through its "outsider" point of view, a radical critique of familial domination in that the actions of the confining parent ruin the castle irrecoverably. They do so not by turning it temporarily into a prison but by revealing imprisonment to be its inevitable function. The difference is thus one of degree. We can see this in the degree of initiative allowed to the heroine in the "outsider" Gothic. Ellinor, for instance, escapes twice from imprisonment in Ireland by putting on men's clothes, while Matilda once escapes from the clutches of her hated husband by substituting the dead body of another woman for her own. Another character, Rose Cecil, is in love with Lord Leicester but imprisoned in the Recess by her father because she will not marry the man he chooses. She escapes to France with Matilda and Leicester. When she discovers that these two are married, she commits suicide. Desperation and action replace patience and submission.

Of course this initiative is not rewarded, and its value is undercut by the reiterated expressions of regret, on the part of Matilda and Ellinor, that they cannot regain as adult women the paradise they knew as children in the Recess. But the lack of reward comes, as it does in *Wuthering Heights*, from the unworthiness of the world from which a reward might be expected and in which it would be lived out. Elizabeth is the reality principle in the novel, and the source of its sexual politics. The heroines, taught from infancy to value retirement from the world, learn that Elizabeth's vigilant eye is potentially everywhere. Mrs. Marlow and Father Anthony are positive parents, but there are laws that thwart their love also. Happiness combined with sexual fulfillment would require, for all the virtuous characters in this novel, a radically different world that cannot be drawn forth out of the body of this one.

Behind this pessimistic vision hovers the absent figure of Mary, whose claim to fame never rested on an achieved balance between reason and passion, and who clearly served as a stronger role model for her daughters than the self-denying Mrs. Marlow. "All blamed her errors," their guardian tells the girls of their mother, "but they pitied her youth, and imputed many of them to inexperience and faults in her education." The exception, of course, is Elizabeth, in whose Satanic heart "every word in [Mary's] praise was a dagger," and for whom "the unfortunate Mary's greatest crimes . . . were the graces she received from nature."[8] Reeve's villain had the same feelings about his older brother. But what makes Mary hateful to Elizabeth is not her claim to the throne of England but her capacity for passion, which leads her to rash acts. The sadness she draws upon herself only makes her more lovable, and thus more of a threat: it "hung over her features and gave them an irresistible attraction" (I, 56).

The key to Mary's power is her artlessness, a quality that involves the inability to foresee the consequences of one's actions. To grow up is to leave it behind, as Jane Austen's heroines learn, since it precludes self-criticism.[9] It is synonymous with angelic behavior in *Paradise Lost*, but in a fallen political context it supports the domination of certain groups by others, thus setting up the very exploitation against which it is supposed to be a defense. It makes Mary the moral superior of her powerful cousin Elizabeth, just as it made Haywood's Amena, who "fell," superior to the scheming woman who was D'Elmont's first wife. It is the innocence that Eve can leave behind only by eating the forbidden fruit. *The Recess* explores the ambivalent status of that gesture, and expands the boundaries of a "cloistered virtue" that is destroyed by contact with evil. It makes Elizabeth's court an inverted Eden, a parody of familial ties like the monasteries we have discussed.

Once this enclosed space has been poisoned, enclosure cannot keep evil out anywhere. For a while, Matilda and Leicester are secretly married, and domestic happiness is theirs. But when Matilda becomes pregnant, they know they cannot keep this a secret from their all-seeing bad mother/monarch. So they flee to France, where Leicester is murdered in his bed by an overly zealous Catholic uncle of Matilda's with whom they are staying. Even when Elizabeth does not root out the secret herself, the very fact of secrecy may come to be felt as an unacceptable moral compromise, and thus incompatible with a true paradise regained. This happens to the Duke of Norfolk, who marries Mary, at which point "her prison becomes a palace to him" (I, 60). But when his sister reproaches him for not attempting to release his bride from her confinement, he is stung into action, forms an unsuccessful plot against Elizabeth, and is executed for it, an act which deprives the two girls of a father. Secrecy is protective, but it is also both shameful and limiting. Therefore the wish to break out of its circle of tranquility is commendable, though it may mean leaving behind the only Eden a heroine will ever know.

Passion enters the Recess in the "corporal form" of Lord Leicester, and Matilda bids farewell to "a tranquility [she] would not have regained, by being unmarried, if [she] could." Separated from him, she finds herself contending with "an involuntary hatred" of the Recess she once loved. "My heated fancy," she laments, "followed my love into court, and the silence and confinement I lived in became more and more odious" (I, 164). Even chaste passion that cannot be acknowledged becomes a source of suffering that can be alleviated only by its public expression. Love has brought to an end Matilda's first self-sufficient paradise and has given her a desire for knowledge of the world in which her husband moves, a knowledge that is forbidden, though unjustly so. Elizabeth stands in, then, for an entire set of patriarchal values that keep women confined to the home on the grounds that they need to be protected from the evils of the world.

It is not passion, then, but secrecy, the supreme subject of the Gothic, that destroys the domestic happiness. Blame for its destruction is placed on those who exercise autocratic, irrational control over their children, whose "lively preferences" are thereby forced underground. In this novel, secrecy renders every interior a haunted space where past repression can be endlessly re-created, where secrets are concealed, but never fully. In each case the secret comes down to a manifestation of sexuality. Ellinor, the sister who is most like her mother, is the most severely affected by this code. When she is brought to court by Elizabeth and meets Essex constantly there, the necessity of concealing her passion for him causes her to be continually haunted by thoughts of him, thoughts which drive her into the most inescapable prison of all, madness.

This is the novel's radical warning to those parents and moralists who would allow passion no place in the bourgeois ideal marriage, who make female sexuality a secret that cannot move out of its hiding place into the world, and who demand obedience from their children in order to further their own worldly interests. The argument put forward in *The Recess* resonates with that put forward by the opponents of the Hardwicke Act: "lively preference" is a better basis for marriage than parental calculations. Curiosity about "the world" followed by true love is not a fall, or would not be under "natural" circumstances. These emotions do not bring evil into the world. Evil in the world is what brings them forth as a fall. And the cause of evil in the world, for Lee as for Blake, is the man-made institutions that attempt to confine sexuality, both male and female. Like the statue of Alfonso, it may break down walled spaces if they serve not to protect it but to keep it concealed.

It has this power, Lee claims, because it is pure, and women are the preeminent possessors of that purity. We have in this novel two mothers who give birth to two illegitimate children apiece and are completely exonerated. Evil grows up in the space where passion is absent and control is all. The five women in the the novel— Matilda and Ellinor, their mother, their governess, and Mrs. Marlow's mother—all discover "how dangerous it is to give way to Passion," yet all but Mrs. Marlow yield to it in defiance of that danger. A very different standard of virtue is being put forward, one that has little concern with reputation and respectability. Even though all the virtuous characters in *The Recess* are Catholic, and thus members, in eighteenth-century England, of an unpopular and persecuted minority, their moral stance calls up the revolutionary core of Protestantism. Applied to the domain of family relations, this stance has subversive implications. Lee's critique looks forward to a feminist critique of the ideology of separate spheres, but also backward. It looks back, first of all, to Milton's rendering of innocent Uriel's inability to defend the Garden of Eden against Satan. In the fallen Gothic world, as in a creation that allows free will to human beings, enclosure cannot prevent the fall of the house set apart from "the world." Thus, what the heroine needs is not the protection of men against the unfamiliarity of the world but a capacity to take the initiative, to face danger and follow her convictions no matter how slim appears the possibility of success. Her lack of power is precisely what fuels her determination to win against a network of oppressive relations that, from her ostensibly unfallen vantage point, are the conditions that make it dangerous "to give way to Passion."

The novel's support of passion looks back still further to an unrealized ideal of matrimony that was displaced by the bourgeois insistence on parental consent, the publishing of banns, and the emphasis on rationality to which the Hardwicke Act aimed to give legislative support. If the arguments put forward by the opponents of that act sound modern, we need to remember that they were defending an earlier set of practices endorsed by English canon law, in which physical union accompanied by a declaration of intent to live as man and wife were the basis for a valid marriage. Though there are certainly problems for women in the definition of marriage that the Hardwicke Act was attempting to replace, it gave Lee a place from which to make a radical critique of the present, one that was carried on, as we shall see, in the writings of Mary Wollstonecraft and Charlotte Smith.

NOTES

1. Michael Sadleir, "The Northanger Novels: A Footnote to Jane Austen," English Association Pamphlet no. 68 (London: Oxford University Press, 1927), 14.

2. Horace Walpole, *The Castle of Otranto* (1764), in *Three Gothic Novels*, ed. E. F. Bleiler (New York: Dover, 1966), 73. Subsequent references will be to this edition.

3. For the early publication history of *The Castle of Otranto* see K. K. Mehrotra, *Horace Walpole and the English Novel* (Oxford: Basil Blackwell, 1934), Appendix A, 173.

4. Clara Reeve, "Preface" to *The Old English Baron* (1778), ed. James Trainer (London: Oxford University Press, 1967), 4. Subsequent references will be to this edition. Originally published without this preface as *The Champion of Virtue, A Gothic Tale* (London, 1777).

5. *The British Critic* 2 (Dec. 1793), 383.

6. Clara Reeve, "Dedication" to *The Exiles, or Memoirs of the Count of Cronstadt* (London, 1788), quoted by James Trainer, "Introduction" to *The Old English Baron*, xii.

7. Sir Walter Scott, "Ann Radcliffe," in *Biographical Notices of Eminent Authors*, in *Miscellaneous Prose Works*, 3 vols. (Edinburgh, 1854), vol. 1, 313–35.

8. Sophia Lee, *The Recess*, 3 vols. (1783–85; rpt., New York: Arno Press, 1972), vol. 1, 50–51.

9. Judith Wilt, in *Ghosts of the Gothic: Austen, Eliot, and Lawrence* ([Princeton: Princeton University Press, 1980], 133–35), contrasts the essential role of self-reproach in the growth of an Austen heroine with the deliberate avoidance of that emotion as a mark of the Radcliffian heroine's virtue.

CHAPTER V

Radical Terror:
Charlotte Smith,
Mary Wollstonecraft

$\mathfrak{T}$HE LIVES and fictions of Mary Wollstonecraft and Charlotte Smith intersect at many points. Both led independent and often difficult lives, supporting themselves by their writing and defying the narrowing codes of behavior that attempted to control what women wrote and read as well as what they did. Both created characters who seriously transgressed these codes and used some of the "machinery" of the Gothic to expand the domain of virtue so as to include these heroines. And both took advantage of the new female audience to attack barriers between their heroines and the happiness they so clearly deserved. These barriers were neither inevitable, nor, in the case of Smith's Adelina, permanent. Rather, it was the task of the woman writer to direct her gift toward changing them. Smith attacked prejudice against women, especially as it appeared in the law. Similarly Wollstonecraft's "main object" in writing *Maria, or the Wrongs of Women*, was "the desire of exhibiting the misery and oppression, peculiar to women, that arise out of the partial laws and customs of society."[1]

In presenting transgressive heroines as vehicles for exhibiting the misery and oppression peculiar to women, Smith and Wollstonecraft faced common problems, which they solved in similar ways. They had, on the one hand, the censorious male critic to contend with, and on the other hand, the powerless reader. Their strategy for dealing with these related problems was to give their heroines virtue in excess, to make them not only beyond reproach but assertive of that fact. Judith Wilt has remarked that the Radcliffian heroine is careful always to avoid self-reproach, and Wollstonecraft and Smith are Radcliffians in this respect.[2] This quality of irreproachability is what makes the Gothic heroine so interesting as an ideological vehicle and so tiresome as a literary character. In Smith and Wollstonecraft, whose expressed aim was not only to expose evil but to inspire protest, excessive virtue in their heroines substituted for actual power to right the wrongs being exposed. An appeal is being made, but it is directed, in the words of the title of a pamphlet by their contemporary, Mary Hays, "to the Men of Great Britain on Behalf of Women." Loosen the bonds of male tyranny (with which women cooperate all too often) and women will become the "angels" into which their culture seeks to make them. It is men who bring Death into the world of Wollstonecraft and Smith.

Nevertheless these two share a profound ambivalence about the ideal of passionlessness, both for themselves and for their heroines. If a woman's heart is pure, why should her "lively preference" not find the worthiest man as its object? Their answer entails a critique of the culture of separate spheres that encourages women, in the name of innocence, to grow up ignorant of the male world, and men, unused to restraint, to express their masculinity in domination and debauchery. The Richardsonian sentimental novel did this too, but without allowing determination to be admitted into the ranks of qualities for which a heroine could be rewarded. The heroines of Smith and Wollstonecraft, on the other hand, struggle, in a world prone to misjudge them, to create adequate objects for their "lively preference," and to defend themselves and others in the exercise of it. Like Lee's Matilda and Ellinor, they grasp the sexual politics under which they are thwarted, and they do taste victory.

The differences in the two writers reflect differences in their lives, but they also show different ways of being a feminist in the eighteenth century. Smith, who was ten years older than Wollstonecraft, was born in 1749 and educated at a finishing school, where her father spared no expense to have his daughter accomplished in music, dancing, drawing, and French. But by the time Charlotte was fifteen, his fortune was apparently depleted, and, ten years a widower, he sought and married a woman with a large fortune. And so, like one of the heroines of her first novel, *Emmeline, the Orphan of the Castle*, Smith found her domestic world "usurped" by a woman she did not like. Spoiled by her father, she resisted the authority of this new member of the household. The solution was found in an eligible young man, the son of Richard Smith, a West Indian merchant and director of the East India Company. Dazzled by these credentials, anxious to please her father, and hostile to her new stepmother, Charlotte married Benjamin Smith in 1765.

Over the next two decades, this man mismanaged his finances so badly that he was imprisoned for debt in 1783, whereupon his wife put her children in the care of her brother and joined her husband in prison. Although he was released, his creditors were pursuing him a year later, and he, like a true Gothic villain, fled the country to a desolate chateau in Normandy where he, his wife, and their nine children, spent a cold, miserable winter in 1785. Then, in 1787, Charlotte decided that the sins of the father, and especially his bad example, should no longer be visited on their children, and she separated from her spouse. Thereafter, she supported herself and her children by writing four volumes of poems, two books of translations, ten novels, five works "intended for the use of young persons," and two other collections of "narratives of various description." She spent many years fighting to obtain for her children the money her father-in-law had left them, over which the law entitled her husband to exercise sole control. She struggled tirelessly in the courts, and won her case just as her last child was leaving the parental household.

In her own life, then, Smith saw herself thwarted in the exercise of property rights because she was a woman. Yet below the anger in her novels directed at lawyers, at fathers who marry their daughters off to unsuitable men, and at public opinion that applied a double standard to the conduct of women and men is a deep antipathy to all restrictive institutions and customs that thwart love in the name of propriety. The fact that she chose, for her first venture into publishing fiction, a translation of Prévost's controversial *Manon Lescaut* (1785) suggests that she was looking for a way to express these politics. Claiming to write not for fame but to support her many children was one way for a woman to avoid offending male critics, and was certainly the truth in Smith's case. But Prévost's novel of a young man's passion for a courtesan was not the sort of thing for which a woman writer, especially a beginner, could expect praise by English reviewers.

Yet though she withdrew her work and reissued it anonymously, her next project was another translation: fifteen tales, some in Old French, from *Les Causes Célèbres*, a 134-volume compilation by Guyot de Pitval of sensational trials. This collection focuses exclusively on a world that fell through Jane Austen's "finely drawn mesh," portraying just the sort of events that Henry Tilney assures Catherine Morland cannot happen in eighteenth-century England. Children are abandoned by their parents; a felon remains silent while another man, falsely accused, is tortured and killed; a daughter is forced into a convent; a legal marriage is annulled and the child it produced is declared illegitimate, but finally vindicated; the now-famous Martin Guerre reclaims his wife from an impostor: these are the materials that Charlotte Smith labored mightily to bring to the English reading public. Wishing to emphasize their *truth* she called her collection *The Romance of Real Life*. If she was seeking to realize a quick profit, or to win favor from (mostly male) critics, she chose her subject matter strangely.

The explanation that makes more sense is that Smith saw in these prototypically Gothic themes a way to bring her growing radicalism into a form that would arouse outrage while instructing her readers. Yet a book cannot instruct if it does not deal with situations that a reader can recognize as existing in the present, and wives were undoubtedly being slowly poisoned in the eighteenth century, as they are now. But the fact that the stories were displaced into the past gave Smith the same freedom to draw moral lessons from her sensational material that it gave a whole generation of Gothic writers whose books began flooding the circulating libraries a few years later. Most important, this freedom does not involve an escape into the more-than-human realm of romance. These stories, Smith tells her audience, really happened.

The first story in her collection begins with a generality intended to set up a framework for the whole collection: "It has been asserted, that there is in human nature a propensity to every kind of evil; and that persons of the best disposition, and most liberal education, may find themselves in situations as will, if their passions are suffered to predominate, betray them into the most frightful excesses, into crimes which cannot be related without horror."[3] This is the side of human nature to which Henry Tilney, and the Enlightenment for which he is a spokesman, gives little space. Its appeal for Smith is an indication of her affinity for Romanticism and radical politics. Her fascination with the criminal justice system was modified as she experienced her own powerlessness at the hand of the law. Her politics changed as English opinion turned against the French Revolution that she defended in her early writings. Yet she remained an opponent of restrictive social institutions and a champion of individuals of both sexes who defied them.

In her lifelong antipathy toward the institutionalized power of men over women, and in her desire to use the written word to challenge it, Smith had an ally in Mary Wollstonecraft, whose early life also made her sensitive to the hypocrisy of men's "protective" stance toward women's virtue. Wollstonecraft's father lacked the "slow diligence" needed to make him a good breadwinner, and his fitful efforts to convert his father's wealth (made in trade) into land led him to uproot his family and flee repeated failure. He squandered his son's inheritance as well as his own, and was physically violent to his wife until her death in 1782. Both before and after she left home to work, first as a companion to an elderly woman and then as a writer in London, Wollstonecraft was thrown into the masculine role of the responsible member of the family, first defending her mother against her father's abuse and later giving financial support, albeit sometimes reluctantly, to her two sisters, Eliza and Everina. Living on her own in London, then with Gilbert Imlay, who later deserted her after fathering her first daughter, Wollstonecraft defied sexual conventions to a far greater degree than the unfortunately married Smith.[4]

This difference in life experience, with Smith having lost a paradise of paternal affection that Wollstonecraft never knew, shows up as differences in the feminism of the two writers. Both were strong defenders of the right of women to be included in the rational discourse of their period. Yet when Wollstonecraft reviewed *Emmeline* for the *Analytical Review* in 1788, she was critical of Smith's "wild scenes."[5] She is referring to the fact that Adelina, one of the novel's two heroines who has been married off at a young age to a man she hates, has a child by a man she loves and is ultimately rewarded with this man as her second husband. The other heroine, Emmeline, and her mentor, Mrs. Stafford, support this young woman against hostile criticism and convert the man who loves Emmeline to their position. The danger that women readers might believe men of her day to be capable of such a conversion disturbed Wollstonecraft greatly, and *A Vindication of the Rights of Woman* can be seen as an outgrowth of this concern.

Throughout her career as a writer, Wollstonecraft was more fearful than Smith of the power of the imagination to destroy happiness, even in virtuous women. "Nature is the nurse of sentiment," she wrote from Sweden in 1795, "yet what misery, as well as rapture, is produced by a quick perception of the beautiful and sublime, . . . how dangerous it is to foster these sentiments in such an imperfect state of existence."[6] The question raised by Wollstonecraft's comment on a fellow radical writer is how to present "the wrongs of woman" so as to avoid discouraging the readers they wished to reach, while at the same time not deluding them with false expectations. It is a question that comes up when writers are living at a time of revolutionary hope, and the responses of Smith and Wollstonecraft to it differed. Wollstonecraft's pessimism deepened over time while Smith, who survived Wollstonecraft by ten years, lost some of her revolutionary hope, though none of her outrage at the situation of women.

Although Charlotte Smith's novels are not set in imaginary medieval landscapes, her deployment of "Gothic machinery" in a recognizably contemporary setting opens up possibilities for a sexual politics that profoundly subverts the status quo. Unlike Wollstonecraft, Smith was immensely popular in her day, and the surprising combination of sexual radicalism and popularity with critics is nowhere more evident than in *Emmeline, the Orphan of the Castle*. In this novel, Emmeline is the rightful heir of the usurped Mowbray castle. Yet the usurpation involves not violence but class pride and a concomitant opposition to clandestine marriages. Emmeline's father, the heir to the castle, fell in love with a poor relation who had been his companion since childhood. Parental antipathy gave rise to a secret marriage. Emmeline's mother died in childbirth, leaving her daughter (subsequently orphaned) under the shadow of illegitimacy. Lord

Montreville then took over the castle as the next in line, and his villainous qualities include reminding Emmeline of her dependency on him as his ward.

The frequent presence of bad parents as Gothic villains gives authors ample opportunity to hold up for criticism overindulgent or negligent mothers and indifferent or authoritarian fathers. Emmeline's problems derive from both her guardian and his wife. First, Lord Montreville, having once established a legal relationship of control over Emmeline, leaves her under the guardianship of a Mrs. Carey and a Mr. Maloney. When Mrs. Carey dies, Maloney makes advances to Emmeline, who appeals to her guardian for protection. He, however, urges his ward to accept the uncouth Maloney, with his presumptuous attitude toward women, because his own son, Lord Delamere, has fallen in love with her. A more violent version of Pamela's pursuer, Delamere has a doting mother who has failed to teach him the value of self-restraint. Consequently he abducts Emmeline and is killed in a duel over her, freeing her to marry Lieutenant Godolphin, the man she loves. But even before Delamere dies, she breaks an engagement to him that she insists was forced on her and has not the consent of her heart. Smith's sexual politics are evidenced by the fact that Delamere is punished and Emmeline is not.

Moreover, Delamere's excessive passion is contrasted to that of Adelina, the second heroine of the novel and the one to whom Wollstonecraft objected. Her situation parallels that of Emmeline and Delamere in that her parents do not provide her with the protection and proper instruction without which children are likely to become victims of their own impulses and those of others. But like Emmeline and unlike Delamere, Adelina is permitted a conventional happy ending, married to the man she loves. Her uncontrolled passion for the remorseful Fitz-Edward, unsanctioned except by her own pure heart, is not punished at all. Not only does Adelina marry him when her husband dies, but she contributes to Emmeline's fortunes in that Emmeline first meets Godolphin, her future husband, while taking her "fallen" friend to Bath to be delivered of Fitz-Edward's child. Godolphin is Adelina's brother, and Emmeline's finest hour comes when she prevails upon her lover to refrain from killing the defiler of his sister. In taking the side of the child against the parent, the woman against the man, the one who offends "the proprieties" against the one who upholds them, Smith expresses a stance that will become characteristic of the Gothic as a genre.

That Charlotte Smith did not find it necessary to kill Adelina, as Elizabeth Gaskell would find it necessary to kill Ruth sixty-five years later, indicates that the narrowing of female sexual possibilities in print that had begun in the middle of the eighteenth century was still in an early stage. Of course, as the sensation novels of the 1860s attest, novels that portray tabooed behavior can be widely popular even as critical denunciation is heaped upon them. But Scott's praise of *Emmeline* is typical of her positive reviews. Looking back thirty years later Scott remembers well "the impression made on the public by the appearance of *Emmeline, the Orphan of the Castle*, a tale of love and passion, happily conceived, and told in a most interesting manner. It contains a happy mixture of humour, and of bitter satire mingled with pathos, while the characters both of sentiment and of manners, were sketched with a firmness of pencil, and liveliness of colouring, which belong to the highest branch of fictitious narrative."[7] Another of her admirers, Sir Egerton Brydges, writing at the time of Smith's death in 1806, was astonished that "a mind oppressed with sorrows and injuries of the deepest dye, and loaded with hourly anxieties of the most pressing sort, could be endowed with strength and elasticity to combine and throw forth such visions with a pen dipped in all the glowing hues of a most playful and creative fancy."[8]

But the subversive element in Smith's novel did not go unremarked. The year after *Emmeline* appeared, Henry James Pye, who the following year became poet laureate, published *The Spectre*, an epistolary novel devoting some forty pages to a discussion of *Emmeline* and containing the following rhetorical question: "Is it the business of the moral writer, who should strengthen the young mind in habits of virtue, to invent situations where every event is supposed to concur in such temptations [as Adelina's] irresistible, and such breach of engagement [as Emmeline's with Delamere] excusable—to draw the characters eminently virtuous, yet contrive to make them err, without incurring our blame for it—to make adultery amiable, and perfidy meritorious, and dismiss the perpetrators of both to respectability, to honour, and to happiness?"[9]

Women writers, whose personal morality was as much on trial as the talents and faculties they shared with male writers, and whose privileged domain was the strengthening of young minds in habits of virtue, were especially vulnerable to criticism of the morals of their characters, and especially of their female characters. Male characters, in Pye's view, ran the risk of being insipid if they resembled Sir Charles Grandison too closely: "But a woman may be drawn perfectly good, and at the same time perfectly interesting, for there is no virtue in the catalogue of moral and Christian duties that is not becoming, and does not give and receive additional lustre, when possessed by that amiable sex. The utmost exertions of patience, and meekness, which at least sink the tragic hero, raise the tragic heroine in our esteem."[10] Emmeline is not a tragic heroine, and this is part of Pye's objection to her. But if Smith did succeed with most of her readers in her portrayal of extraordinary heroinely initiative, what were her strategies? One that we have seen, displacement backwards in time, appears not to have interested her. But she did use two others that characterize the feminine Gothic within which she was working.

First, she leaves her readers with absolutely no doubt that Emmeline *is* "perfectly good." She does this partly by stressing the artlessness, the state of being untouched by "culture," that Emmeline epitomizes from the moment we see her, "perfectly unconscious of those attractions which now began to charm every other eye." One consequence of this artlessness is that "the ignorant rustics, who had seen Emmeline grow up among them from her earliest infancy, and who now beheld her with the compassion as well as the beauty of an angel, administering to their necessities and alleviating their misfortunes, looked upon her as a superior being, and throughout the country she was almost adored" (5). Emmeline thus prefigures the heroine whose popularity would grow in the nineteenth century—Victor Frankenstein's mother is another example—culminating in "angels" such as Esther Summerson who move among the poor, first in the countryside and later in the Satanic city itself, and who, through exemplary sweetness and generosity, embody a fantasized healing of England's widening class divisions.

Emmeline augments her perfectly Rousseauean natural goodness with a cultivation of mind that is entirely self-administered.[11] Raised by two servants, she "had a kind of intuitive knowledge; and comprehended everything with a facility that soon left her instructors behind her." Neglected by her guardian, "she would have been left in the most profound ignorance, if her uncommon understanding, and unwearied application, had not supplied the deficiency of her instructors, and conquered the disadvantage of her situation" (2). But she needs, in addition to "intuitive knowledge" and "unwearied application," an interaction with equals, and this she gets from Mrs. Stafford, a woman who remains tranquil despite mistreatment and then desertion by an abominable husband.

If this were all there was to Emmeline, she would not be a heroine who challenged a sexual code that equated female virtue with "exertions of patience and meekness." It is where Emmeline defies the sexual code enunciated by Pye that Smith introduces the emotion whose representation served to separate out the Gothic as a genre, terror. A phrase from the review of *Desmond*, Smith's fourth novel, suggests that it was Smith's ability to elicit from her readers this response, combined with pity for the heroine's perfect goodness, that was the source of her critical acclaim. The reviewer praised the concluding scenes of the novel for being "worked up with so much terror and pathos, as to fix the rank of this last work of Mrs. Smith's in the very first class."[12] It is by adding "terror" to the sentimental formula that Smith made room for the expression of radical ideas inside a genre, the novel, that was scrupulously watched over by reviewers for possible corrupting influences. It was not the only way of using the novel as a vehicle for "dangerous" sentiments, but it was one particularly suited to women writing for a female audience.

In *Pamela*, terror becomes a vehicle through which the heroine can express a wish to leave and to stay at the same time. When Mr. B. has Pamela carried off and imprisoned, she greets him on his arrival thus: "Sir, said I, clasping his knees with my Arms, *not knowing what I did*, and falling on my Knees, Have Mercy on me, and hear me, concerning this wicked Woman's Usage of me."[13] Pamela is in a situation where she is powerless, but terror lifts the overactive superego, the internalized parents to whom Pamela is writing, to the point of allowing her to express the conflicted feelings for her tormentor that she has to deny, but whose presence is essential in bringing Mr. B. to the point of giving in to her demand for respectability. Where a woman can never acknowledge "a wish to yield," men's superior power encourages them to universalize every "no" into a "yes." Terror therefore does not always open the space for sexual choice for women. However, within a set of conventions that proscribe any but the vaguest knowledge on the basis of which women might make such a choice, terror stands in for the forbidden sexual specificity, and thus inscribes sexuality into a situation in which it cannot be mentioned directly.

Terror appears in *Emmeline* when she is confronted with sexuality, and thus with a need to assert herself, but without losing her claim to innocence and virtue. Terror is thus the place of transgression, either of others upon Emmeline or on the part of Emmeline herself. Usually the first calls up the second, as in the scene near the beginning of the novel when Mrs. Carey dies and Emmeline finds herself alone in the castle in the presence of death. But this produces no terror in her since her spirits "were yet unbroken by affliction, and her understanding was of the first rank." The "garden" of her consciousness, in other words, has not yet been invaded. "Instead therefore of giving way to tears and exclamations, she now considered how she could best perform all she could now do for her deceased friend." But then she realizes that the garden has fallen, and that flight may be necessary. Mr. Maloney, whose forwardness has annoyed her in the past, is in the area and "might now, she feared, approach to a more insulting familiarity; to be exposed to which, entirely in his power, and without any female companion, filled her with the most alarming apprehensions: and the more her mind dwelt on that circumstance, the more she was terrified at the prospect before her; insomuch as she could have immediately quitted the house—but whither could she go?" (6). Terror comes in the presence not of death but of the need for initiative and self-assertion. Emmeline does go beyond the limits of patience and meekness in that, acting on the knowledge that her terror represents, she rejects her guardian's choice of Maloney as a marriage partner for her.

Emmeline's "entrance into the world" takes the form of an unspecified realization that she is a target for rape wherever she is. Without "voluntary spies" to intervene on behalf of powerless women, to move about without the protection of a family, husband, or chaperon, is to expose herself to this danger. She faces it again when, on a walk in the woods near the castle, her rapport with nature is interrupted by Delamere. He in turn, impetuous though he is, "could not see her terror without being affected." He therefore takes her arm in his and offers to walk her home, thus risking being seen by his father, who opposes a match between his son and an ostensibly poor relation. "To this Emmeline in vain objected. To escape was impossible. To prevail upon him to leave her equally so." Yet fearing to be blamed for a situation she neither provoked nor desired, her response is not irritation but terror. Finally, as she is packing to flee the castle, she hears footsteps near her door. "Amazed to find it so late, her terror increased; yet she endeavoured to reason herself out of it, and to believe it was the effect of fancy." Delamere bursts through the door and throws himself at her feet, at which point Emmeline is "infinitely too terrified to speak" (32).

This scene is followed by one of those Gothic flights along the corridors of a castle that readers like Catherine Morland expected to find in "horrid novels," flights in which broken steps lead to bolted doors and a sudden gust of wind blows out a candle at the crucial moment. At last, "breathless with fear," Emmeline knocks on a door, hoping to arouse Lord Montreville, then faints on discovering that she has knocked on the wrong door and awakened Delamere's friend Fitz-Edward instead. Nor is Fitz-Edward an entirely safe choice as a midnight companion. When Delamere later abducts Emmeline, he is on the scene and helps his rash friend attain his object, not because he is villainous but because he is one of those innocents who forward evil. In this case, he cannot believe that Lord Montreville's opposition to the match will not disappear in time or that his friend could possibly do anything to compromise such a fine girl as Emmeline.

What is remarkable about a Gothic flight such as this is the amount of physical contact with a man it allows a heroine even as she is demonstrating her purity. In this instance, Fitz-Edward supports Emmeline, who cannot walk back to her room herself, and who at one point clasps his hand and entreats him not to leave her. Yet all this is perfectly virtuous, since, as Burke points out, in arguing for terror as a route to the sublime, "the mind is so entirely filled with its object that it cannot entertain any other."[14] Transmitted to a reader who identifies with Emmeline, it deflects the realization that, in a "wild scene" such as this one, where two people of opposite sexes are clasping each other at two in the morning, sexuality might break through at any moment. It thus gives a heroine, as Ellen Moers has pointed out, opportunities for "adventures" that do not "offend the proprieties."[15]

When she is faced with the sexuality of others, Emmeline's terror emanates from an impulse toward self-preservation. But what is problematic in novels of this period is not the heroine's aversion but her own "lively preference." In *Emmeline,* terror indicates that the heroine has moved outside the bounds for virtuous behavior prescribed for her sex, though not quite in the same way that it does for Pamela. When Pamela and Mrs. Jewkes are getting ready for bed, for instance, and Mr. B. has hidden himself in Mrs. Jewkes's closet, Pamela's plea to Mrs. Jewkes not to leave her alone with her master comes as much out of a fear of what she herself might do in a moment of weakness as of what he will do to her. In the first half of the novel, she is never far from the edge of her own self-control, which is why she must constantly invoke assistance from present and absent others to reimpose it.

Smith is much more explicit about Emmeline's feeling for her lover, describing her as "one who fancied that in retirement she might conceal, if she could not conquer, her affection for Godolphin, (tho' in fact she only languished for an opportunity of thinking of him perpetually without observation)" (400–401). Terror comes up for her and for Adelina around the issue of Adelina's illegitimate child. Her brother has taken her in and agreed to raise the child, but only if she refuses to see Fitz-Edward. A mysterious figure begins to "haunt" the house. Inevitably Adelina recognizes him and faints, and Fitz-Edward, commenting that "her brother has terrified her into madness," carries her into Godolphin's house, and into his presence. Godolphin comments that Emmeline is "almost terrified to death." Then after a moment, "excess of terror now operated to restore, in some measure, to Emmeline the presence of mind it had deprived her of. She found it absolutely necessary to exert herself; and advancing towards Lady Adelina, by whose side Fitz-Edward still knelt, she took one of her hands" (481).

Fitz-Edward insists that Godolphin is a "cruel and unrelenting brother, who has persisted in wishing to divide" him from his beloved even though Adelina's husband is now dead. Godolphin is infuriated by this disregard of public opinion, whereupon Emmeline cries out: " 'I must leave you, indeed I must, Mr. Godolphin! If you would not see *me* expire with terror, and entirely kill your sister, you must be cool.' She was indeed again deprived nearly of her breath and her recollection by the fear of their instantly flying to extremities" (482). Fitz-Edward is finally persuaded to leave and Godolphin is persuaded to an interview with him the following day. "Tell me," Emmeline asks Fitz-Edward, "before I die with terror—tell me with what intention you come tomorrow?" Fitz-Edward replies that he intends to ask Godolphin for his sister's hand in marriage "which in fact [he has] no right to prevent" (484).

Terror seems to be associated here with the possibility that Godolphin may do something that would run so contrary to Emmeline's unconventional but deeply held moral position that he would forfeit her love. It comes up in the presence of transgression: Fitz-Edward is not supposed to be near Adelina, nor is he supposed to insist on a right that eighteenth-century English society did not grant to adulterers. In the situation with Maloney, too, terror arose when Emmeline realized she would have to take responsibility for her "innocence" even if it meant repulsing a suitor and defying her guardian. If we think of Clarissa and Evelina, to take two of the most popular heroines of the period, such latitude of action would have rendered them, as Lord Orville says of Congreve's Angelica, too conscious of their own power.

In the scenes just described, Emmeline is uncertain of her power to bring about a reconciliation between Godolphin and

Fitz-Edward, but she is conscious of a moral imperative that she do so. Terror is produced by the juxtaposition of these two feelings. It gives rise to unconsciousness of the transgression involved in her assertion of moral superiority to her lover, whom she creates in her own image, just as Maria created Darnford. Thus at the very moment of her triumph, when Godolphin, Fitz-Edward, and the illegitimate child of the latter are embracing, Godolphin "took the hand of Emmeline. 'Why this terror? why this haste?' said he, observing her to be almost breathless. 'I thought—I imagined—I was afraid—' answered she, *not knowing what she said*. 'Be not alarmed,' said Godolphin—'We go together as friends' " (492, my italics). Terror has opened up possibilities for the heroine to assert herself where Evelina would have fainted long ago. It gives Godolphin room to reassert a dominant, protective stance after being corrected by the morally superior sex.

Like *The Old English Baron* and *The Recess, Emmeline* involves a contest over a circumscribed space. The secret concealed in Mowbray castle is the fact of Emmeline's legitimate birth. It is written on a piece of paper in a casket that she has had in her possession all along, but a faithful servant telling her the circumstances of her birth must intervene before she can avail herself of the valid form of this information, a written document. Lord Montreville, to whom the castle had passed on the assumption that his brother left no heir, is not a villainous second son. His usurpation is unwitting, like that of Reeve's Baron Fitz-Owen. Yet in allowing the castle to fall into disrepair during the sixteen years of Emmeline's growing up, in refusing to give her the benefit of the doubt and treat her as a legitimate niece, and therefore, at the very least, an appropriate object for his son's affections, he demonstrates not so much his opposition to domesticity as his inability to perform the role of good parent it requires.

This is because, in relation to their son, both he and his wife are blinded by class pride, a mild form of the ambition to stay on top that we saw in Walpole's Manfred. Lord Montreville does not go so far, in violating the "natural" order of things, as Manfred did: he does not try to seduce Emmeline himself. But he stands by while his wife indulges Lord Delamere's every whim, and is in fact "equally fond of him; and looked up to the accumulated titles and united fortunes of his own and his wife's families as the point where his ambitious views would attain their consummation" (29). Consequently, Delamere contrasts unfavorably with the self-effacing Godolphin, throwing himself at Emmeline with the irrationality of a nature unused to restraint. Her virtue, on the other hand, springs partly from "nature" and partly from the fact that she had no parents to rely on, but also none who can thwart her development either by excessive severity or by excessive indulgence.

Smith's message to parents is therefore cautionary in two directions, using Delamere and Adelina as examples of children equally wronged by parents who, whether they be indulgent or repressive, express their ambition through their children's marriage prospects. On the positive side, Emmeline is an example to parents of what a truly virtuous daughter can attain if she is allowed to develop her "natural" understanding with a minimum of external constraints. Three times in the novel she is told that the only protection she can have against the overtures of one man she does not want is marriage to another, and each time she rejects the idea that an unmarried woman cannot say "no" to a man without risking her safety and her future. Her conviction that virtue is conferred from within rather than from without is as subversive of established morality as the Protestant analogue of this individualistic stand is subversive of established religion.

What is more, her reward for this firmness entails nothing less than a complete redefinition of the social hierarchy she enters at the top. We have seen how the terrified heroine expands the space for virtuous female action beyond the limits imposed in "the world" of social interaction under normal circumstances. We have seen also how such a state of emotional disarray allows a man to take control even after his "general manners, disposition, and conduct" has been "improved" by the society and example of the other sex. But the careful economic and moral calculus that we find at the end of an Austen novel, in which the man with the most money weds the woman with the greatest capacity for integrity and growth, is not present here at all. There must be money, of course, and in Gothics, as we shall see, this often comes from the female side. But how the heroine gets it involves not merely a fairy-tale ending but some bending of the patriarchal legal system that Smith hated so much.

For one thing, no court in eighteenth-century England could have awarded a girl in her position the title to an estate and the privileges that went with it. Her parents may have married, but it was clearly one of those clandestine affairs that the Hardwicke Act of 1753 was drawn up to delegitimate. Then Emmeline's mother was a commoner, however beautiful and virtuous. Her daughter's nobility, like that of Burney's heroines, is moral rather than legal. Yet unlike Evelina, she has neither a father nor an aristocratic lover to confirm that nobility. Her lover is a professional soldier and proud of it, one who says that "a man of my age ought not surely to waste in torpid idleness, or trifling dissipation, time that may be usefully employed" (314). Together, however, they gently displace the undeserving representatives of the old aristocracy, and not only the "ignorant rustics" but the aristocrats themselves rejoice at the event. A more explicit acting out of the aesthetic and political program of the later Gothic revival would be hard to imagine.

Wollstonecraft's *Maria, or The Wrongs of Woman* takes some of its details from its author's own biography: a violent father whose declining and erratic fortunes were coupled with domestic tyranny, a weak mother at whose deathbed her daughter presided, and an older brother whose preferential treatment, in terms of money as well as love, gave Mary at an early age a deep sense of injustice. Wollstonecraft supplements Maria's story with that of Jemima, her keeper while she is in jail, and with an incident in the life of Peggy, the sister of her old nurse, to show the devastating effects on innocent women of male power that is unrestrained by law or custom. But Maria's marital disappointment, and her explanation for having given herself in marriage to Mr. Venables, a man she came to detest to the point of leaving, could have come from a biography of Charlotte Smith.

Wollstonecraft's novel protests the power of men to imprison their wives in order to defraud them of money they cannot get at in any legal way. Maria tells how her uncle "had left the greater part of his fortune to my child, appointed me its guardian; in short, every step was taken to enable me to be mistress of his fortune, without putting any part of it in Mr. Venables' power."[16] Charlotte Smith's father-in-law did the same for his grandchildren, though Charlotte had to engage in years of legal haggling to benefit from this method of getting around the absolute power of a husband over his wife's money. The narratives of Jemima and Peggy, and Maria's own story of how she was brought to the prison in which the novel is set, dramatize the marginality of women and their helplessness before the power of irresponsible men whose behavior is supported by custom and law.

This motif of imprisonment and female victimization links *Maria* to the Gothic novel. But the most radical part of the work, though less openly stated, is her defense of female sexuality: what Maria calls her "delicacy." Writing the story of her life for the daughter from whom she has been separated by her husband, Maria warns of the danger to a woman of complying out of a sense of duty with the sexual demands of the man to whom she is legally bound. She tells her daughter how, after an absence in which she had gone home to take care of her father's botched finances, her husband attempted without success to reawaken her love for him. "My husband's renewed caresses then became hateful to me," she comments. "[H]is brutality was tolerable compared to his distasteful fondness." But then, "compassion, and the fear of insulting his supposed feelings, by a want of sympathy, made me dissemble, and do violence to my delicacy" (101). Thus she followed what she calls "my principles, till the improvement of my understanding has enabled me to discern the fallacy of prejudices at war with nature and reason" (114).

Reflecting on this aspect of women's oppression, often and easily concealed, Maria makes the following observations to a daughter who will need to understand sexuality in a light beyond the one her hypocritical culture provides:

When novelists or moralists praise as a virtue a woman's coldness of constitution, and want of passion, and make her yield to the ardor of her lover out of sheer compassion, or to promote a frigid plan of future comfort, I am disgusted. . . . [Such women] may possess tenderness; but they want that fire of the imagination, which produces *active* sensibility and *positive* virtue. How does the woman deserve to be characterized, who marries one man, with a heart and imagination devoted to another? Is she not an object of pity or contempt, when thus sacrilegiously violating the purity of her own feelings? Nay, it is as indelicate, when she is indifferent, unless she be constitutionally insensible; then indeed it is a mere affair of barter; and I have nothing to do with the secrets of trade. . . . Truth is the only basis of virtue; and we cannot, without depraving our minds, endeavor to please a lover or husband, but in proportion as he pleases us. (101–2)

Of course moralists and novelists from Richardson onwards were representing virtue in the "corporal form" of a woman who, in another of Wollstonecraft's telling phrases, "sentimentalized herself into stone." In her insistence that purity include a sexuality that stems from a "lively preference," Wollstonecraft's unfinished novel can be read as a gloss on the Gothic novels of her day, as well as a comment on the sentimental fiction from which they, in certain crucial respects, departed.

In the previous chapter I distinguished between two kinds of Gothic: one that reclaimed the castle by expelling its usurping owner, the other that viewed the castle from the point of view of a very Satanic rebel. Although *Maria* was unfinished when Wollstonecraft died, her notes indicate that she intended Maria's romantic happiness to be temporary, and that her disappointment should drive her to suicide. But what keeps domestic life a pleasure not for her ordained is not Maria's own sin but the sin of a society that denies women their rights as equal persons. Using one of the "negative spaces" that had become part of the world of the Gothic, the asylum, Wollstonecraft created a heroine whose life negates the claims made for a world divided into "separate spheres." Not only is a sequestered world not safer for women, it makes impossible the kinds of relationships between men and women on which that safety must depend. The critique she levels at her society is that its actual practice with respect to women makes the ideal of "home" a cruel lie.

The concern with the power of the written word that we saw in Wollstonecraft's early review of *Emmeline* is found again in her last work. While in prison Maria is prepared to fall in love with Darnford through the medium of the written word, that is, through the books he lends her and the marginal notes he has written on them. "She read them over and over, and fancy, treacherous fancy, began to sketch a character, congenial with her own, from these shadowy outlines" (34). Looking out the window in vain for the owner of the books, "She was ashamed of feeling disappointed, and reflected, as an excuse to herself, on the little objects which attract attention when there is nothing to divert the mind; and how difficult it was for women to avoid growing romantic, who have no active duties or pursuits." (35) As Janet Todd has insightfully observed, the asylum "is a metaphor for more than the external tyranny of men."[17]

At issue is the status of imagination in the lives of women. "What a creative power has an affectionate heart!" Wollstonecraft exclaims. "There are beings who cannot live without love, as poets love; and who feel the electric spark of genius, wherever it awakens sentiment or grace" (35). Clearly, Mary is to be seen as one of these people, and to be admired as such. In the next chapter, which deals with the development of Maria's love for Darnford, she goes on to talk about "the electric spark of genius" as it relates to women: "The youths who are satisfied with the ordinary pleasures of life, and do not sigh after ideal phantoms of love and friendship, will never arrive at great maturity of understanding: but if these reveries are cherished, as is too frequently the case with women, when experience ought to have taught them in what human happiness consists, they become as useless as they are wretched" (49). The wonderful Darnford that Maria experiences simply enters the space in which her imagination has created him.

As long as the two remain in prison, this creative power of Maria's converts the prison into an Eden on earth. "So much of heaven did they enjoy, that paradise bloomed around them; or they, by a powerful spell, had been transported into Armida's garden" (51).[18] Yet the imagination is not intrinsically an enemy to women's happiness, nor are its fruits contemptible. "What are we," Wollstonecraft asks rhapsodically, "when the mind has, from reflection, a certain kind of elevation, which exalts the contemplation about the little concerns of prudence!" It enables women to transcend the chicanery and self-interest which she criticizes in *A Vindication of the Rights of*

Woman, even though they are not free beings. "We see what we wish, and make a world of our own—and, though reality may sometimes open a door to misery, yet the moments of happiness procured by the imagination, may, without a paradox, be reckoned among the solid comforts of life." The paradise is real inasmuch as women are allowed to "rule," as they sometimes are in enclosed spaces. It is so for Maria in her prison, who, "imagining that she had found a being of celestial mould—was happy,—nor was she deceived.—He was then plastic in her impassioned hand—and reflected all the sentiments which animated and warmed her" (139).

But of course Darnford out in the world is a different story. Like Gilbert Imlay, he shuns the woman who has taken him "as a husband." Wollstonecraft's notes have Maria succeeding in the suicide she herself attempted when she faced the end of her alliance with Imlay. Women imprisoned within patriarchal institutions "can make a heaven of hell," but by directing all their powers toward this end, they make themselves unfit to survive in the world. There is thus a point to the alternation of Wollstonecraft's comments on Maria's imagination as it creates Darnford and the condition of the inmates around her, of whom "the playful tricks and mischievous devices of their disturbed fancy, that suddenly broke out, could not be guarded against, when they were permitted to enjoy any portion of freedom; for, so active was their imagination, that every new object, which accidentally struck their senses, awoke to phrenzy their restless passions" (33). Through juxtaposition, each state of mind becomes a comment on the other.

An enclosed paradise created at the price of liberty for those in it is a contradiction, as Milton's God understood when he made his blest pair "free to fall," foreknowing that they would. When Maria comments that "marriage had bastilled me for life" (103) she is using a metaphor that underlies the whole of her uncompleted novel. Her marriage to George Venables is a prison not simply because he drinks or because his "fondness" is a sham. Male control of women is so deeply harmful to them that love in that context is as disabling as the lack of it. The radical critique in *Maria* is directed not simply against the misuse of power by fathers, as it is in the feminine Gothic. Though the Gothic "happy ending" has far-reaching implications for that fundamental social institution, the family, Mary

Wollstonecraft, like Sophia Lee, saw the separation of "home" and "world" undermining domestic happiness even when the partners had chosen each other. When Mary Shelley came to write *Franken-stein* twenty years later, she would begin where her mother's unfinished manuscript left off.

In their treatment of passion as an expression of female virtue, Smith and Wollstonecraft pit "nature" against entrepreneurial capitalism, as did the conservative opponents of the Hardwicke Act, whose position their plots endorse. So the support of clandestine marriage, be it between Maria and Darnford, whom she received "as her husband," or in *Emmeline* between the heroine's aristocratic father and commoner mother, is not simply an opposition of the new and the old. Rather, it takes an unfulfilled promise of the old order—in this case "natural" unions of passion that know not class distinctions— and makes it the future toward which the new order is unfolding. Ann Radcliffe, as far as we know, had no connection to radical politics. Yet we see in her novels the same critique of prevailing patriarchal arrangements made from the standpoint of an earlier, unrealized marital ideal.

NOTES

1. Mary Wollstonecraft, "Author's Preface," to *Maria, or the Wrongs of Woman* (1798), ed. Moira Ferguson (New York: Norton, 1975), 21. Smith's preface to *Marchmont; a novel* (London, 1796) shows her characteristic desire to alter the power relations that work to deprive women of their rights. She will not have written in vain, she declares, if her novel's representations "should deter any individual, who has a drop of manly or human blood in his heart, from sharpening the fangs of one of these scourges of the earth against the innocent and defenceless" (xiv).

2. Judith Wilt, *Ghosts of the Gothic: Austen, Eliot, and Lawrence* (Princeton: Princeton University Press, 1980), 134.

3. Charlotte Smith, *The Romance of Real Life*, 3 vols. (London, 1787), 1.

4. Biographical information on Charlotte Smith may be found in Sir Walter Scott, "Charlotte Smith" in *Biographical Memoirs of Eminent Novelists* (Edinburgh, 1834), vol. 2; Florence May Anna Hilbish, *Charlotte Smith, Poet and Novelist (1749–1806)* (Philadelphia, 1941); Ann Henry Ehrenpreis, "Introduction" to Charlotte Smith, *The Old Manor House* (London: Oxford

University Press, 1969). For Mary Wollstonecraft see William Godwin, *Memoirs of Mary Wollstonecraft*, ed. W. Clark Durant (London: Constable, 1927); Eleanor Flexner, *Mary Wollstonecraft* (New York: Coward, McCann and Geohegan, 1972); Clare Tomalin, *The Life and Death of Mary Wollstonecraft* (New York: Harcourt Brace Jovanovich, 1974).

5. *Analytical Review* 1 (May–Aug. 1788), 333. Ralph M. Wardle identifies Wollstonecraft as the author of this anonymous review in "Mary Wollstonecraft, *Analytical* Reviewer," *PMLA* 62 (1947), 1000–1009.

6. Mary Wollstonecraft, *Letters Written during a Short Stay in Sweden, Norway and Denmark*, ed. Sylvia Norman (Fontwell, Sussex: Centaur Press, 1970), 71.

7. Scott, "Charlotte Smith," 60.

8. Sir Egerton Brydges, *Censura Literaria*, 10 vols. (London, 1805–7), vol. 4, 77–78.

9. Henry James Pye, *The Spectre* (London, 1789), vol. 2, 92. Anne Ehrenpreis, in her introduction to *Emmeline, the Orphan of the Castle*, ed. Anne Ehrenpreis (London: Oxford University Press, 1971), identifies Pye as the author of this anonymously published novel. Subsequent references to *Emmeline* will be to this edition.

10. Henry James Pye, *A Commentary Illustrating the Poetics of Aristotle* (London, 1786), 16.

11. Mary Lascelles, in *Jane Austen and Her Art* (Oxford: Clarendon Press, 1939), makes a case for Smith's novel being the basis for Austen's portrait of Catherine Morland.

12. *Critical Review*, 2d series, 6 (Sept. 1792), 100.

13. Samuel Richardson, *Pamela or Virtue Rewarded*, ed. T. C. Duncan Eaves and Ben D. Kimpel (New York: Houghton Mifflin, 1971), 161 (my italics).

14. Edmund Burke, *A Philosophical Inquiry into the Origin Of Our Ideas of the Sublime and the Beautiful* (London, 1757), p. II, sect. I.

15. Ellen Moers, *Literary Women: The Great Writers* (New York: Doubleday and Co., 1976), p. 126.

16. Wollstonecraft, *Maria*, 130.

17. Janet Todd, *Women's Friendship in Literature* (New York: Columbia University Press, 1980), 210.

18. For a discussion of Tasso's Garden of Armida as an artificial, and therefore dangerous, enclosed space, see Lillian S. Robinson, *Monstrous Regiment: The Lady Night in Sixteenth-Century Epic* (New York: Garland, 1985), 271–85.

CHAPTER VI

"Kidnapped Romance"
in Ann Radcliffe

W̶E HAVE BEEN speaking up to now about the way in which women
writers took up *The Castle of Otranto* and turned its innovations into
vehicles for the concerns that were thought to be appropriate for
women readers. Yet Clara Reeve, for all that she brings Walpole's
plot "within the utmost verge of probability," does not offer any
insights that her female readers could generalize into their lives.
Her only woman character, Emma, is entirely passive, and total
passivity could get a lady into compromising situations in a "world"
being reconstituted by cities and trade. Lee and Wollstonecraft tell
their female readers that, in a society where men's first loyalty is
not to their families, happiness for women is impossible. Smith
sought to expose the customs and institutions that produced unhappiness for women—forced marriages, economic control by parents
in any form, the whole legal system that supported these practices.
Her heroes and heroines pit themselves against social abuses and
triumph over them.

The novels of Ann Radcliffe offer something new to the Gothic
tradition still in formation. Working in the domain of romance, which
had less prestige even than the novel, she transformed the features
of romance on which the novel was thought to improve—its remote,
extravagant settings, its reliance on conventions and "fancy" rather
than close observation of "nature," its use of coincidence—into in-
struments of didacticism whose lessons addressed real problems of
"entering the world." Her protagonists exist entirely inside parameters of virtue with which "young persons of both sexes" could identify
without risk. Yet they respond to difficulties with rationality and,

most important, independent initiative, opening the sphere of virtuous endeavour but without appearing to do so. This feat is particularly characteristic of her heroines, who took the lead in expanding the domain of virtue while seeming not to insist that the whole social order must be modified to accommodate it.

This is because they display their rationality and independence within a context in which the thrill of observing "wild" nature—steep precipices, vast forests, sudden thunderstorms and such—can in a moment become terror in the face of the apparently supernatural. Isolated in this setting, Radcliffian heroines can exhibit a hypersensitivity to God's hand working through what seems to be the most intense disorder in nature, thereby exhibiting a quality that became a mark of virtue to a class that did not work outdoors. Then, having established their virtue in this way, they can assert their rationality as a response (though invariably a delayed one) to a supernatural that is "wild nature" in its most extreme form. Thus they could be fiercely rational without really moving outside a definition of femininity that denied this resource to women.

The respectability of Radcliffe's Gothic has to do with the fact that "real contradictions" of eighteenth-century life are so close to the "medieval" surface of her novels. The feudal ties that bind Reeve's and Walpole's characters are supplanted by sixteenth- and seventeenth-century settings, the beginning of the period of early capitalist accumulation that continued through her own time, and one of the lessons to be found throughout Radcliffe's work is the proper attitude to be taken to the very real uncertainties of the marketplace. Her villains see the possibility of capitalism for making money out of money, and chafe at the "slow diligence" that smacks of the old order of agricultural accumulation, with its dependence on nature. This attitude is what brings "death into the world" of the Radcliffian Gothic. Not only Eden as "home" but Pandemonium as "world" have been placed in the embattled realm of eighteenth-century economic life, where the virtues needed to resist the forbidden fruit are precisely those needed to survive there—thrift, prudence, and stoicism.

Exemplary in this respect are Emily St. Aubert and her father in *The Mysteries of Udolpho*. St. Aubert lives in the country, but his relationship to his tenants is not a feudal one: he collects rent and invests it. He gives this money to a M. Motteville, whom he considered worthy of his confidence. Nevertheless "a variety of circumstances have concurred to ruin him," St. Aubert tells his daughter, "and I am ruined with him."[1] Upon hearing this, Emily repeats back her father's wisdom to him. Poverty "cannot deaden our taste for the grand and the beautiful, or deny us the means of indulging it; for the scenes of nature—those sublime spectacles, so infinitely superior to all artificial luxuries! are open to the enjoyment of the poor as well as the rich. Of what, then, are we to complain, so long as we are not in want of necessaries?" (40). This, then, is the value of the exaggerated sensitivity to nature that virtuous Radcliffians display. It indicates an independence from the market without which virtue can turn in a moment into its opposite. Radcliffe's Gothic pastoral uses the city, on the one hand, and art, on the other, to represent those desires which only the marketplace can satisfy, drawing the weak beyond the limits set by nature in a world of agrarian self-sufficiency.

The relationship to money exemplified in Radcliffe's virtuous characters served a didactic function for the reading public of her day, particularly for the women whose leisure time for reading was supported by men whose work took them into the "world" of early industrialization. The message is that nothing desirable is to be found in that world. True happiness is attainable, therefore, only when one is adequately protected from its influence, both mentally and physically. Her villains, male and female, crave the stimulation of meteoric profits and conspicuous consumption. In the country there are not enough people to impress, and they see its isolation only in terms of its opportunities to recoup their financial and emotional reverses illicitly and unobserved. Caught up in "art" and urban life, Radcliffian villains are unable to appreciate nature transmuted into "scenery," that is, nature emptied of its economic content as producer of food and thus (for agricultural laborers) a place for work as well as (for large landowners) a source of capital.

Radcliffe's ideal is therefore not a retreat from capitalism back into feudal relationships, as it would be for later Gothic revivalists. Her Eden is not a place that included work, as it did for Milton, but a place removed from moneymaking, a haven for self-improving leisure supported by a group of M. Mottevilles of Paris and backed up by the same garrulous but faithful servant class we saw in Walpole and Clara Reeve, as well as agricultural laborers (recompensed we do not know how) who will bring simple "necessaries" from out of the ground, from off the trees, from the dairy, the kitchen, and the slaughtering place of domestic animals. The household established at the end of a Radcliffian Gothic then becomes a microcosm of the larger societal ideal the novel presents: the home with its (mostly female) defenders, its assailants of both sexes, and its two harmoniously integrated classes, masters and servants. Here are the forms of an earlier ideal, unrealized under feudalism, that become a goal for the future and a place from which to point out the inadequacies of the present.

In her first novel, *The Castles of Athlin and Dunbayne*, Radcliffe announces near the beginning two themes that she will take up repeatedly throughout her immensely successful career. The first is the polarities of innocence and knowledge, youthful sensibility and mature judgment, and the necessity of gaining the second without losing the first. The second, related to it, is the necessity of leaving our first Eden and the danger of so doing. Our prelapsarian state is described as follows:

> When we first enter on the theater of the world, and begin to notice its features, [the] young imagination heightens every scene, and the warm heart expands to all around it. The happy benevolence of our feelings prompts us to believe that every body is good, and excites our wonder why every body is not happy. We are fired with indignation at the recital of injustice, and at the unfeeling vices of which we are told. At a tale of distress our tears flow a full tribute to pity; at a deed of virtue our heart unfolds, our soul aspires, and we feel ourselves the doer.

This capacity for what Mrs. Barbauld calls "virtuous sympathy" represents the zenith of a character's development in a sentimental novel. Radcliffe thus sees "sensibility" in developmental terms, a valuable quality that must be supplemented, as one grows older, by others.

But Radcliffe, like Blake her contemporary and Milton her predecessor, sees beyond such a fugitive and cloistered virtue, one that feels but cannot act. Innocence (even in a female) must sally forth and meet the world of experience. What happens then is the true measure of a character's virtue or villainy. Nor is it possible to avoid this encounter; it is part of growing up. For as we advance in life

> imagination is compelled to relinquish a part of her sweet delirium; we are led reluctantly to truth through the paths of experience; and the objects of our fond attention are viewed with a severer eye. Here an altered scene appears;—frowns where late were smiles; deep shades where late was sunshine; mean passions, or disgusting apathy stain the features of the principal figures. We turn indignant from a prospect so miserable, and court again the sweet illusions of our early days; but ah! they are fled for ever! Constrained, therefore, to behold objects in their more genuine hues, their deformity is by degrees less painful to us. The fine touch of moral susceptibility, by frequent irritation, becomes callous, and too frequently we mingle in the world, till we are added to its votaries.[2]

The world, for Radcliffe, does more than give us a taste for expensive luxuries, thereby making us dependent on money rather than on nature to supply what we think to be our wants. Our moral being "becomes callous," or "hardened," as Ruskin would later put it. Yet Radcliffe would not have accepted Ruskin's assertion, from which he drew the conclusion that a man should guard "the woman from all this," of a world that *always* hardens. We may become its votaries, but we may also develop a Blakean vision of "experience." Such a vision is, in fact, a precondition for entering into the earthly paradise where the happy ending of her novels is situated.

The need to leave behind "the sweet illusions of our happier days" in order to survive is a lesson learned by Julia, the heroine of Radcliffe's second novel, *A Sicilian Romance*. Julia's father, the Marquis of Mazzini, has imprisoned his wife under the east wing of the castle and then told his son and two daughters that their mother was dead. His motive is not direct financial gain, but rather lust for the pleasures of the city and for a woman who shares his jaded tastes. The girls live quietly with their governess, Mme de Menon, who warns them of the dangers of "the world," using her own experience of ill-fated passion as an example. Initially, then, life in the castle is represented as a simple, self-sufficient existence from which men are excluded, the marquis having taken his young son and his mistress to Naples.

But "the world" enters anyway, in the "corporal form" of the marquis, his now-adolescent son, Ferdinand, and Hippolitus, the friend of Ferdinand who, as an "outsider," upsets the peaceful stasis into which the women have settled. Catching sight of him for the first time, "Julia trembled in apprehension, and for a few moments wished the castle was in its former state."[3] But this cannot be, not only because of her own awakened sexuality but also because her father sees in her an opportunity to advance his own fortune by an arranged marriage to the Duke de Luovo, a man much like himself. In no time Julia is plotting flight with Hippolitus, and when her first attempt is foiled, leaving Hippolitus wounded, she tries again without him. This time she succeeds in escaping with her maid, whose lover has stolen a set of keys from another servant. She then wanders, as a Gothic heroine should, until she meets her old governess, who has been so shocked by the behavior of the marquis that she cannot remain under his roof.

Obviously, a higher morality than obedience to one's father or master is at work here. "Believe me," says Ferdinand when his sister consults him about the propriety of her proposed flight, "that a choice which involves the happiness or misery of your whole life, ought to be decided only by yourself" (I, 144). Hippolitus is even more emphatic. " 'Fly,' said he, 'from a father who abuses his power, and assert the liberty of choice, which nature assigned to you' " (I, 141). Hippolitus assumes that a "bond of nature" draws Julia and himself together, and that nature is above the man-made laws of a fallen patriarchal world. If God and nature "bid the same" (as they did before the fall) in the "true home" that Gothic heroines create wherever they go, then they can issue forth, like Milton's waters of creation, and, "with Serpent error wand'ring, [find] thir way" (VII, 302). Even when this wandering takes them, as it does Julia and her governess, into a monastery where instead of sanctuary they find a prison, the reader can expect good to be brought out of this evil. A romance plot is superimposed upon the mythological underpinning of a particular culture, and reshapes it.

Once in the monastery, Julia finds that the loyalty of the "Abate" is to her father rather than to her when he makes her entrance into a monastic life a condition of his continued protection. But Ferdinand helps Julia escape, and she runs into a cave where Hippolitus, who has been pursued by bandits, has also taken refuge. Julia finds a doorway in the cave and enters through it an underground dungeon where she is recognized by her mother. Hippolitus is caught by the duke as he defends the entrance to this cave, but he escapes and follows Julia into the castle from below. Ferdinand is imprisoned in the upper part of the castle by his father, but is freed when the marquis has such a violent quarrel with his mistress that she poisons him and then kills herself. These two deaths transform the castle from a multileveled prison into a home, an Eden where sexuality is no longer connected to abuses of power. All the members of the younger generation have a hand in bringing this transformation about, but it is Julia's "courage never to submit or yield," be it to her father, the Church, the duke, or to reverses of fortune, that moves it from one point to the next.

What distinguishes virtuous determination from the Satanic parody of it that we see in Radcliffian villains is that, like Satan, a villain never really wanders in the positive sense of that word. *Wander* is related to the Old English *windan,* meaning "to turn, wind, twist," and comes to mean "to move aimlessly about" with no negative connotations.[4] But being aimless, like being poor, takes on negative connotations in the sixteenth century, and the nonjudgmental use of the word is restricted to "poetic" usage from that time on. So it is important that Julia's wanderings be aimless, even as she is determined not to submit to the abbot, her father, or the man he has chosen for her. As with all Radcliffian heroines, her impetus to flight is to get away from what she does not want, but she does not take the further step of seeking her lover out. The fact that they meet by chance in a cave denotes the hand of Providence sanctioning their union, rather than the unguided human will through which a Gothic villain seeks to control his fortunes.

However, in the two subplots of this novel, each with an unhappy ending, Radcliffe shows passivity to be a greater contributor to female unhappiness than an excess of initiative. In these two stories, virtuous female characters fail to act at a crucial moment and thus experience the fate of sentimental heroines. The first, which doubles the "brother's friend" motif of the main plot, involves Louisa, Julia's mother, and her friend from childhood, Mme de Menon. This virtuous woman and her brother, Orlando, were orphaned and adopted by Louisa's father. Orlando fell in love with Louisa, but "a sentiment of delicacy and generosity kept him silent. He thought, poor as he was, to solicit the hand of Louisa, would be to repay the kindness of the count [her father] with ingratitude" (I, 239). Instead, he went off into the army, and came back for a visit with a friend who became Mme de Menon's husband. They returned to the army, a quarrel ensued between them, and Orlando was killed by his friend, whereupon Louisa, indifferent to the world, married her present husband.

Telling this story to her two charges, the daughters of her unhappily married friend who is now imprisoned in the very castle they find so protective, Mme de Menon says of her husband's return to the army with Orlando: "Had I accompanied him, all might have been well, and the long, long years of affliction which followed had been spared me" (I, 73). But the army is a world of men, and though the presence of women might have changed the course of history, and of this story in particular, Mme de Menon chose to stay with her friend Louisa—both victims of conventions which they let stand unchallenged. For had Louisa dared to speak her love, and thus defy the convention of female silence that, in such situations, denotes virtue, the story might have taken, at that point also, a more fortunate turn.

The other subplot concerns Cornelia, the virtuous daughter who sacrificed herself so that her brother could inherit his father's entire, meager fortune. She was in love with Angelo, but his family was "noble—but poor!" So when her father opposed the match, "he immediately entered into the service of his Neapolitan majesty, and sought in the tumultuous scenes of glory, a refuge from the pangs of disappointed passion" (II, 35). Rebellion of the sort that Hippolitus suggests and Julia carries out is not possible for these two because Cornelia reveres her father, as sentimental heroines often do, even though his behavior is in fact no different from that of Julia's father with respect to his daughter's heart. If only all heroines had villainous fathers, they could all rebel without compromising their virtue, and their real feelings. But "good" Cornelia has remained silent, and so, when a rich suitor comes along, her father, unaware of his daughter's feeling and thus thinking he is doing no harm, gives Cornelia a choice between this suitor and the veil.

Then her brother, who turns out to be Hippolitus, discovers her love for Angelo and persuades his well-meaning father to consent to the marriage. Hardly has this happened, however, when a rumor reaches Cornelia's ears to the effect that Angelo is dead. Believing it, she takes the veil. Then Angelo learns what has happened to his beloved, becomes a monk, and the two lovers pine away in adjacent convents. This subplot points up the complexity that accompanies a woman's barely recognized right to have the final word in "a choice which involves the happiness or misery of [her] whole life." Again, neither one did anything wrong by conventional standards. Yet Cornelia believed immediately the rumor that Angelo was dead, whereas Julia, who saw her lover wounded and carried away before her very eyes the first time she attempted to flee from her father, clings to the hope that he is alive somewhere and finally, quite literally, *runs* into him.

This fidelity of Julia's is in reality a fidelity to herself. It is this that is tested in the course of her journey from castle to monastery to cave and back again to the castle. These tests all involve resistance to coercion at the hands of those who are clearly more powerful than she is. Her triumph, like Osbert's, is the triumph of the weak and inexperienced over the stronger devotees of the world and its power. Like the children of Athlin, the two daughters of the marquis begin in a sham Eden that is untroubled as long as its master keeps his distance. It is when the marquis returns that his children become concerned with the evidence that the castle is fallen, the glimmering light in the east wing that turns out to come from the place where their mother is imprisoned. But with the marquis comes Hippolitus, who awakens in Julia those feelings that signal the end of her innocence by presenting an opportunity (in fact, the necessity, from her perspective) of disobedience.

Julia at least has a prelapsarian childhood, however limited it might have been, before she is cast out into the arena of testing. In Adeline, the heroine of Radcliffe's next novel, *The Romance of the Forest,* the author gives us a heroine who has no such experience to draw on. Thus the object of Adeline's quest is not simply the marriage partner of her choice, but a set of parents from whom she can learn what a domestic space can be. All of the characters in this novel who are not Adeline's age peers function as parents, good or bad, for the heroine. Her release into a home of her own comes only after she has found a set of adequate surrogate parents and learned that her real parents were the unfortunate but blameless victims of the Marquis de Montalt, the villain who is attempting to marry her for her fortune. Thus the novel is about parenting as much as it is about mating, taking up the theme that we have examined in Charlotte Smith: what are the requisite qualities that will bring forth the founding members of the triumphant bourgeois order?

The parent figures in the novel can be arranged in three groups: one at the bottom of the moral continuum, one in the middle, and one at the top. The leader of the first group is the Marquis de Montalt, a younger son who bends all his efforts toward gaining the fortune of his brother's wife. This woman died giving birth to Adeline, so the fortune passed to her husband, whom the marquis slowly killed in a dungeon below a deserted abbey he owns. He then placed the orphaned Adeline in a convent until she refused to take the veil, whereupon he placed her with one of his henchmen, who raised her as his daughter. But when the marquis ordered this man to kill Adeline, he could not do it. Instead he brought her to an isolated dwelling where La Motte, in flight from his creditors, had taken refuge. The owner of this fortuitous sanctuary also refused to kill Adeline, and instead forced La Motte to take her with him. These henchmen are not Satanic like the marquis, but they are much too afraid of his power to do more for Adeline than pass on to someone else the responsibility for her safety. (One of them had in fact been paid by the marquis to kill Adeline's father, and had done so.)

La Motte and his wife occupy the middle position of good-bad parents. Their function in the plot is to bring Adeline to the ruined abbey where her real father was murdered by the man she believes to have been her male parent. At a crucial moment La Motte puts Adeline's safety ahead of his own, being a man "whose passions often overcame his reason, and for a time, silenced his conscience."

Yet Adeline's presence does have an improving effect on him because, "though the image of virtue, which Nature had impressed upon his heart, was sometimes obscured by the passing influence of vice, it was never wholly obliterated."[5] He and his wife are the first people who show her love unmixed with greed or guilt. Mme La Motte "loved her as her child, and La Motte himself, though a man little susceptible to tenderness, could not be insensible to her solicitudes." They even have a son who falls in love with her, though unrequitedly.

But all is not harmonious in this found family. La Motte's avarice follows him out of the city and into the forest. In an impulsive moment he robs the marquis, and becomes sullen and withdrawn. Mme La Motte, "being unable to assign any other motive for his conduct, . . . began to attribute it to the influence of illicit passion; and her heart, which now outran her judgement, confirmed the supposition, and roused all the torturing pangs of jealousy" (46). This jealousy proves stronger than her maternal feelings for Adeline, and she in turn withdraws from Adeline, to the distress and bewilderment of the latter. Similarly, La Motte's paternal feeling for her gives way in the presence of his fear of the marquis. So when he finds out that Adeline is planning to flee rather than give in to the demand of the marquis for her hand, La Motte betrays her into the hands of her persecutor. He gets a second chance and allows her to escape, submitting to the consequent arrest and possibility of death. But under pressure both he and his wife are transformed inexplicably, from Adeline's perspective, from being good parents to being bad ones.

People who undergo such sudden shifts cannot provide the domestic models Adeline needs. But having given her her first vision of human goodness, their later behavior tests the strength of Adeline's belief in that goodness. When she hears that La Motte has decided to hand her over to the marquis, and that his wife has not taken her side and given her a warning, she declares: "How had my imagination deceived me! . . . what a picture did it draw of the goodness of the world! And must I then believe that every body is cruel and deceitful? No—let me be still deceived, and still suffer, rather than be condemned to a state of such wretched suspicion" (150). Adeline seems to be trying to "court again the sweet illusions of our early days," but in fact she is moving through a conflict necessary to the birth of adult virtue. Specifically, she refuses to condemn Mme La Motte, attempting instead to grasp the situation of a well-meaning person in a world where evil is no illusion. In this spirit "she now endeavoured to extenuate the conduct of Mme. La Motte, attributing it to a fear of her husband. She dare not oppose his will, she said, else she would warn me of my danger and assist me to escape from it. No—I will never believe her capable of conspiring my ruin. Terror alone keeps her silent" (150). What confirms Adeline's belief to be more than a "sweet illusion" is the fact that she is right about her good-bad mother. Solidarity among women can be broken by men, but this not sufficient reason to deny its existence altogether.

The ideal family to which her quest for domestic models now takes her is one where the father, named La Luc, functions as father and mother to both a daughter, Clara, and a son, Theodore. The fact that it is La Motte's servant who brings her to her new "father," the husband of his sister, gives Adeline's journey a providential shape, tracing a line from the home of her father's murderer to the place where he was murdered and finally to the home of La Luc, her future father-in-law. Adeline's growing capacity for initiative is shown by the fact that she ends her second captivity in the marquis's castle by jumping out the window. From there she runs into Theodore, who has heard of her plight and left his regiment to rescue her. The terror of her situation sweeps away considerations of "the proprieties," yet there are still obstacles to a matrimonial finale. Adeline does not know who his family is, nor does she know her own origins.

La Luc's credentials as a parent are encapsulated in a short narrative concerning a lute he has given to his daughter, Clara. Overjoyed at her new possession, Clara plays it all day long and neglects her duties, including her duty to care for the poor in the neighborhood. Her aunt (her mother being dead) wants to reprove her, but "La Luc begged she would be silent. Let experience teach her her error, said he; precept seldom brings conviction to young minds" (249). Clara soon perceives the consequences of her neglect, and vows to put her lute aside. But temptation again overcomes her, and she begs her father to take his present back. "The heart of La Luc swelled as she spoke," Radcliffe comments: " 'No, Clara,' said he, 'it is unnecessary that I should receive your lute; the sacrifice you would make proves you worthy of my confidence.' . . . 'Dear Sir,' said she, tears of pleasure swelling in her eyes, 'allow me to deserve the praises you bestow, and then I shall indeed be happy.' . . . 'You do already deserve my praises,' said he, 'and I restore your lute as a reward for the conduct which excites them' " (253). La Luc is following the method articulated by Locke, of internalizing guilt by conferring and withdrawing expressions of affection: "If therefore the father caress and commend [his children] when they do well, and show a cold and neglectful countenance to them upon doing ill, and this accompany'd by a like Carriage of the mother and all others that are about them, it will, in a little Time, make them sensible of the Difference; and this if constantly observ'd, I doubt not but will of itself work more than threats or blows."[6] This substitution of the disciplinary use of affection and its withdrawal in the home, which developed alongside parallel discourses on the prison, the school, the asylum, is the code underlying the formation of a "guilt culture."[7] The maternal gaze, here assumed by La Luc since his children have lost their mother, has the power to constitute its charges as "good" or "bad."

Effective training is the means whereby the child/inmate/pupil registers the power of that gaze and internalizes it. So, for instance, the two children in Mary Wollstonecraft's *Original Stories from Real Life* are taught by Mrs. Mason, who had as one of her rules that "when they offended her, that is, behaved improperly, to treat them civilly, but to avoid those marks of affection which they were particularly delighted to receive." Consequently, she, like La Luc, "was never in a passion, but her quiet, steady displeasure made them feel so little in their own eyes, they wished her to smile that they might become something, for all their consequence seemed to arise from her approbation." We see that Mrs. Mason's strategy has worked when one sister says to the other: "I declare I cannot go to sleep, said Mary, I am afraid of Mrs. Mason's eyes—would you think, Caroline, that she who looks so good-natured sometimes, could frighten one so?"[8]

However, Adeline needs more than a good surrogate father to complete her mythic progress toward a recovered Eden. La Luc may occupy the highest rung in this novel's ladder of paternity, inasmuch as he extends his benevolence beyond the home, and "the people of his parish looked up to him as a father" (44, 93). But for the formation of an adult self Adeline needs to know the secret of her parentage concealed beneath the ruined abbey to which the La Motte family has magically brought her. She finds a hint one day when she notices in her room in the abbey an arras concealing a door. She enters the passageway behind it, and there discovers a manuscript written by someone who was being slowly tortured. We will learn before the novel ends that this man was her father and that his murderer was the man to whom she was given by the marquis to be brought up. But when Adeline discovers that this man is not her real father, it looks for a while as though the marquis himself may be the missing parent, who abandoned her in the convent on the death of her mother and is now trying to force her to marry him. The threat of incest is the false secret which, like the manifest content of a dream, hides the real one—Adeline's aristocratic parentage and her eligibility to inherit the family fortune.

The importance of wealth that rightly belongs to the heroine, an issue we have seen in *Emmeline* and will see again in *Jane Eyre*, is a Radcliffian theme that is particularly prominent in *The Mysteries of Udolpho*. A fortune that fell into female hands would legally become the property of a heroine's husband upon her marriage. But it enables Adeline and Theodore to settle down in the country near La Luc, and frees Theodore from the need to support himself by the male profession of soldiering. The rural endings of the Radcliffian Gothic move away not only from the industrial economy being created by the bourgeoisie but also from the extremes of the accompanying ideology of separate spheres. This shift, as I will argue in more detail in discussing the Brontës, is the trajectory along which the feminine Gothic moves toward its Lewisite antithesis.

If difficult beginnings were a prerequisite to being a heroine, then Emily St. Aubert of *The Mysteries of Udolpho* would be as unqualified as Austen's Catherine Morland. If anything, her task can be framed in terms of a situation that is the opposite of Adeline's. Emily's parents are so overwhelmingly virtuous, so wise in their precepts toward her, that the question for her is how she can continue to be worthy, after they die, of the high expectations they have placed on her. Her father, in particular, is so anxious to protect her innocence that he enjoins her, before he dies, not to look at certain of his papers which would give her disturbing information about the violent death of her aunt. With respect to the bourgeois family, the implicit context of Radcliffe's novels and the object of her didacticism, the problems of Adeline and Emily represent two sides of a coin. Either parents refuse to recognize (sometimes even going to the extreme of abandoning) their children, seeing in them only obstacles to their own advancement, or else they overwhelm and overprotect then, obstructing in that way their development toward autonomy.

Just before he dies, St. Aubert gives his daughter the injunction, coupled with a summing up of all the knowledge she will need to retain her innocent virtue and keep out of trouble:

> Above all, my dear Emily, said he, do not indulge in the pride of fine feeling, the romantic error of amiable minds. Those, who really possess sensibility, ought early to be taught that it is a dangerous quality, which is continually extracting the excess of misery, or delight, from every surrounding circumstance. And, since, in our passage through this world, painful circumstances occur more frequently than pleasing ones, and since our sense of evil is, I fear, more acute than our sense of good, we become the victims of our feelings, unless we can in some degree command them. (79–80)

St. Aubert's remarks touch directly on the index of maturity that Emily slowly acquires in the course of this long novel, an ability to "command" her feelings. The way of the sentimental heroine represents a danger to her, a barrier to learning the secret in her past that throws over her own birth a shadow of mystery. Specifically, she must learn to command her tendency to respond with terror and supernatural explanations to unusual "surrounding circumstances" which prove, upon rational examination, to be *heightened nature* guiding her wanderings in the direction of the truth she seeks.

St. Aubert thus leaves his daughter "sufficient to [stand]" but, like Milton's Adam and Eve, free to fall. But like the God of

Genesis, St. Aubert makes one piece of knowledge off-limits for Emily. It is, moreover, knowledge that Emily needs if her faith in the absolute goodness of her parents, and her consequent certainty about her authentic blood tie to them, is to be a rational faith rather than a blind one. The "forbidden fruit" is made concrete form after Emily's mother has died and she and her father are about to set out toward the south for the sake of St. Aubert's health. That night Emily sees her father sighing deeply over a miniature that is not her mother. The mystery is deepened when St. Aubert commands her to burn his papers unexamined. Emily attempts to honor his dying words, though her eye does land, in doing so, on a few disturbing phrases that rouse her curiosity about the miniature. The truth that he places off-limits, for the sake of preserving the "sweet illusions" of Emily's earlier days, is that the woman depicted in the miniature is his sister, murdered by her husband for the same reason that the Marquis of Mazzini imprisoned his spouse: he had a mistress, Signora Laurentini of Udolpho.

The fact that a scrap of this forbidden knowledge comes to Emily involuntarily suggests a higher power at work similar to the one we saw in Osbert's disobedience to his mother. In this novel one method of that higher power lies in giving Emily partial knowledge sufficient to create a mystery and then having her wrestle with, and overcome, the excesses of "fine feeling" occasioned by its presence. The form that these excesses take in her is terror, an emotion she experiences for the first time after she has destroyed those disturbing papers: "As she mused she saw the door slowly open, and a rustling sound in a remote part of the room startled her. Through the dusk she thought she perceived something move. The subject she had been considering, and the present tone of her spirits, which made her imagination respond to every impression of her senses, gave her a sudden terror of something supernatural. She sat for a moment motionless, and then, her dissipated reason returning . . ." At first, she thinks it is simply "one of those unaccountable noises, which sometimes occur in old houses." "The same sound, however, returned; and, distinguishing something move towards her, and in the next instant press beside her into the chair, she shrieked; but her fleeting senses were instantly recalled, on perceiving that it was [her dog] Manchon who sat by her, and who now licked her hands affectionately." The interval between the onset of terror and the return of reason is usually more drawn out than this, and evidence of the good intentions of the "something supernatural" never again take a form as tangible as licking her hands affectionately. Nevertheless this scene can stand as a structural model for a succession of others, each increasingly challenging, that occur between St. Aubert's death and Emily's apotheosis as a practitioner of her father's precepts concerning sensibility.

Terror also denotes transgression, as we observed in the case of Smith's heroines. Emily has, in fact, looked at the papers she was supposed to burn unread. By refusing to tell his daughter about her murdered aunt, St. Aubert plants in Emily's mind the very intimation of evil from which he has sought to spare her: a suspicion that the relationship she had with her mother was a false one, and that it is his own infidelity that St. Aubert is trying to conceal, a past that haunts him in the form of the miniature and the papers he wants Emily to burn. It is as if transgression itself is the source of Emily's terror, and the "fine feelings" she must "command" are the trepidations she has about moving beyond the limits of innocence her father has set for her. Error is occasioned, in other words, by a vague sense of guilt, a consciousness of transgression that Smith's heroines—more rebellious but also more righteous—do not experience.

Yet the "wand'ring steps and slow" that lead away from the Eden of her birthplace, though never directed to a particular destination, and over which she has almost no control, do take Emily to the two haunted castles that between them conceal the identity and fate of the woman in the miniature. When father and daughter set out, with no more of a destination than that of going south for St. Aubert's health, they find themselves at the monastery where his sister lies buried. Moreover, they are lodged, just before his death, with a peasant, le Voisin, who gives Emily the first piece of the story her father has withheld from her, namely that the neighboring Chateau-le-Blanc was once owned by the Marquis de Villeroi and is now haunted. Emily experiences the convent itself as "haunted" by strange music, and she turns out to be right. The music is made by the now-mad Laurentini, coconspirator with the Marquis de Villeroi in the murder of Emily's aunt. Some force, which Radcliffe and her Christian readers called providence and Freudians call the return of the repressed, is clearly drawing Emily's father into the presence of the tree he has labeled forbidden knowledge.

In their first wandering steps, Emily and her father are alone, but soon they meet on the road a young man who describes himself as "only a wanderer here" (32). "I, too, am a wanderer," St. Aubert replies, "but neither my plans nor my pursuits are exactly like yours." Valancourt, the young man, appears to be hunting, but has not had much success. "[N]or do I aim at it," he adds. "I am pleased with the country, and mean to saunter away a few weeks among its scenes. My dogs I take with me more for companionship than for game. This dress, too, gives me an ostensible business, and procures me that respect from the people, which would, perhaps, be refused to a lonely stranger, who had no visible motive for coming among them." Like St. Aubert, Valancourt does not have to provide his own "necessaries." The estates of his family belong to his elder brother but are sufficiently large to make him known in the neighborhood, and to St. Aubert. "Wandering" after the fall, in Radcliffe's Gothic world, denotes an economic position. The aristocracy are too dissipated to appreciate nature as "scenery" in the way that Valancourt is doing. But those who depend on it for food are too predatory: their "aim" is deadly to animals. They are too-visible reminders of God's curse to Adam: "in the sweat of thy face shalt thou eat bread." Only the middle class appreciates nature while positioning itself at a sufficient distance from it.

This unfallen mode of wandering is not the only allusion to the Genesis myth in this early part of the novel. St. Aubert, as we have seen, is a conservative on matters of female innocence. He is also antipathetic to "the city," that symbol of modernity par excellence. The scenes and interests that it offers "distract the mind, deprave the taste, corrupt the heart, and love cannot exist in a heart that has lost the meek dignity of innocence. . . . How then," he asks, "are we to look for love in great cities, where selfishness, dissipation, and insincerity supply the place of tenderness, simplicity, and truth?" (49–50). Valancourt, who "has never been to Paris," takes the old (in fact, dying) man back to his youth, awakening "a remembrance of all the delightful emotions of his early days, when the sublime charms of nature were first unveiled to him." When he sees Valancourt with his daughter, "they appeared like two lovers who had never strayed beyond these their native mountains, whose situation had secluded them from the frivolities of common life, whose ideas were simple and grand, and who knew no other happiness than in the union of pure and affectionate hearts" (49). This could be a prose portrait of Milton's "blest pair" with St. Aubert urging them to "sleep on . . . and know to know no more."

Yet Valancourt does see Paris before the novel is over. He is parted from Emily after the death of her father, whose will makes his sister, Mme Cheron, Emily's legal guardian. This woman is not impressed with the credentials of Valancourt, a mere second son, and Emily dutifully refuses to see him. Then Mme Cheron is herself the object of a proposal, and Montoni, her new husband, takes the two women to his castle, Udolpho, whereupon Valancourt, in despair, throws himself into the dissipation of Paris life. Once she has escaped from the clutches of Montoni Emily must learn, if she is to forgive her former partner in purity, that love *can* exist in a heart that has lost the meek dignity of innocence. At first, she accords with her father's view of things and refuses to see the contrite Valancourt. But when she discovers that he has used money he won in gambling to rescue an innocent man from jail, she has to reject the idea that actual participation in the life of "great cities" inflicts inevitable and permanent damage. Or, as Milton put it, that

> Evil into the mind of God or Man
> May come and go, so unapprov'd, and leave
> No spot or blame behind:
>
> (V, 117–19)

The reason she can come to this conclusion is that by the time she meets Valancourt again after his fling she herself has spent considerable time in contact with dissipation, not in Paris but as a prisoner in Udolpho. Montoni's interest in her is purely financial: he wants the estates her father left her, extracting a deathbed promise from her never to sell them and to make it an article in her marriage contract "that the chateau should always be hers" (78). To the end of gaining this control he tries to marry her to his friend, Count Morano, who in turn tries to effect her escape with him. Each time the pressure becomes too much, she thinks of Valancourt and of a marriage in which her fortune will presumably be the primary source of income. Finally she gives in, only to find Montoni unwilling to keep his part of the bargain and leave her alone. Constantly anguished because she cannot lock her bedroom from the inside, she endures a life of terror without losing "her virtue" or mentioning why it is the security of her bedroom about which she is so concerned.

But there comes a point when fortitude becomes foolishness, and when Emily's aunt is killed by Montoni for *her* fortune, and the castle fills up with ladies of questionable virtue, she escapes with a young man, Du Pont, who had fallen in love with her back in the days when she lived innocently in La Vallée with her mother and father. Back then he provided a bit of mystery by carving some verses to her on the wainscot of a nearby fishing hut and appropriating a bracelet of her mother's with her picture on it. Since then he had followed her, and Montoni had imprisoned him thinking he was Valancourt. By revealing himself (in a note) to be the author of the verses, the possessor of the bracelet, and the source of a mysterious serenade that Emily has heard, Du Pont solves an old mystery and also a more recent one concerning the singing, which had let Emily know that someone with sensibilities like hers was in the vicinity of the castle. Finally the threat to her virtue in the castle outweighs the impropriety of traveling alone through the countryside with a strange male her own age. So they *wander* together toward the shore and into a boat that carries them to the very place where St. Aubert and his sister lie buried.

With these two washed up on the shore near the very place where Emily needs to be to complete the puzzle of her birth, thrown into doubt by her father's excessive scrupulousness, Radcliffe now has the problem of having Emily track down this information, and thus give a rational explanation to the mystery surrounding the miniature, without actually seeking the knowledge her father defined as forbidden. In directing Emily's verbal "wanderings" toward the solution to the false mystery, Radcliffe has her heroine learn a middle way between capitulating to the excesses of "fine feeling" her father warned her about and dismissing the possibilities that terror opens up to her simply because they look strange in the light of common day. She has to become attuned, in other words, to a natural supernaturalism through which the ways of God are revealed to his chosen.

We see Emily struggling with this problem when, after her father's death, her peasant host and informer, le Voisin, drops dark hints to her concerning the former owner of the neighboring Chateau-le-Blanc. She mentions some strange music she has heard, and he tells her he has heard it too. " 'You doubtless believe this music to have some connection with the chateau,' said Emily suddenly, 'and are, therefore, superstitious' " (86), implying, of course, that she is not. But le Voisin's superstitions, disembodied though they are for Emily at this stage, point to a true connection between the convent and the castle that rationally explains the mystery surrounding both spaces. The musician is the murderess, Laurentini, who wanders over the grounds of the convent in a state of guilt-ridden derangement. The clues provided by superstition are thus not present simply as tests for the heroine's sensibility. Their function is to strengthen her command over her imagination and at the same time to alert her to the need to penetrate below the surface of certain phenomena which, when subjected to the probe of reason, provide guidance that is simultaneously "natural" and divine but not, finally, terrifying.

Emily's probing has to be careful, however, not only because of her father's injunction, but also because her inquiry might lead to the discovery of indiscretion, at best, on his part, and the painful knowledge of her illegitimacy—not a subject for a lady to raise in conversation, or even to appear to be interested in. Therefore, when le Voisin responds to her charge of superstition by saying, "It may be so, Ma'amselle, but there are other circumstances, belonging to that chateau, which I remember, and sadly too," Emily bows to a convention to which even Gothic heroines are subject. "Delicacy restrained the curiosity these revived, and she enquired no further."

After her stay at Udolpho, Emily is less restrained, though still conscious of the need to be careful. When she accidentally drops the miniature she had found (and did not burn) with her father's papers, and Dorothée, an old servant, identifies it as her now-dead mistress, Emily suspects that Dorothée may have information about the marchioness that relates to her father's papers. "But with this supposition," Radcliffe notes, "came a scruple, whether she ought to enquire further on a subject, which might prove to be the same, that her father had so carefully endeavoured to conceal." She had a similar scruple when she found the miniature initially, but then assured herself that she need not burn it, that her father had spoken only of "papers."

Yet Radcliffe apparently felt the need to assure her readers that Emily would not have yielded to the impulse of curiosity

> had she been certain that the history of that lady was the subject of those papers, or, that such simple particulars only as it was probable Dorothée could relate were included in her father's command. What was known to her could be no secret to many other persons; and since it appeared very unlikely, that St. Aubert should attempt to conceal what Emily might learn by ordinary means, she at length concluded, that, if the papers had related to the story of the Marchioness, it was not those circumstances of it, which Dorothée could disclose, that he had thought sufficiently important to wish to have concealed. She, therefore, no longer hesitated to make the enquiries, that might lead to the gratification of her curiosity. (497–98)

This sounds rather like Milton's Eve persuading herself that God could not possibly forbid his children what would make them wise. Dorothée does not, of course, have the whole story. Yet once Emily breaches her vow of silence in this equivocating way, the information she needs flows in. Moreover, she herself generated the evil supposition her father did not want her to have. Clearly the forces guiding Emily toward the identity of the woman in the miniature are working from a concept of innocence that St. Aubert's cloistered virtue did not fully grasp.

The person who leads Emily to the final unfolding of the truth is an abbess of the convent where St. Aubert and his sister are buried. Though the Catholic Church in the Gothic functions mostly as a provider of parodies of family life, there are exceptions, and this convent is one of them. This abbess does not go so far in a Protestant direction as the superior of the Santa della Pieta in *The Italian*, who "conformed to the customs of the Roman Church, without supposing a faith in all of them to be necessary to salvation."[9] But when Emily came to the convent to bury her father, the abbess "suffered [Emily] to weep without interruption, and watched over her with a look of benignity, that might have characterized the countenance of a guardian angel." She calls Emily "my daughter," and introduces her to the other nuns saying, "This is a daughter for whom I have much esteem. Be sisters to her" (85).

These familial appellations are not intended to be taken ironically, as they are when the convent is being used to imprison a heroine. Rather, they suggest that this abbess takes over as Emily's good mother while her relationship to her original one is under a cloud of uncertainty. It is worth noting, therefore, that Radcliffe gives this woman the task of conducting Emily along that part of her journey that her father on his deathbed had specifically enjoined the abbess (through a messenger) not to let his daughter take. Female wisdom is higher than male wisdom, and in this spirit the abbess tells Emily whose daughter she is. Laurentini, who is known at the convent as Sister Agnes, shows Emily a miniature of the Marchioness de Villeroi that is just like St. Aubert's, and tells Emily that she, Emily, is that unfortunate woman's daughter. But the abbess knows that Laurentini is guilt-ridden and confused by Emily's resemblance to her dead aunt. She therefore reveals to Emily Laurentini's role in the death of the woman she so resembles.

The Mysteries of Udolpho is the most female-centered of Radcliffe's novels. The secrecy that St. Aubert would maintain with respect to the miniature, the fact that Emily sees him contemplating it in such a state of distress, Emily's resemblance to the woman depicted on it, and the rumor that she was secretly in love with, and perhaps even secretly married to, another man before she was forced to accept the marquis, all combine to suggest that St. Aubert was this secret love and that Emily is the child of that union. Like Julia, therefore, but unlike Adeline, Emily is seeking not a lost father but a lost mother. In the abbess she finds a new mother who can give her what her father could not: information that is at the same time about herself and about the effects of unrestrained passion, and that situates her in a world where good can be brought out of evil as well as destroyed by it.

Once Emily incorporates this forbidden knowledge she can forgive Valancourt and accept him as her husband, the step that brings her to the end of her journey. She is able, that is, to transcend her father's belief in the inevitable "hardening" that the capitalist world engenders, with the consequent necessity of protecting women from it. This view of innocence, which constitutes one-half of the central paradox of *Paradise Lost,* had become, by the time Ruskin gave his speech about the true home, enshrined in the ideology of "separate spheres" as the whole nature of woman. Writing in the 1790s, Radcliffe deconstructed this ideology. Her heroines find male protection at best a mixed blessing, at worst an intolerable limitation. By clothing in the romance elements of "accident and superstition" many of the actions that propel her protagonists forward, by having, for instance the mad Agnes/Laurentini tell Emily a mixture of truth and erroneous conjecture that the abbess must then rectify with the whole truth ("Emily, however, thought she perceived something more than madness in the inconsistencies of Agnes"), Radcliffe inscribes the "deep subversive impulse" underlying their journeys, presenting it as part of the natural order, the work of providence.

Finally, *The Mysteries of Udolpho* is woman-centered not only in its mythic dimension, where women are magically guided beyond the limits imposed by men, but in the domain of economics as well. This is true also of *The Romance of the Forest,* where Adeline, to whom "the rich estates of her father were restored" with the discovery of her true parentage, marries a soldier, a mere "son of an ancient family of France, whose decayed fortunes occasioned them to seek a retreat in Switzerland." Indeed not only La Luc *fils* but all the male characters in *The Romance of the Forest* have married women whose incomes are greater than theirs. Both the marquis and La Motte have dissipated the doweries of their wives, though only the marquis has raised his level of villainy from petty to grand by murdering to gain the "superior fortune" that Adeline's mother brought into her marriage to the virtuous Henri. Marrying a wealthy woman is not a crime per se in Radcliffe's world. What matters is not how much wealth you have, but whether or not you want more, and what you do to get it.

In *The Mysteries of Udolpho,* the struggle between good and evil is fought over the estates which passed from St. Aubert to Emily and those which will (and do) go to Emily on the death of her aunt, Mme Cheron. What is notable about the economics of Radcliffe's medieval world is that money and property do not automatically revert to a husband when a woman marries. This appears, in fact, to have been historically accurate for women on the Continent, particularly aristocratic women. By contrast, an eighteenth-century English husband did not have to resort to murder to acquire his wife's estates, since it was a long-established custom, undone by the Married Woman's Property Act of 1837 and subsequent legislation, that they became his on marriage. Sharply contrasting to this we have, in *The Mysteries of Udolpho,* a determination on the part of Emily and her aunt to preserve inheritance in the female line, behind which lies a conviction that without their consent there is nothing Montoni can do to become the legal owner of their property.

But Montoni does go to great lengths. Like the Harlowes in *Clarissa,* he wants to marry Emily to a man from whom he can later extract Emily's estates. Thus he attempts to "sell" Emily to Count Morano, whom he thinks to be a member of the Italian aristocracy. He is actuated "by motives entirely selfish, those of avarice and pride, the last of which would be gratified by an alliance with a Venetian nobleman, the former by Emily's estates in Gascony, which he had stipulated as the price of his favor" (273). If Morano could acquire Emily's property automatically through marriage, we would have to assume that Montoni could have avoided the long process of torture by which he wears Mme Cheron down to the point of her death. But if a woman's consent is necessary, then Montoni's plan involves delegating some of the persuading and forcing to Morano, leaving him to concentrate on Mme Cheron while making sure he gets the fruits of Morano's efforts with Emily.

The need for such machinations suggests considerable economic power on the part of Radcliffian women. Even when Montoni does finally force Emily to sign over her estates to him after the death of her aunt, that document, Du Pont assures her later, will not necessarily be binding in a court of law. The legal system of *Udolpho* protected women to a degree that did not occur in England until half a century after the novel appeared. Before this is proven true, however, Emily sees no possibility of marriage to Valancourt once her property is gone. The question of how she will survive is not even raised. But Montoni dies "in a doubtful and mysterious manner," so Emily inherits not only Udolpho (usurped by Montoni from Laurentini, who wills it to Emily, who in turn gives it away) and the "chateau" of her childhood, La Vallée. She also buys from the relatives who had tried to modernize it the family residence where her father had grown up. These arrangements would be called by anthropologists matrilineal and matrilocal: the husband joins his wife's kin group rather than her joining his.

The Italian is not as female-centered, economically speaking, as *Udolpho* because Vivaldi, its hero, unlike Theodore and Valancourt, is an eldest son of a very wealthy family. His parents therefore do not wish him to marry Ellena, who is beautiful, passive, and poor. The discovery of her true parentage does not bring wealth with it, but merely enables her to marry Vivaldi without crossing class lines. Written in response to Matthew Gregory Lewis's *The Monk*, which claimed inspiration from *The Mysteries of Udolpho*, this last Gothic work of Radcliffe's has more of the features of a realistic novel— credible situations, "mixed" (or as we would now say, "round") characters—and fewer instances of coincidence and other forms of magical guidance that characterize the romance genre.

What makes this an unusual Radcliffian Gothic is that its center of developing consciousness is not the heroine but the villain. Engaged by the Marchesa di Vivaldi to murder her son's sweetheart, Schedoni, her confessor, comes to believe that Ellena is his own daughter by a woman who is now, herself, retired to a convent. He believes this because, at the point at which he is about to murder Ellena, he sees a miniature of himself that Ellena's aunt, Signora Bianchi, had given to her niece. Ellena has been taught that this man is her father, but the truth is that her father is Schedoni's elder brother, whom he has murdered. He also believes he has murdered his wife in a fit of jealousy when in fact this virtuous woman escaped and gave her daughter to her sister.

But why would Bianchi keep a miniature of a man who attempted (and as far as she knows, succeeded in) the murder of her sister? Clearly the miniature has a life of its own, a purpose that will be revealed at the right moment. It is preserved in Bianchi's drawer for some higher destiny, and falls into Ellena's possession precisely so that it can save her from death at the hands of the man it represents. But it saves Schedoni as well as Ellena, making him into a much more complex figure than those almost allegorical figures of evil named Malcolm, Mazzini, de Montalt, and Montoni. For though Schedoni has all the crimes, the flaws, and the birth order that characterize a Radcliffian villain, he too is traveling toward a truth he does not fully know, and it is this journey, rather than those of the virtuous Ellena and Vivaldi, that constitutes for the reader the center of consciousness in the novel. Radcliffe was writing to show her public how *The Monk* ought to have been written, but she is as much, and as little, "of the devil's party" as Milton was.

What makes Schedoni such a complex, appealing villain is that though he is, by reason of his past and his profession, an exile from the circle of domesticity, he is drawn to it, however perversely. His relationship to the marchesa, Vivaldi's mother, certainly stretches the meaning of the word "confessor." She opens up her heart to him on topics she cannot mention to her husband. "My mind is perpetually haunted by a sense of my misfortune," she tells him. "It has no respite; awake or in my dream, this ungrateful son pursues me! The only relief my heart receives is when conversing with you—my only counsellor, my only disinterested friend" (171). We can understand in psychoanalytic and feminist terms the marchesa's feelings of rejection by a son who is in love with another woman, and her obsession with vengeance against the young and beautiful Ellena. What is more subtle is the way Schedoni falls in with her need for a person who can give her the sympathy and attention that neither her husband nor her son is willing to give her.

Schedoni has not yet discovered his own incestuous feelings for the young woman who will later appear to be his daughter. But the marchesa is right in suspecting that, of all the characters in the novel, he is uniquely capable of understanding her pain. Schedoni's own sexuality is caught in the familial net, despite the fact that he has repudiated both by becoming a monk. Yet if we go back to Schedoni's own family we see that he saw himself as an outsider there as well. First, the size of his patrimony as a younger son caused him to suffer "full as much resentment towards [his brother] from system, as he did from passion." It is in his resentment "from system" that Schedoni most resembles the heroic side of Milton's Satan, who objected more to the idea of Christ's elevation than to any consequent change in heavenly arrangements. Secondly, this brother's move to cut off "further aid than was sufficient for [Schedoni's] absolute necessities" pushes the second son's extravagance and reinforces his outsider status. Finally, the economic aspect of sibling rivalry is augmented, as it is in *The Old English Baron*, by sexual jealousy. "That brother had a wife," Schedoni confesses. "She was beautiful—I loved her; she was virtuous, and I despaired" (339).

Yet even when Schedoni has attained the object of his passion he cannot be happy. Seeing his wife in the mere act of talking to another man throws him into such a rage that he stabs her instead of the man, his intended victim. Schedoni's problem is not that he is contemptuous of, or disbelieving in, domestic happiness in the manner of the eighteenth-century rake. Rather, he is obsessed with it. He "trusted to have equall'd the most High," that is, his older brother, and had hopes he might surpass him in the eyes of the woman they both loved. Unable to accept second place in anything, he sees in the Vivaldi family a substitute for his original domestic relations, one in which he can have power over *their* only son, and therefore be "the most High." Having made himself indispensable to them in their need to control their son's marriage choice, he is willing to go as far as committing murder to secure the preeminence he has won in the eyes of this second family. In return, he looks to them for the advancement in "the world" that his own family did not adequately provide for him.

Yet there is plenty of room for remorse as well as moments when Schedoni becomes "stupidly good," in the manner of Milton's Satan catching sight of Eve before he tempts her (IX, 465). When Schedoni sees Ellena walking near the Adriatic, for instance, her innocent appeal to him for help against his henchman Spaletro brings out a fatherly compassion he had not expected. Ellena has fainted, and

> as he gazed upon her helpless and faded form, he became agitated. He quitted it and traversed the beach in short turns; he came back again, and bent over it—his heart seemed sensible to some touch of pity. At one moment he stepped towards the sea, and taking water in the hollow of his hands, he threw it upon her face; at another, seeming to regret that he had done so, he would stamp with sudden fury upon the shore, and walk abruptly to a distance. . . . He who had hitherto been

insensible to every tender feeling, . . . even he could not now look upon the innocent, the wretched Ellena, without yielding to the momentary weakness, as he termed it, of compassion. (223)

We see here, as in the later scene where he comes into Ellena's bedroom and pauses, on the verge of murder, at the sight of the miniature, that Schedoni's tender feelings are most strongly aroused when Ellena is not conscious.

Nevertheless this scene shows that, even before he has seen the miniature, Schedoni has a range of feelings we find in no other Radcliffian villain. Confronted with the "stupid goodness" that gave Milton's Satan momentary pause at the sight of Eve (IX, 465), he girds himself for action as Milton's villain did: "Am I awake! Is one spark of the fire, which has so long smouldered within my bosom, and consumed my peace, alive! Or am I tame and abject as my fortunes? . . . Shall the spirit of my family yield forever to circumstances?" (223). There are no more references to the spirit of the di Bruno family so we do not know directly what it is that Schedoni is referring to. It seems likely, however, that "courage never to submit or yield" was not their response to reverses of fortune, as it was not St. Aubert's, and that such indifference to the perils of early capitalist accumulation is the source of Schedoni's bitterness.

Radcliffe plays up Schedoni's incipient virtue, allowing him to become as genuinely fond of Ellena as a monk in a Gothic novel can be fond of anything good. Unlike Lewis's Ambrosio, against whom she was writing, he is never taken over entirely by evil. He is, rather, the site of a struggle between his old family and his new one, between the di Brunos, who yield forever to circumstances, and the Vivaldis, who are so determined to control their fortune that they will murder a penniless girl. Ellena is the point of connection between these two families, and it is when Schedoni realizes he might have killed his own daughter that "stupid goodness" becomes more than a fleeting deterrent to crime. It becomes the mark of the "outsider," the exile from domestic happiness whose point of view is represented in the masculine or Lewisite Gothic, toward which the feminine Gothic, with its "deep subversive impulse," is developing.

Notes

1. Ann Radcliffe, *The Mysteries of Udolpho* (1794), ed. Bonamy Dobrée (London: Oxford University Press, 1970), 59. Subsequent references will be to this edition.

2. Ann Radcliffe, *The Castles of Athlin and Dunbayne* (1790), 2d edition (Philadelphia, 1796), 6–7. Subsequent references will be to this edition.

3. Ann Radcliffe, *A Sicilian Romance*, 2 vols. (1792; rpt., New York: Arno Press, 1972), vol. 1, 35. Subsequent references will be to this edition.

4. For Milton's use of the word "wander" see E. W. Tayler, *Milton's Poetry* (Pittsburgh: Duquesne University Press, 1979), esp. 90–104.

5. Ann Radcliffe, *The Romance of the Forest*, in *The British Novelists*, ed. A. L. Barbaud, 50 vols. (London, 1810), vol. 43, 2–3.

6. John Locke, *Some Thoughts Concerning Education*, ed. Peter Gay (New York: Teachers College Press, 1964), 37. See also Isaac Kramnick, "Children's Literature and Bourgeois Ideology: Observations on Culture and Industrial Capitalism in the Later Eighteenth Century," *Studies in Eighteenth-Century Culture*, 12 (1983), 11–44.

7. This distinction comes from Ruth Benedict, *The Chrysanthemum and the Sword* (New York: Houghton Mifflin, 1946).

8. Mary Wollstonecraft, *Original Stories from Real Life* (London, 1971), 53.

9. Ann Radcliffe, *The Italian* (1797), ed. Frederick Garber (New York: Oxford University Press, 1971).

PART III

Outsider Narratives

"Such mistakes," he added, interrupting himself, "are unavoidable, since we have eaten of the tree of knowledge. But Paradise is bolted, and the cherub is behind us; we must make a voyage around the earth, and see if, perhaps, it is open again at the back."

"Therefore," I said, somewhat confused, "we would have to eat again of the tree of knowledge to fall back into the state of innocence." "To be sure," he replied. "That's the last chapter of the history of the world."

HEINRICH VON KLEIST

CHAPTER VII

The Outsider's Revenge:
Matthew Gregory Lewis

In the Radcliffian Gothic, we see that female virtue coupled with initiative is capable of prevailing over its enemies. It must be strengthened through tests, until knowledge that was nominally forbidden comes to the surface as evidence of the guiding hand of providence, concurring finally with the heroine's own voice of reason. The revelation of evil, that is to say, never overwhelms her, but rather propels her to a point where it "makes sense" as part of a larger scheme in which good triumphs. Her misfortunes thus fall within the parameters of Milton's idea of a fortunate fall. To be sure, the entire Gothic genre moves beyond the traditional assumption of the Genesis myth that female innocence without a male protector was not "sufficient to have stood." Heroines from Walpole's Isabella onwards have had sufficient knowledge of evil to know the difference between a sickly Conrad and a scheming Manfred, and once they decide to break with the commands of an authority figure they once obeyed, they develop some "courage never to submit nor yield" of their own.

But once a protagonist goes beyond flight from evil and actively takes matters into his or her own hands, it is not innocence that prevents a fall. Agnes and the peasant Marguerite are both rewarded with domestic happiness at the end of their respective stories in *The Monk*, Agnes being reunited with her lover, Don Raymond, Marguerite with her aged father. Yet both have borne illegitimate children, and Marguerite has killed her persecuting husband with her own hands. The passive Antonia, on the other hand, is an almost willing victim of the lascivious Ambrosio, drawing along with her a mother who kept her daughter ignorant of the differences between men and women. Insofar as the journey toward an earthly Eden is taken up in the novels of Lewis and his followers, that journey follows a trajectory that leads away from unfallen innocence. In this sense, the Lewisite Gothic extends, rather than counters, the Radcliffian. As Robert Platzner has put it in a recent debate on the nature of the Gothic: "Lewis' marginally pornographic romance is but an actualization of the incipient or imagined horrors of an Emily or an Adeline. To put it another way, the paranoid apprehensions of the Radcliffian heroine become the real crimes of an Ambrosio."[1]

Written from the point of view of an outsider, one who has been "hardened" by encounters with the "rough world,"the Lewisite novel focuses on the experience of exile from the domestic world and on the desire for revenge called forth by the experience. The revenge plot contrasts with the Radcliffian marriage plot in three specific ways. First, providential guidance gives way to a pull in the opposite direction. Victor Frankenstein's "fatal" attraction to science is an obvious example of this pull, but all Gothic outsiders are driven, as Robert Hume puts it, "into a tangle of moral ambiguity for which no meaningful answers can be found."[2] Finding themselves beyond the pale of the domestic order, they perform their own harrowing of hell without the hope of a resurrection at the end.

Related to this is a search for a counterpart, someone with whom to share not the pleasures of legitimate wedded love but the pain of one's exiled state. What causes this suffering is what causes suffering in the "hardened" man in a rigidly gendered society: he is at core friendless, denied not only the refuge of domestic life but the company of his own kind. This is what makes the eternal life of the Wandering Jew so terrible, the bond that draws Ambrosio to the novice Rosario, Walton to Victor Frankenstein, Heathcliff to Catherine. By emphasizing the absence of "kind" in the protagonist's life the author elicits the sympathy of the reader in the presence of manifestly horrendous crimes. The crimes of the Lewisite outsider are the same sorts of assaults against the family that we found in the Radcliffian villain. Yet in their isolation those outsiders appear to be more sinned against than sinning, and the burden of blame is shifted toward social institutions and away from the villains themselves.

These three themes, then, the counterprovidential pull exerted on the protagonist as he or she pursues justice through revenge, the desire for a counterpart with whom to share that experience, and the author's endorsement of the protagonist's counter-quest, contribute to a thorough undermining of the vision of innocence that is at the heart of the ideology of separate spheres. And no author has gone further, nor been more vehemently criticized for his critique of innocence as an ideological given, than Matthew Gregory Lewis. His narrative delivers not so much an unreliable narrator as an entire society that perceives itself unreliably. Those deemed most virtuous, most earnest in their dedication to irreproachable conduct are exposed as inadequate at best in the battle against evil, and at worst a deceptive surface behind which the most gruesome passions imaginable are harbored and acted upon.

The contamination of innocence is apparent in the very opening scene of *The Monk*. In fact, nothing is as it appears. We are in a church awaiting the arrival of Ambrosio, the monk of the title who is famed for his asceticism. Yet is is primarily a place where the women come "to show themselves, the men to see the women." Consecrated ground has been changed into a sexual meeting place, a fallen garden totally invaded by "the world." Most ambiguous of all is Antonia, following her aunt through the crowd "with timidity and silence," but nevertheless "profiting by the exertions of her conductress." She wears a veil, but "the crowd had deranged it sufficiently to discover a neck which for symmetry and beauty might have vied with the Medicean Venus," while her virginal white dress "just permitted to peep out from under it a little foot of the most delicate proportions."[3] Deliberately, Lewis compares her to a statue, not of the Virgin nor of a saint but of the pagan goddess of love. The seductive quality of her charms is emphasized by the now-you-see-them-now-you-don't manner in which they are presented to the reader.

Antonia's behavior is as ambiguous as her appearance. She says she never unveils in public, yet "whenever her eyes accidentally met Lorenzo's, she dropped them hastily upon her rosary; her cheek was immediately suffused with blushes, and she began to tell her beads." This is surely suspect behavior for a fifteen-year-old who claims, two pages later, that she "knows not in what consists the difference of man and woman." Lorenzo, though smitten, cannot decide whether her silence proceeds "from pride, discretion, timidity, or idiotism," and Lewis does not resolve his quandry for us. Rather, this titillation is all in preparation for Antonia's "awakening" at the sight of the monk she does not know to be her brother. Her response to his sermon is romantic rather than religious: "Dwelt she also in his heart?" she asks, and then, "as the door closed after him, it seemed to her as she had lost some one essential to her happiness" (46–47). That this awakening comes to her in a unconscious, "involuntary" manner underlines the commonality between the two siblings.

Ambrosio has been protected from "forbidden" knowledge by an institution believed (by the anti-Catholic English especially) to be hostile to sexuality. But Antonia has been protected by her mother, Elvira, and it was Lewis's depiction of Elvira's attempts to protect her daughter from sexual knowledge that aroused his critics. The first edition of *The Monk* appeared anonymously, and critical reception was, on the whole, rather favorable.[4] It was only after Lewis signed his name to the second edition, and affixed the initials M.P. to it, that the storm of criticism began to mount, compelling Lewis to expurgate his third edition. The contemporary case against Lewis is best summed up in the remarks made by Coleridge in the *Critical Review* for February 1797. Though he finds in the novel marks of a writer of genius, he deplores the "libidinous minuteness" with which the temptations of Ambrosio are described, making them "a poison for youth and a provocation to the debauchee."

What he and other critics found unpardonable was the scene in which Antonia is reading the Bible. " 'How!' said the Friar to himself, 'Antonia reads the Bible, and is still so ignorant?' "

> But, upon further inspection, he found that . . . that prudent mother, while she admired the beauties of the sacred writings, was convinced that, unrestricted, no reading more improper could be permitted a young woman. Many of the narratives can only tend to excite ideas the worst calculated for a female breast: every thing is called plainly and roundly by its name; and the annals of a brothel would scarcely furnish a greater choice of indecent expressions. . . . Of this Elvira was so fully

convinced, that she would have preferred putting into her daughter's hands *"Amadis de Gaul"*, or *"The Valiant Champion, Tirant the White"*; would have sooner authorized her studying the lewd exploits of *Don Galaor*, or the lascivious jokes of the *Damsel Plaze di mi vida*. She in consequence made two resolutions respecting the Bible. The first was, that Antonia should not read it until she was of an age to feel its beauties, and profit by its morality. The second, that it should be copied with her own hand, and all improper passages either altered or deleted. (258)

This attitude of wariness toward knowledge in the name of preserving virtue has implications, as I will show, for Ambrosio's own "innocence."

Doubting that a Christian could have written such "blasphemies," Coleridge goes on to assert: "We believe it not absolutely impossible that a mind may be so deeply depraved by the habit of reading lewd and voluptuous tales, as to use even the Bible in conjuring up the spirit of uncleanliness. The most innocent expressions might become the first link in the chain of association, when a man's soul has been so poisoned; and we believe it not absolutely impossible that he might extract pollution from the world of purity, and, in a literal sense, turn the grace of God into wantonness."[5] He is speaking as an enlightened male of his age, a time in which the cultural assessment of women had undergone within his memory a profound change. One sign of that change is that women's greater purity is not attacked as a façade concealing corruption but instead is taken seriously. But Coleridge is also profoundly suspicious of the novel, going so far as to declare, later in his life, that "where the reading of novels prevails as a habit, it occasions in time the utter destruction of the powers of the mind."[6]

I am suggesting that it is this very attitude toward the danger of popular reading that is the object of Lewis's attack, using Elvira, the apparently perfect mother, as an example of it. The entire novel might then be read as critique of these attitudes toward reading through which a woman's sphere was demarcated. Clearly, Elvira would not have agreed with Mrs. Barbauld that it was better that a woman "in the retired scenes of life" encounter a bad character "in the pages of a fictitious story, than in the polluted walks of life."[7] Consequently, Antonia in her ignorance is defenseless against her own feelings of attraction to Ambrosio, and responds, when he describes to her the sensations of erotic love and asks her if she has felt "all this," with the words, "Certainly I have: the first time that I saw you, I felt it" (260).

Nevertheless, to place "blasphemies" about the Bible in the mouth of an oversolicitous mother, and to make that oversolicitous behavior a cause of a daughter's loss of innocence, could be read as an outburst of eighteenth-century misogyny that is part of a long tradition of writing about women going back to Augustine and Jerome. Without the second plot, the story of Agnes and Raymond, *The Monk* might well be of a piece with the mild or vociferous outrage of a Pope or a Swift that women in the flesh did not live up to the emerging ideal of "true womanhood" that was being constructed throughout the eighteenth century.[8] But by surrounding Antonia, in all her "learned helplessness," with other women characters, some stronger and some more deceiving in their appearance than she, the argument of the novel is considerably more complex.

The women in *The Monk* can be ranged on a scale according to the degrees of agency they exercise in their lives. At one end is Antonia, whose excessive innocence prevents her from having control over anything. At the other is Matilda, the demonic seducer of Ambrosio, who tries to know all, and to control all. Agnes is close to the median in this ranking. In her immediate surroundings are two women who take female initiative to dangerous extremes. One is her aunt, Donna Rodolpha, who "governed her husband with despotic sway," and conceives a passion for Raymond, to the latter's intense disgust. The other haunts the castle of Lunenberg as "the Bleeding Nun," formerly Beatrice de las Cisternas, an ancestor of Raymond's who murdered her husband and was in turn murdered by her lover, the husband's younger brother and a second son.

Agnes extricates herself from the castle controlled by these women, and survives as well the cruelty of the prioress of the convent to which her relatives have committed her. Far from being too pure to know the difference between a man and a woman, she has met secretly with Raymond while confined in the convent and increased the wrath of her captors by becoming pregnant. After she is rescued she confesses: "I have been frail and full of error: but I yielded not to the warmth of constitution. . . . I was too confident of my strength: but I depended no less on your honour than on my own" (397). That is to say, she did not flee from temptation, as she accuses Ambrosio of doing. But neither did she allow passion, superstition, or "warmth of constitution" to drive her into irrationality. Nor did she allow these possibilities to warp her, as has happened in the case of the vengeful prioress, who shows her novice no mercy, or, in a comic mode, Leonella, the vain aunt of Antonia.

Three women in the novel are rewarded with domestic happiness in some form. Virginia de Villa Franca, the beautiful novice at the convent where Agnes has been imprisoned, helps Lorenzo find his sister and wins his heart after he has recovered from the shock of Antonia's death. Marguerite, as I mentioned earlier, is reunited with her father after bearing two children to a man who would not marry her and from there falling into the hands of a vicious murderer. Yet she, like Agnes, denies that she is a "fallen woman" in the conventional sense: "Yet though my passions overpowered my virtue, [she says] I sunk not into that degeneracy of vice but too commonly the lot of women who make the first false step. I loved my seducer, dearly loved him! . . . Even at this moment I lament his loss, though 'tis to him that I owe all the miseries of my existence" (137). It is thus active virtue, and not a more fugitive and cloistered variety, that is rewarded by a joyful reunion with a long-lost father or a marriage to a virtuous hero.

We first see Agnes in the same church where Antonia encountered Ambrosio, and again it is being used as the setting for contact between the sexes. Lorenzo, smitten only hours earlier by Antonia, has just had an ominous dream about his beloved and has come to the church, the setting of the dream. There he meets his friend Don Christoval, who says to him,

"Oh! Lorenzo, we shall see such a glorious sight! The prioress of St. Clare and her whole train of nuns are coming hither. . . . We shall see some of the prettiest faces in Madrid!"

"In truth, Christoval, we shall do no such thing. The nuns are always veiled."

"No! No! I know better. On entering a place of worship, they ever take off their veils, from respect to the saint to whom 'tis dedicated." (55–56)

The bantering attitudes of these cavaliers are the same that caused Antonia to turn "involuntarily, and cast back her eyes toward Lorenzo."

At the same time a much more serious level of lovemaking is taking place between Agnes, who is one of the nuns, and Don Raymond. A clandestine correspondence, which Ambrosio intercepts, is being carried on between the two. Its aim is to release Agnes from the bondage of a convent to which she was consigned before her birth by her superstitious mother. Since Agnes (unlike Radcliffe's Ellena) has already taken her vows this step is one that defies the authority of church and family at once, and Agnes is no less actively engaged in putting the plan into effect than her determined lover. She pursues it, however, only after more orthodox methods have failed. When she first meets Raymond in Lunenberg castle, the home of her aunt, she recommends caution: "Be generous, Alphonso [Don Raymond's assumed name], you possess my heart, but use not the gift ignobly. Employ not your ascendancy over me in persuading me to take a step at which I should hereafter have to blush. Take pity on my unprotected situation. Instead of seducing me to an action which would cover me with shame, strive rather to gain the affection of those who govern me" (146). This approach is foiled when Raymond succeeds all too well in gaining the affection of Donna Rodolpha, who vows revenge on learning that her niece has won the heart she thought was hers.

Agnes's reaction to this blow of fate is anything but passive. She writes her lover a note telling him to conceal himself in the neighborhood until her aunt has left the castle. She then sets up a midnight meeting with him where they can plan her escape. In the meantime she has procured a nun's habit from a neighboring convent and has worked out a plan to flee to Raymond and an awaiting coach, disguised as "the Bleeding Nun." When that plan fails, it is Don Raymond's turn to take the initiative. Disguised as a gardener's assistant, he gains access to her in her convent, where she sets up the meeting at which, "in an unguarded moment, the honour of

Agnes was sacrificed" to the passion of her lover. One could hardly call this a providentially guided act, yet it propels the relationship to move beyond the barrier of Agnes's respect for her father, who has "sacrificed his dearest interests to his scruples, and would consider it an insult to suppose him capable of authorizing his daughter to break her vows to heaven" (192).

Despite the severe punishment for her "fall" inflicted on her by the prioress, Agnes takes a positive view of the living reminder of that encounter that she carries inside her, "on whom, though un-born, I already doted" (391). Her description of her fingers "ringed with the long worms which bred in the corrupted flesh of my infant" denotes serious derangement. But it also shows her aware of the life-sustaining powers of an object to love. Jane Eyre observes this need also in her childhood self. "To this crib," she narrates, "I always took my doll; human beings must love something, and in the dearth of worthier objects of affection, I contrived to find a pleasure in loving and cherishing a faded graven image, shabby as a miniature scare crow."[9] This ability of Agnes to draw strength from past love, however painfully terminated, recalls the use to which Emily St. Aubert puts her memory of Valancourt during the period of their separation. But it also serves as a point of contrast between Agnes and Marguerite, the survivors, and Antonia and Elvira, the victims.

Elvira had married for love the eldest son of the noble family de las Cisternas, against the wishes of his father. When their secret was found out, the couple fled to the Indies, taking with them an infant Antonia, but abandoning their two-year-old son. The husband died and the old marquis refused to see his daughter-in-law, but set her up with a small pension in an old castle in Murcia. One might say she had not done badly for the daughter of "as honest a pains-taking shoemaker as any in Cordova."

Yet Elvira views the difficulties of her married life not as manifes-tations of unjustified parental hard-heartedness, but as just punish-ments for the "imprudent step" she took. "Taught by experience, that a union contracted against the inclinations of families on either side must be unfortunate," she assumes that Lorenzo will not be able to do what her husband could not. "There being little probabil-ity of such a union taking place," she tells him, "I fear that it is desired but too ardently by my daughter. You have made an impression upon her young heart which gives me the most serious alarm: to prevent that impression from growing stronger, I am obliged to decline your acquaintance" (221). Her assessment of her daughter is right: Antonia needs a guardian to ward off "temptation" just as Eve did. There is no such thing as a fortunate fall in her scheme of things: good is not brought out of evil but rather the reverse. She therefore becomes an overprotective parent like St. Aubert, but with much more disastrous consequences.

It is not just an unfortunate coincidence, then, that Elvira's good intentions, both in her life and after her death, precipitate her daughter's demise. It is because Antonia responds to the sight of her mother's ghost by falling deathly ill that Ambrosio is summoned to a situation that is ideal for putting into effect Matilda's plan to drug Antonia into a simulated death. Lacking a parent who would lecture her on the dangers of excessive sensibility, she is very much the kind of daughter St. Aubert warned against, one who "still nourished a superstitious prejudice in her bosom" (309). She has not been encouraged by her mother to overcome this trait through the exercise of her intellect, however. At the age of fifteen she has only just been allowed to read her mother's expurgation of the Bible.

Elvira thus exemplified those attitudes of Lewis's day that Mary Wollstonecraft excoriated, attitudes that sacrificed women's intelligence on the altar of "simplicity" and made virtually all knowledge forbidden. Radcliffe's Emily, though her father had given her "a general view of the sciences, and an exact acquaintance with every part of elegant literature," is similarly circumscribed by her father's notion of forbidden knowledge. But Emily has enough spirit to glance "involuntarily" at her father's papers, and thus makes for herself a necessary opening out of her overly defended garden. But Antonia, who is accustomed to confide in her mother her "most secret thoughts," lacks even minimal independence from Elvira, and therefore has precious little self to defend.

We see this when Lorenzo, in response to Elvira's wish that he withdraw from Antonia's sight, attempts, "by occasional serenades, to convince his mistress that his attachment still existed." This stratagem, Lewis tells us, "had not the desired effect." "Antonia was far from supposing that this nightly music was intended as a compliment to her. She was too modest to think herself worthy of such attention; and concluding them to be addressed to some neighbouring lady, she grieved to find that they were offered by Lorenzo" (291). While Emily's parents were still alive, she had a similar experience in the form of verses on the wainscoting of the fishing hut near La Vallée. Because "she had no leisure," Radcliffe tells us, "to suffer this circumstance, trifling at first, to swell into importance by frequent remembrance, [t]he little vanity it had excited (for the incertitude which forbade her to presume upon having inspired the sonnet, forbade her also to disbelieve it) passed away."[10] But at least Emily thinks she *might* have inspired the devotion of an unknown admirer, whereas Antonia assumes a rejection from a man she has met and likes. She therefore cannot draw strength from a constancy she cannot envision sufficiently to claim.

Antonia's paradoxical habit of confiding in her mother her "most secret thoughts" denotes a relationship that we would now call symbiotic. Elvira suspects that this symbiosis has been broken, but fears "to inspire her daughter with notions to which she might still be a stranger." Like Mrs. Marlow in *The Recess*, Elvira draws on her own experience to conclude that the entrance of these notions into the prelapsarian female mind brings with it a train of woe. Finally Elvira breaks their mutual silence and Antonia agrees, "without hesitation, though not without regret," to banish from her thoughts the person who had made a portion of them truly secret. The part that remains secret even after this promise is Antonia's "partiality" for Ambrosio. Nevertheless "the strong prepossession in his favor still existed, which she had felt for him at first sight: she fancied, yet knew not wherefore, that his presence was a safeguard to her from every danger, insult or misfortune" (318). After the appearance of her mother's ghost, she tells him, thinking herself to be on her deathbed, that among those few who she will leave behind, "I lament for none more than for yourself; but we shall meet again, Ambrosio! We shall one day meet in heaven: there shall our friendship be renewed, and my mother shall view it with pleasure" (331). A star-crossed lover's cry, if ever there was one.

Antonia's enthusiasm for Lorenzo is but the outer layer of an "awakening" that goes much deeper, a "love that never can be told," ostensibly because "he is separated from the world," as she tearfully observes the first time she sees Ambrosio, but in reality because he is her brother. The basis of this incestuous pull towards him is presented indirectly through Elvira's "memory" of her son. "His fine and full-toned voice struck me particularly; but surely, Antonia, I have heard it before. It seemed perfectly familiar to my ear; either I must have known the abbot in former times, or his voice bears a wonderful resemblance to some other, to whom I have often listened. There were certain tones which touched my very heart, and made me feel sensations so singular, that I strive in vain to account for them" (250). Having been separated from her brother as an infant, Antonia has no such "memory." Yet she keeps speaking about him to her mother as if she did. "I know not why," she says, "but I feel more at my ease while conversing with him, than I usually do with people who are unknown to me. I feared not to repeat to him all my childish thoughts; and somehow I felt confident that he would hear my folly with indulgence."

Perhaps what resonates in Antonia's mind is the prelapsarian world they shared before being driven out and separated by their tyrannical grandfather. In this world "childish thoughts" are not judged by an adult standard. Sex roles have yet to be prescribed, and love has yet to be narrowed into the gender-specific responses by which each culture creates its own meaning of male and female. The fall imaged in the Genesis myth encompasses actually two separations: this one between brother and sister as well as the division between parent and child. The point at which they intersect, the "fall" itself, is the experience of sexual shame. In *Paradise Lost* the separator is not the onset of sexual responses, but rather those responses combined with a sense, however vague, that they must be "secret thoughts" uncommunicable to a parent.

Antonia's feelings for Ambrosio never reach this threshold. What so surprises Ambrosio about them is that they are, quite literally, shameless. This is particularly true when he draws from her the "secret" that she has indeed seen the man she wished to be her husband, and that that man is himself. But Lewis makes this point through repeated small touches as well. For instance, one evening after the Monk has visited the ailing Elvira, Ambrosio looks for Antonia and finds her in her room. She gets up, but Ambrosio, "taking her hand, obliged her by gentle violence to resume her place." Lewis goes on to say that "she complied without difficulty; she knew not that there was more impropriety in conversing with him in one room than in another" (257). This is, in part, a portrait of the eighteenth-century heroine who does not know the rules of "the world." But there is also the overconfidence that led Eve to her downfall. "She thought herself equally secure of his principles and her own; and having replaced herself upon the sopha, she began to prattle with her usual ease and vivacity," unaware of the equally disruptive possibilities of desire and rejection.

Once her overprotective parent dies, Antonia is in a situation common to Gothic heroines from Smith's Emmeline to Brontë's Jane Eyre. Yet Lewis's point is that she has relied too much on "the excellent morals which she owed to Elvira's care, the solidity and correctness of her understanding, a strong sense of what was right, implanted in her heart by nature" (256). For Ambrosio's hold on her reaches into areas that Elvira has treated "with caution, lest, in removing the bandage of ignorance, the veil of innocence should be rent away" (262). Antonia is thus truly defenseless after her mother's death. She writes a letter to the Marquis de las Cisternas, and, in accordance with her mother's command, resolves not to see the friar. But then Elvira does the very thing that undermines these tentative steps toward self-preservation. She appears to her daughter announcing that "yet three days, and we shall meet again!" Antonia falls ill with fright, her maid Jacintha summons the friar, and Antonia is delivered into his power.

The reclosing of the symbiotic union between his two victims is sealed by Antonia's last utterance: "Mother, I come!" Freedom, autonomy, sexual pleasure, love beyond the familial circle—these options have all been closed to her, and there is no way left but to return to the union that annihilates all differences: to enter paradise by way of hell itself. These last words of Antonia's provide an illuminating contrast to the invocation voiced by Jane Eyre the night before she leaves Thornfield. Jane, whose motherlessness has been insightfully discussed by Adrienne Rich, calls out to the spirit of her mother, imaged in the moon shining through her window, at the point where she is drawing away from a relationship that would annihilate her separate personhood.[11] "My daughter, flee temptation," says the moon, and Jane replies, "Mother, I will" (281).

If Agnes and Antonia, taken together, embody a critique of Radcliffe's innocent, providentially guided heroines, Ambrosio represents a challenge to her concept of villainy, and one that she took up in writing *The Italian.* It has been argued, in a study of the influence of German sources on *The Monk,* that Lewis does not share the critique of society that animates the "storm and stress" writers whose work his novel in some respects resembles. Syndy Conger comments that "the author who depicts his Faustian figure as an awesome tragic figure, suffocated by a small-minded society, is very apt to be a *Sturmer und Dranger,* an intellectual rebel himself who admires rebellion in others. On the other hand, the author who assumes his Faustian character is a sinful overreacher who essentially causes his own demise is most apt to be a conservative rationalist, one who fears any kind of unorthodoxy, whether religious or social."[12] This idea, which comes from the German critic Otto Rommel, is certainly useful in highlighting Lewis's ambivalent attitude toward Ambrosio. Yet if my analysis of the depiction of Antonia is valid, it would follow that Lewis's critique of society is not more muted than that of Goethe and his fellow countrymen, but rather aimed in a different direction.

If we compare *The Monk* with *Faust,* for instance, we find not only two very different seducers but two very different victims. Margaret, like Antonia, lives with her mother in straitened circumstances. But she has a more rebellious spirit, chafes at her poverty, admires herself in the jewels that Mephisto has left in her clothes chest, and is annoyed when her mother gives them to the church. And when Faust asks her

> Will there never be
> At your sweet bosom one hour of rest
> When soul touches on soul and breast on breast?

She knows exactly what he is talking about, and replies

> Had I my own room when I sleep,
> I should not bolt the door tonight;

But Mother's slumber is not deep,
And if she found us thus—of fright,
Right then and there I should drop dead.

(3503–9)

Goethe condemns a society that persecutes the likes of Margaret for a response that is so pure and loving.

Lewis's criticism is directed toward the other side of this same coin: a society which, in the name of innocence, makes such a response unavailable to "good" women, while at the same time leaving them utterly unprotected from the consequences of masculine designs. Moreover, when we turn to Ambrosio, we see that his crimes arise, not from original sin nor from some innate masculine predilection toward violence against women. Lewis makes at some length the point that blame lies in the friar's external circumstances.

It was by no means his nature to be timid: but his education had impressed his mind with fear so strongly, that apprehension was now become part of his character. Had his youth been passed in the world, he would have shown himself possessed of many brilliant and manly qualities. He was naturally enterprising, firm, and fearless: he had a warrior's heart, and he might have shown with spendour at the head of an army. There was no want of generosity in his nature: the wretched never failed to find in him a compassionate auditor: his abilities were quick and shining, and his judgement vast, solid, and decisive. With such qualifications he would have been an ornament to his country: that he possessed them he had given proofs in his earliest infancy, and his parents had beheld his dawning virtues with the fondest delight and admiration. Unfortunately, while yet a child, he was deprived of those parents. . . . His instructors carefully repressed those virtues, whose grandeur and disinterestedness were ill suited to the cloister. . . . Add to this, that his long absence from the world, and total unacquaintance with the common dangers of life, made him form of them an idea far more dismal than the reality. While the monks were busied in rooting out his virtues, and narrowing his sentiments, they allowed every vice which had fallen to his share to arrive at full perfection. He was suffered to be proud, vain, ambitious and disdainful: he was jealous of his equals, and despised all merit but his own: he was implacable when offended and cruel in revenge. (237–38)

Two and a half more pages follow in this vein.

Lewis does not need to be a follower of Rousseau, believing that all institutions corrupt man's inherent goodness, to hold that some institutions do precisely this. For the eighteenth-century Gothicist, the monastery was the quintessential repressive institution, exerting its corrupting influence at a safe distance, both temporally and spatially, from the English present. Writing about this Catholic institution gave these writers a way of speaking about abusive power not in the public but in the private sphere. In this passage, Lewis's concern is with the socialization of children, with "modelling the human mind during the early stages of its growth, and fixing," as Gisborne put it, "while it is yet ductile, its growing principles of action." From what we know about the abusive traditions of the English public school system, much of what Lewis says about the Capuchin method of bringing up Ambrosio might be equally applicable to a school like Westminster, which Lewis attended from his eighth to his fifteenth year.[13]

To this we need to add the fact that Ambrosio was subjected to this soul-shriveling experience because his parents abandoned him to "a relation, whose only wish about him was never to hear of him more" (238). That it was not their intention to do so matters little to the one who was thus deserted, from whose point of view this account of Ambrosio's childhood is being written. The medieval practice of sending children to spend their pre-adult years as apprentices in the households of others had by this time given way to a system of child labor for the poor and boarding schools for those who could afford them. But if, as Aries says, "the eighteenth century in England appears as a period of violence and brutality" in the annals of education, the developing concern for the rights of children that we saw in the criticism of primogeniture raised questions about the effectiveness of such practices as daily flogging. One can only speculate that in view of the increasing acceptance of the family as a center of affective ties, with discipline based on the subjective phenomena of guilt and confession rather than shame and coercion, the child sent off to a school or college, where the latter methods still held full sway, might have felt abandoned by his parents, however well-meaning.

Threats of earthly and heavenly punishment are the principal disciplinary methods of the Capuchins, and the fate of Ambrosio warns against the use of overt and covert violence in the education of the young male. This criticism makes him, unlike Radcliffe's Schedoni, a victim as well as a villain. When Matilda tells her protégé, after he has killed Elvira, that "he had only availed himself of the rights which nature allows to everyone, those of self-preservation," we are not supposed to take this argument seriously. But since sexuality in a context of mutual love is a right for which a virtuous Gothic hero or heroine is prepared to take grave risks, we might say that Ambrosio, in his amatory dealings with Matilda and then with Antonia, is engaging to an extreme form of this risk-taking behavior, attempting to secure "the rights which nature allows to everyone" in the only way he can. Since he cannot enter paradise legitimately he must make a voyage down into the depths of hell to see if, perhaps, he can enter it from below.

If eating of the tree of knowledge brings with it sexual shame, then the return to paradise would involve the loss of that shame. If shame (as opposed to guilt) involves a painful recognition of the limits of another's approval, then one way to obliterate it is to push those limits as far as they will go. Alternatively, one can try to be so virtuous that those limits are never encountered. Ambrosio's behavior in the convent prior to meeting Matilda conforms to this latter pattern. His body is a garden whose walls no temptation has been able to surmount. But this condition, according to Lewis, is an acquired, not a natural, state, and issued in "a contest for superiority between his real and acquired character [that] was striking and unaccountable to those unacquainted with his original disposition" (239).

One place where this conflict arises, unknown to those around him, is when he contemplates the image of the Madonna hanging on his wall. Resistance to temptation is overlaid with a longing for it when he exclaims: "Oh! if such a creature existed, and existed but for me were I permitted to twine round my fingers those golden ringlets, and press with my lips the treasure of that snowy bosom!

gracious God, should I then resist temptation? Should I not barter for a single embrace the reward of my sufferings for thirty years?" (65). This from a man who is reputed to "know not in what consists the difference of man and woman." Moments after this outburst Ambrosio makes the prophetic statement: "What charms me, when ideal and considered as a superior being, would disgust me, become woman and tainted with all the failings of mortality." Yet this is simply a version of the double standard so extreme as to put sexuality out of reach at either end of the scale.

Lewis could be talking about any middle-class man down through the nineteenth century when he observes that "for a time spare diet, frequent watching, and severe penance cooled and repressed the natural warmth of his constitution: but no sooner did opportunity present itself, no sooner did he catch a glimpse of joys to which he was still a stranger, than religion's barriers were too feeble to resist the overwhelming torrent of his desires" (239–40). This regimen was a standard treatment for "the heinous Sin of Self-pollution," as it was called in the first popular English pamphlet on masturbation, issued in 1710.[14] As for what happens when "religion's barriers" prove "too feeble to resist the overwhelming torrent," scholars of nineteenth-century sexuality tell us that Ambrosio's problem is not limited to the inhabitants of monasteries.

The counterprovidential pull that draws him downwards into the vaults of St. Clare, where Agnes is confined and Antonia buried, is a determination "to eat again of the tree of knowledge to fall back into the state of innocence," that innocence he enjoyed with his parents and sister before he was abandoned to the power of his grandfather and the Capuchin order. It is interesting to note that Agnes's downward journey takes her to more or less the same subterranean space. For it is by this device that Lewis makes his final point: that it is she, who "opposed seduction" rather than fleeing from it, who can rise again and enter paradise by way of its typological antecedent, the home, and the unfallen love it was built to contain. In *The Monk* it is not yielding to temptation that bars a character from paradise, but rather what happens after the fall. Agnes, who stands midway between the defenseless passivity of Antonia and the uncontrolled licentiousness of Ambrosio, can encounter the limits of others' approval and transcend the shame that accompanies that experience.

But since the protective wall around Ambrosio's "innocence" is the public's belief "that the smallest stain is not to be discovered upon his character," he would be totally undone by public disapproval. This is why Antonia, once she becomes a party to his guilty secret, cannot be allowed to return to the world. She must become an accomplice to his need for approval, a fellow prisoner behind the walls that shield him from the public gaze. Here we have Lewis's version of a theme that runs through the "outsider" Gothic: the exiled hero-villain's search for a companion to share in his exiled condition. This theme becomes paramount in the vampire genre that we shall discuss in the following chapter. Here we should note that one feature of that genre pervades the entire "outsider" Gothic, of which it is a part: the fact that the vampire-exile is not only doomed to sustain himself off the blood of his victims but compelled to confine his infernal visitations to those beings he loved most while upon earth, those to whom he was bound by ties of kindred and affection.

Lewis and his followers were apparently fascinated by the idea that "each man kills the thing he loves." In Ambrosio's case, he kills because he cannot tolerate obstacles to that love that arise because his access to paradise is now barred. It can now be unbolted only by the kind of "courage never to submit nor yield" shown by Agnes holding her rotting infant in the crypt of St. Clare's. The middle-class dream of an inviolable home is violently exploded: children enclosed and kept from knowing "in what consists the difference in man and woman" grow up to become the perfect match. The culture of separate spheres urges the man to heights of sadism, the woman into a complementary victimization. Only those who can survive the horrors of hell can turn the home into anything else.

NOTES

1. Robert L. Platzner, " 'Gothic versus Romantic': A Rejoinder," *PMLA* 86 (1971), 270.

2. Robert D. Hume, "Gothic versus Romantic: A Revaluation of the Gothic Novel," *PMLA* 84 (1969), 288.

3. Matthew Gregory Lewis, *The Monk*, ed. Louis F. Peck (New York: Grove Press, 1959), 37. Subsequent references will be to this edition.

4. See André Parreaux, *The Publication of "The Monk": A Literary Event* (Paris: Michel Didier, 1960), esp. 87–91.

5. *Critical Review*, 2d series, 19 (Feb. 1797), 198.

6. Samuel Taylor Coleridge, *Lectures on Milton and Shakespeare* (London: Chapman and Hall, 1856), 3.

7. See John J. Richetti, "Women in Eighteenth-Century English Literature," in *What Manner of Woman: Essays on English and American Life and Literature*, ed. Marlene Springer (New York: New York University Press, 1977), 65–97, esp. 79–85.

8. Anna Laetitia Barbauld, "On the Origin and Progress of Novel-Writing," preface to *The British Novelists*, 50 vols. (London, 1810), vol. 1, 51.

9. Charlotte Brontë, *Jane Eyre*, ed. Richard Dunn (New York: Norton, 1971), 24. Subsequent references will be to this edition.

10. Ann Radcliffe, *The Mysteries of Udolpho*, ed. Bonamy Dobrée (London: Oxford University Press, 1970), 8.

11. Adrienne Rich, "*Jane Eyre:* The Temptations of a Motherless Woman," in *On Lies, Secrets and Silence: Selected Prose 1966–1978* (New York: Norton, 1979), 89–106.

12. See Syndy M. Conger, *Matthew G. Lewis, Charles Robert Maturin and the Germans: An Interpretive Study of the Influence of German Literature on Two Gothic Novels* (Salzburg: Institut für Englishe Sprache und Literatur, 1977), 40.

13. See Louis F. Peck, *A Life of Matthew G. Lewis* (Cambridge: Harvard University Press, 1961), 5–7.

14. See Lawrence Stone, *The Family, Sex and Marriage in England 1500–1800* (New York: Harper and Row, 1977), 515.

CHAPTER VIII

Men as They Are:
William Godwin

THE RECONCEPTUALIZATION of womanhood that is being argued out in the subtext of the Gothic novel engendered a parallel discourse about men. The privileging of the home as a place where paradise was regained, or never lost, made men's participation problematic, since they went out every day into a world that was undergoing a costly industrialization. In the work of the three male authors I have chosen to discuss in this study, the plots turn on the issue of male innocence. Lewis in *The Monk* attacks purity in excess, which lies at the root of Antonia's victimization as well as Ambrosio's villainy. The monastery, behind whose walls Ambrosio preserves his innocence of the world, is invaded by a female serpent, and Ambrosio's much vaunted innocence makes her victory easier, not harder. Caleb Williams in Godwin's novel of that name, and Alonso de Moncada in *Melmoth the Wanderer* protest their exclusion from domestic life, insisting that they are *innocent*. The wanderer protagonists of the masculine Gothic are obsessed with innocence and its loss.

One way to read *Caleb Williams* is as a dramatization of conflicts between opposing ideals of masculinity. Godwin's novel has, to be sure, a Gothic heroine, and one who fits perfectly into the pattern we have seen in the feminine Gothic. But the real struggle is not between masculine evil and feminine purity. It is between, and among, men. Falkland, his enemy Tyrrel, Tyrrel's victim Hawkins, his henchman Grimes, Falkland's half-brother Mr. Forester, the peasant who has been egged on by his enemy's insults to his fiancée, and Caleb himself, live by different codes of masculine behavior which can be arranged on a continuum. At one end is Falkland's obsession with other people's perceptions of himself, with his reputation, his honor defined entirely in public terms. At the other end is Caleb, whose conviction of his innocence lives entirely within him, independent of public recognition.

In this novel, we can see clearly a struggle between the two modes of defining transgression that I have been calling "shame culture" and "guilt culture." In the first, wrongdoing is entirely a public matter which, when expiated in the eyes of others, leaves "no spot or blame behind." Guilt, on the other hand, is an inwardly generated sense of transgression which, though learned, operates independent of public opinion. Guilt is a part of the Protestant ethic, though not confined to Protestant countries. Foucault speaks of the way in which the scope of confession increased, after the Council of Trent, as a shift took place away from sexual acts and toward "all the insinuations of the flesh: thoughts, desires, voluptuous imaginings, delectations, combined movements of the body and the soul, from behavior that was visible to that which might never becomes so."[1]

Now the point of the conflict, as of the Gothic more generally, is that public honor is always "haunted" by private knowledge, by the things no one knows about, by one's best kept secrets. But Godwin adds to this the converse: that private conviction, no matter how firm, is nothing better than a ghost if it is locked inside the walls of the self. In *Caleb Williams*, the haunted castle is the mind itself, obsessed with what it cannot include. "Locking in" and "locking out" become metaphors for interpersonal nexuses, as Falkland tries at first to keep Caleb out of the domain of his secret, while Caleb, fascinated by his master and eager to know everything about him, invades Falkland's guarded privacy, only to discover that he has forgone his freedom in satisfying his "innocent curiosity."

So we have, as in other Gothics, the drama of the fall, with the correlative point that one can be locked *in* by trying to maintain one's innocence, as Caleb does, just as surely as one can be locked out of paradise by guilt. For a time, Falkland is alone with the knowledge that he has killed his neighbor Tyrrel and caused the death of Tyrrel's proud tenant Hawkins, who is hanged for the crime. But once the secret is "out" in Caleb's consciousness, even if Caleb lives up to his promise never to tell another living soul, Falkland can never be "home" again. He must constantly be "out of his mind," trying to control knowledge that he has forbidden, but that is no longer his exclusive possession. He can only accuse Caleb of stealing some of his actual possessions and then see to it that no one will believe Caleb's claim to be innocent of any crime against his master. Since his home is no longer a truly private place, Falkland turns the world (or at least the British Isles) into a prison where Caleb is wholly controlled by the master he once revered.

After confessing the murder of Tyrrel to Caleb, Falkland declares to his terrified servant, "You might as well think of escaping from the power of the omnipresent God, as from mine."[2] Yet this self-appointed God feels he has been deprived by Caleb of something to which he, and particularly he as a man, feels he has a right: the right to withdraw from the ever-prying public eye into a place of safety and security. This "right" is not part of the code of chivalry and romance with which Falkland's conception of his honor is bound up. It is an eighteenth century possibility, one of the rights (that of privacy) that constitute the individual, that is discursively circulated alongside the discourse of the female-centered home. Individualism presupposes a specific view of the self, one that can be the focus of scrutiny by the speaking subject or by others. Such a notion of the self underlies the experience of guilt, with its Protestant emphasis on self-examination and private conscience, its elevation of the private over the public as the source of the "true self."

In his *Letters on Chivalry and Romance*, Richard Hurd enumerated the qualities found in medieval knights as depicted by Malory and others. Their "passion for arms" and for "the rewards of valour . . . their eagerness to run to the succour of the distressed, and the pride they took in redressing wrongs and grievances" partake of a warrior ethic except that the wrongs they seek to address do not besmirch the honor of their clan.[3] Rather, any damsel in distress (of a particular class) deserves rescue simply because she is a woman. Thus "the courtesy, affability, and gallantry, for which these adventurers were famous" encodes a variant on the warrior ethic that is tied to clan loyalty. Falkland, who was steeped in his youth in the writings of Tasso, embodies this variant. "His polished manners were particularly in harmony with female delicacy" (19), but he carries within him also an individualized masculine code that emphasizes direct action against those who have slighted one's individual honor, or masculinity.

Tyrrel is motivated by this latter code, and it includes attitudes toward women that hark back to a "clan" mentality. In his attitude toward his cousin Emily Melville he is more generous than his mother, who "conceived that she performed an act of the most exalted benevolence in admitting Miss Emily into a sort of equivocal situation, which was neither precisely that of a domestic, nor yet marked with the treatment that might seem due to one of the family" (38). She is, in other words, an eighteenth-century Mrs. Reed. For Tyrrel, "habit had rendered [Emily] necessary to him," so that while she is not an object of lust, he regards her as his property in the manner of a typical Gothic villain. When she gives her heart to Falkland, he regards his "rival" as someone who has stolen from him, just as Falkland later regards the "innocent" Caleb as a thief. A man does not passively suffer his property to be made off with by another man.

Tyrrel's anger is compounded by a shift in standards of masculinity coming from women. "Every mother taught her daughter to consider the hand of Mr. Tyrrel as the highest object of her ambition," Godwin comments, adding that "one of the qualifications that women are early taught to look for in the male sex, is that of a protector" (18–19). But when Falkland appears on the scene, the ladies desert their former ideal. "It was in vain that Mr. Tyrrel endeavoured to restrain the ruggedness of his character. . . . [H]is courtship was like the pawings of an elephant" (21). Therefore he chooses as his "engine," his "instrument" of revenge upon Emily, a man even more contemptuous of women than he is. Falkland, not Emily, is the object of this revenge: the occasion for the struggle is a woman, but the relationship that requires it is between two men. So Tyrrel finds an ally, Grimes, whose contempt for female helplessness is the antithesis of the chivalry Falkland demonstrates when he rescues Emily, first from a burning building and later from the pursuit of Grimes.

Another bearer of a code of beliefs about masculinity is Hawkins. When we first see him, he appeals successfully to Tyrrel for help against his landlord. This landlord, Mr. Underwood, demanded of his tenant that he vote for a particular candidate, and Hawkins refused, whereupon Underwood proceeded to torment Hawkins on the grounds that such a denial of the rights of landlords over their tenants would threaten the whole system of patriarchal privilege. Certain men have a right to dictate the behavior of other men, and this view conflicted with Hawkins's view of the rights of men. He then clashes with his new landlord, Tyrrel, when Tyrrel wants to show preferment to Hawkins's son by taking him into his service. For Hawkins independence is at the core of his sense of himself as a man. His father was a clergyman, he tells Tyrrel, and he cannot bear to see his son go into service. The ensuing clash between two deeply felt masculine principles almost destroys Hawkins, the less powerful of the two, and sets him up to be falsely convicted as Tyrrel's killer.

Thus honor is very much connected with male power, in that challenges to one's power by those perceived to be weaker or less deserving of public approbation are taken by the men in this novel as slights to their honor and therefore appropriate occasions for retaliation. The consequences of Hawkins's refusal of Tyrrel's "favor" to his son, or Emily's refusal to marry Grimes, show that law supports the power of men rather than restricting it, as Henry Tilney assured Catherine Morland that it would. The degree of Hawkins's fondness for his son causes him to resist the common feudal practice of sending one's children to serve in the houses of others.[4] His unwillingness to relinquish his boy to Tyrrel problematizes his relationship to a masculinity whose economic base has shifted, and he becomes the scapegoat that keeps its code intact.

Even those who resist are caught up in this code, as in the story of the murderer whose case Falkland is called upon to adjudicate.

[H]e and his sweetheart had gone to a neighbouring fair, where this man had met them. The man had often tried to affront him, and his passiveness, interpreted into cowardice, had perhaps encouraged the other to additional rudeness. Finding that he had endured trivial insults to himself with an even temper, the deceased now thought proper to turn his brutality upon the young woman that accompanied him. He pursued them; he endeavoured in various manners to harass them; they had sought in vain to shake him off. The young woman was considerably terrified. The accused expostulated with their persecutor, and asked him how he could be so barbarous as to persist in frightening a woman? He replied in an insulting tone, Then the woman should find someone able to protect her; people that encouraged and trusted to such a thief as that deserved no better. (128)

Here a masculine code has gone awry, as it has in various ways throughout the novel.

As for Caleb, he is innocent, in both senses of the word, when he enters upon a world already constructed around conflicting notions of honor. Throughout the novel he emphasizes his youth: his "youthful mind," his "youthful curiosity," his "raw, unfriended youth." Like Falkland, his character was formed by "books of narrative and romance." He is admitted into Falkland's home in the capacity of secretary, and, hired to write, gets too involved in Falkland's "story." He looks to Falkland to take his father's place, and regards him at the beginning of the novel, and again at the end, "as a being of a superior nature." Caleb's desire to merge with his "father" begins with the eye, with his decision "to place [himself] as a watch upon [his] patron." His "crime" is that he wants to stand in the place of Falkland, to appropriate his story, to become one with his desire, the "desire of the other." Forbidden knowledge is knowledge of the world from the place of the other, the place of the parent into whose consciousness the child has not yet grown.

All of this suggests the transference of therapy, where the patient relives his "innocent" attachments and the therapist, by refusing to cooperate, helps the patient to create a fully separate self. This self is particularly important for the male psyche in an individualistic culture where strength is often equated with being, as Caleb is, "indifferent . . . about the good opinion of others." He constructs an ego through his narration, an ego that he hopes will have "that consistency, that is seldom attendant but upon truth" (3). The more intensely Caleb is persecuted, the more he discovers, and congratulates himself upon, his strength. In fact, being helped by others causes his courage to waver. "[W]hile I had no one to depend on but myself," he comments, "I possessed a mine of seemingly inexhaustible fortitude, yet no sooner did I find this unexpected sympathy on the part of another, than my resolution appeared to give way, and I felt ready to faint" (213). Once he succeeds in vindicating his version of who he is, this ego collapses. It lives only in isolation and opposition, nowhere at home.

Caleb begins with a desire to vindicate his character, and ends by having no character that he wishes to vindicate. By the end of the novel, he realizes the cost of the personality structure that he has taken on in order to deny his wish to merge with his father surrogate: "I affirm that he has qualities of the most admirable kind. It is therefore impossible that he could have resisted a frank and fervent expostulation, the frankness and the fervour in which the whole soul poured out. I despaired, while there was yet time to have made the just experiment; but my despair was criminal, was treason against the sovereignty of truth" (323). Similarly, his relationship with Laura Denison, another parent who "adopts" him and whom he honored and esteemed "like a mother," is destroyed because he did not trust her enough to tell her his story before she found it out from other sources. Unable to acknowledge his dependency on, and fear of separation from, these two who stand in the place of parents to him, he is not even aware, until the end, of trust as a possible alternative. He acts on his worse fears, and in doing so brings them forth.

The theme of adoption, or rather misadoption, is persistent in the novel, though submerged. Tyrrel's mother has adopted Emily, and Tyrrel becomes resentful when he realizes that her affections have strayed beyond the family circle. He also wants to adopt Hawkins's son, and turns vengeful when his offer is rejected. Caleb considers himself as having "removed into Mr. Falkland's family" (108). His curiosity then goes to work not upon a distant object but upon "family secrets." While he is on the run he is taken into (only to be thrust out of) several families: the robbers, headed by Mr. Raymond, the Denisons, headed by Laura, Mr. Spurrel, who had lost an only son who resembled Caleb in one of his disguises. Yet in an individualistic culture, the development of an authentic identity, and especially an authentic male identity, requires expulsion from the net of family ties. The growing importance of individualism brings with it a redefinition of familial bonds, one that requires not only certain acts but certain thoughts and feelings. This new set of obligations constitutes a "guilt culture." If the key word in a shame culture is honor, denoting a set of ritualized public procedures for establishing and preserving a man's reputation, the key word of a guilt culture is secrecy. Negative thoughts that are concealed literally haunt the individual in a guilt culture. Who knows what evil lurks in the hearts of men?

Godwin's Falkland stands at the intersection of these two cultural configurations. In a pure shame culture, taking revenge into one's own hands was what a man was supposed to do. Falkland could have acknowledged killing Tyrrel and been proclaimed a hero, one who had rid the community of a pestilence. Yet Falkland too is implicated in the masculine code that creates this pestilence. The male code of honor that allows Mr. Underwood, Hawkins's first landlord, to control the votes of his tenant farmers also gives Tyrrel a right to dispose of Emily as he wishes. Falkland's persecution of Caleb is hardly less brutal than these, but he is persecuting his secretary not out of a sense that he has a right to control the behavior of an "inferior" but purely on the basis of what Caleb has inside him—his thoughts and feelings.

In our Gothic paradigm, the villain has a secret and operates from within the norms of a shame culture in which secrets are irrelevant. His defeat is a victory for a culture based on guilt, one of whose requirements is that there be no secrets. This prohibition applies particularly among family members—husbands and wives, parents and children. The nuclear family, as Eli Zaretsky has pointed out, is supposed to be a place where one can be one's true self, casting off the masks that the outside world requires.[5] To have secrets destroys the home as haven. In Mary Shelley's *Frankenstein* we see the implications of this ban on secrets worked out in a romance that has been "kidnapped" to become part of our cultural mythology. In *Caleb Williams*, but even more so in his second novel, *St. Leon*, Godwin had a hand in the birth of his daughter's achievement.

At one point on Caleb's journey toward the discovery of Falkland's secret, he pleads with his master: "For God's sake, sir, turn me out of your house. Punish me in some way or other that I may forgive myself" (119). In fact, Falkland does just that after accusing his spying servant of robbing him. But because Caleb is literally innocent of the crime of which he is accused, he refuses to acknowledge his wider guilt, and therefore cannot forgive himself until he forgives his master. Human beings have boundaries which impose limitations on what they can know. But once one person in a relationship keeps something secret from the other, doubt and suspicion bring evil into the world of that relationship. The radical edge of Godwin's critique of his culture's gender arrangements lies in his interrogation of secrecy, first in *Caleb Williams* and then again in *St. Leon.*

Secrecy is engendered, in both these novels, by the family constituted as a separate sphere and "ruled" not by force but by surveillance. We are not told that Falkland's early life was idyllic, though in his taste for romantic reading he resembles Godwin's daughter's Robert Walton and Victor Frankenstein, brought up under the "feminine fosterage" of sisters and more-than-sisters. We know only that he was a youthful medievalist. In *The Return to Camelot,* Mark Girouard sets forth a strand of Gothic revivalism in which the medieval knight modeled a specifically English code of male behavior from the end of the eighteenth century to World War I.[6] Falkland is certainly an example of this appropriation, as well as an illustration of its limits as a strategy for countering the power of surveillance and scrutiny.

When Caleb penetrates his gentlemanly externality—and part of the ideology of individualism is that everyone has a secret, a "true self" behind the external mask—Falkland turns Caleb's scopophilia back upon him until the whole world becomes for Caleb a classic Foucaultean institution of confinement, a place where utter isolation is coupled with an incessant scrutiny that slowly destroys in an inmate the constituting private self that insists on its own innocence. Inflicting pain, Foucault notes, is no longer essential to this kind of punishment, as it was in the spectacle of public torture. "The body now serves as an instrument or intermediary; . . . From being an art of unbearable sensations punishment has become an economy of suspended rights."[7] The punisher no longer needs to be present, as Caleb discovers. In fact, his invisibility is part of his effectiveness.

What is effected by this unreturnable gaze is nothing less than the reconstitution of the inmate from within: "Alone in his cell, the convict is handed over to himself; in the silence of his passions and of the world that surrounds him, he descends into his conscience, he questions it and feels awakening within him the moral feeling that never entirely perishes in the heart of man."[8] This descent has the same effect on Caleb: having become "an object of punishment always vulnerable to himself and to the Other," he acknowledges his status as object, and in doing so "return[s] to his awareness as a free and responsible subject."[9] For Foucault, this reconstitution of the subject denotes a more invidious expression of power than that of the torturer, and readers of *Caleb Williams*, with the support of Godwin's preface, have seen in Caleb the victim of an instance of "domestic and recorded despotism."[10]

An interpretation of Caleb at the end of the novel as an emblem of achieved freedom is thus a deliberate misreading, but one in the same direction as Godwin's revision of the ending, with its substitution of Caleb with "no character to vindicate" for the self-pitying speaker of the first ending. Rather than being constituted by the gaze of his master, first parental and approving and then parental but accusing, Caleb now sees Falkland always before him, a constant reminder that secrecy can be eliminated between two people only through total isomorphism. The scrutiny here is male, but its original is the maternal gaze studied by Winnicott and other object-relations theorists.[11] Read thus, Caleb's flight is impelled by fear that his scopic power, and the secret it has revealed to him, could annihilate his constituting parent. In deciding to turn Falkland in, he acts despite this fear, and in doing so, he is able to see his master not as the Other, but as an other, a mortal human being like himself.

In Godwin's second novel, published in 1799, he returns to these complex and difficult themes. Briefly, the novel recounts the adventures of St. Leon, whose father dissipated the family fortune, and whose mother, he says, "loved my honour and my fame more than she loved my person."[12] After his mother's death he falls into gambling, is rescued by marriage to a flawless woman, and undergoes a series of reversals that bring his family to the brink of starvation. At that point he meets a stranger who, in return for friendship, protection, and a burial according to his instructions, gives St. Leon the philosopher's stone on condition that he tell no one about it. He thus gains access to unlimited wealth and life without end, but the immense disproportion of power that this gift creates between him and the rest of the human race, coupled with the secrecy he must maintain in order to keep it, destroys the trust between him and his wife, ruins her health, alienates him from his eldest son, and turns whole populations against him when he tries to put his powers at their service. To escape persecution he becomes twenty again, and is accidentally reunited with his son Charles. But because he arouses his son's jealousy by spending too much time with Charles's fiancée, he is forced to give up this "friendship" and console himself that he is the father of a true hero.

By loving her son's honor and fame more than she loved his person, St. Leon's mother inscribed him into a masculine code in which a man's honor and fame count for everything. The impulse to gamble is a complicated one, but it can be seen as a logical expression of the Protestant ethic and the spirit of capitalism. It makes money out of money, requires a willingness to take risks, and when successful, draws providence in on the side of the male breadwinner. It rejects "slow diligence," but this quality is not really the secret of successful capitalist enterprise. For the man caught up in this vision of success, family ties mean nothing. Mary Shelley's Walton and (for a while) Victor Frankenstein get caught up in the masculine ethic, and so, despite an exemplary family, does St. Leon. Godwin's point, and later Shelley's, is that the feminine power of influence, the only power allowed to women in the paradigm of separate spheres, is at best minimal, and at worst can make life worse for men rather than better.

The relationship between St. Leon and his wife, Marguerite, modeled on Godwin's relationship with Mary Wollstonecraft as he describes it in his *Memoirs*, is perfect in every respect, which makes it only the more surprising that St. Leon ever strays from this ideal garden.[13] And he does resolve repeatedly to "seek no happier state, and know to know no more." Yet when he takes his son to school in Paris, the lure of the gambling table becomes too strong for him. And because his wife "did not partake of [his] vices, an ill-judged forbearance and tenderness for [his] feelings did not permit her effectually to counteract them" (52). On returning home he confesses that "instead of being weaned by the presence of this admirable woman, from my passion for gaming, it became stronger than ever" (66). Consequently "the arms of my wife, that were about to embrace me, suddenly became to me a nest of scorpions."

By this time he has lost his entire fortune, and an uncomplaining Marguerite takes over the management of the family's finances. He determines not to mourn the loss of material wealth, and to "revel in the luxury of domestic affections." Yet he cannot do this. "I might learn to be contented," he says, "[but] I was not formed to be satisfied in obscurity and a low estate" (101). Then further catastrophe deprives this "haven in a heartless world" of even bare necessities. At the sight of those whom he has brought so low engaging in acts of self-sacrifice, "avarice descended," he says, "and took possession of my soul" (118). The more his wife and children act as models of uncomplaining submission, the more guilt he feels at the fact that they are sharing in the calamities he has caused. The more they draw together in their distress, the more alienated from them he feels.

It is at this point that the stranger enters and makes his offer, with the condition of secrecy. When St. Leon objects that he has never had any secrets, he is accused of failing to be a real man: "Feeble and effeminate mortal! Was ever gallant action achieved by him who was incapable of separating himself from a woman? Was ever a great discovery prosecuted, or any important benefit conferred upon the human race, by him who was incapable of standing, and thinking, and feeling, alone?" (126). This is the challenge that Walton and Victor Frankenstein will wrestle with, just as St. Leon does. Opposing it is his wife's view of marriage as an equal partnership. "But to this equality and simple humanity," she laments, "it is no longer within your power to return" (208). One could say the same to a capitalist who owns ships or factories, and who therefore has power over large numbers of people. Yet power is difficult to give up, and St. Leon refuses. Situated in the sixteenth century, he is a firm believer in the transformative power of money. Man has always been interested, he notes in the opening paragraph of the novel, in "the art of multiplying gold, and of defying the inroads of infirmity and death" (1).

In his determination to keep his source of wealth despite the catastrophe brought on by the stranger's condition of secrecy, St. Leon truly embodies the spirit of capitalism. "No man despises wealth," he observes, "who fully understands the advantages it confers" (138). He holds this view even after the bond of his marriage has been broken and his wife has lost her health and her respect for him, even after his son has rejected him, believing his father to have acquired his new wealth by dishonorable means. Above all, he persists despite the fact that he originally wanted the money not for himself but in order to do for his family what a good husband and father is supposed to do. "All opposition and hostile appearance give way," he insists, "before him who goes calmly onward, and scorns to be dismayed" (200). Calamities are nothing more than secular tests of his faith.

Moreover, St. Leon's efforts to put the fruits of his secret, and by analogy those of industrial technology, to the cause of making a better world are presented much more ambivalently than Victor's efforts in the same direction. St. Leon settles on the banks of the Arno and begins conducting experiments in a grotto near his house. When this becomes known, the villagers burn down St. Leon's house and persecute him as a sorcerer, leading him to comment: "No sooner did a man devote himself to the pursuit of discoveries, which, if ascertained, would prove to the highest benefit of his whole species, than his species became armed against him" (290). His rise is thus as paradoxical as Adam's "fortunate fall." Money and technology, linked together in the alchemical image of the philosopher's stone, have potential for good as well as evil that needs to be recognized.

Godwin maintains this ambivalence in the novel's ending. If its hero epitomizes the spirit of capitalism and of the technological revolution that continues to support it, then we leave him, if not entirely domesticated, at least within sight of the domestic circle formed by his son's happy marriage. In contrast to Shelley's monster, who disappears "into the howling darkness," we see St. Leon forgiven by his son and enjoying, vicariously if with some regret, "pleasures not for him ordain'd." This is because, though Godwin calls into question the whole basis of the myth of the fall, its forbidden knowledge, unquestioned obedience, and the rest of the

Christian apparatus that explains the coming of evil into the world, he believes that human society is capable of constituting itself rationally, that is, along lines where freedom would not simply be a choice between falling and remaining "innocent."

NOTES

1. Michel Foucault, *The History of Sexuality*, vol. 1, trans. Robert Hurley (New York: Pantheon, 1978), 19.

2. William Godwin, *Caleb Williams*, ed. David McCracken (New York: Norton, 1977), 144. Subsequent references will be to this edition.

3. Richard Hurd, *Letters on Chivalry and Romance* (1762), ed. Hoyt Trowbridge, Augustan Reprint Society, nos. 101–2 (1963), 11, 13, 15.

4. See Alan Macfarlane, *Marriage and Love in England: Modes of Reproduction, 1300–1840* (Oxford: Basil Blackwell, 1986), 82–87.

5. Eli Zaretsky in *Capitalism, the Family, and Personal Life* (New York: Harper and Row, 1976) observes "the split between the public and the private . . . recreated within the family. As in the 'outside world,' people feel that they are not known for themselves, not valued for who they really are" (75).

6. Mark Girouard, *The Return to Camelot: Chivalry and the English Gentleman* (New Haven: Yale University Press, 1981).

7. Michel Foucault, *Discipline and Punish: The Birth of the Prison*, trans. Alan Sheridan (New York: Vintage, 1979), 11.

8. Ibid., 238.

9. Michel Foucault, *Madness and Civilization* (1964), trans. Richard Howard (New York: Vintage, 1973), 247.

10. Godwin in his preface argued that "It is now known to philosophers that the spirit and character of the government intrudes itself into every rank of society. But this is a truth highly worthy to be communicated to persons whom books of philosophy and science are never likely to reach. Accordingly it is proposed in the invention of the following work, to comprehend, as far as the progressive nature of a single story would allow, a general review of the modes of domestic and unrecorded despotism, by which man becomes the destroyer of man."

11. W. D. Winnicott, "The Mirror Role of the Mother and Family in Child Development," in *Playing and Reality* (London: Tavistock, 1971), 111–18.

12. William Godwin, *St. Leon; A Tale of the Sixteenth Century* (1799; rpt., London: Coborn and Bentley, 1835), 3. Subsequent references will be to this edition.

13. William Godwin, *Memoirs of Mary Wollstonecraft*, ed. W. Clark Durant (London: Constable, 1927), 66.

CHAPTER IX

The Self under Siege:
Charles Robert Maturin

𝕴N THE WORLD of the masculine Gothic as mapped by Godwin, it is a person who is haunted, not a place. Exiled from the home reconstituted as earthly paradise, the Gothic wanderer demands that the fall be revoked immediately, that linear time, brought into being by "man's first disobedience," release its hold on him, and that he be recognized as unfallen, or "innocent." In *Caleb Williams* the man locked out is coupled with the man locked in, but the novel directs our attention primarily to Caleb, the exile. Maturin's vision of gender, and of the consequences of separating male and female spheres, is even more subversive than the sensationalism of Lewis or the radicalism of Godwin. All three writers explore the distinctly masculine problem of the threshold, engendered because men not only can but must move back and forth between the male and female spheres. But Maturin is particularly fascinated by the man who can't get out, who is locked into a sphere coded female.

Ruskin describes the male condition in a world divided into "spheres" as one of being "always hardened." But one can be hardened excessively, and then unable to shed the protective shell the world demands, as St. Leon is. Or one can fail to develop sufficient armor, like the youthful Caleb. Both conditions represent crises of masculinity under particular historical conditions. But the man locked out, excessively "hardened," is the more typical result of Western industrial and postindustrial male socialization. Maturin was drawn to the darker side of the picture, to the man stripped of the gender attributes to which he has, he believes, a right. So while Melmoth's appearances and disappearances are the thread connecting the concentric narratives of enclosed speakers in *Melmoth the Wanderer,* it is the narratives, not the thread, that form the body of the novel and focus the reader's attention on the experience of "unnatural" male powerlessness.

In Maturin's first novel, *The Fatal Revenge; or, The Family of Montorio,* there are three immobilized male characters, Count Montorio and his two sons, Annibal and Ippolito, members of an illustrious family reknowned for its devotion to the black arts. The count fits the pattern of the Gothic second son. He is extravagant, undisciplined, and in love with the woman his brother marries. This older brother, Orazio, is driven into the position of the more typically Satanic wanderer villain, and it is the relationship between these two male subject possibilities that propels Maturin's plot along its path. That this path is difficult to follow, that one feels at points in grave danger of getting lost, is precisely Maturin's method of representing at the level of form a subversion of the tidy eighteenth-century map made even more so by its narrowing gender politics.

The younger Montorio harbors the secret of his jealousy until he makes a discovery that allows him to transfer that serpent from his own bosom to Orazio's. What he learns is that Erminia, his brother's wife, also has a secret. She secretly married a cavalier her family disapproved of, and bore him a child. When the cavalier went off to war and was reported dead Erminia bowed to her family's wishes and married Orazio. Naturally the cavalier reappears years later, and the spurned younger Montorio tells Orazio that the two are carrying on—a lie, of course. In a fit of rage, Orazio kills the cavalier, forcing Erminia to watch, whereupon she dies on the spot and her two young children disappear. Orazio also disappears, and is believed to be dead and buried in the family vault.

In reality, he flees to the East and develops the power to control the minds of others. He then returns to Italy and uses this skill to "haunt" his nephews, Annibal and Ippolito, invading their dreams and waking lives alike to the point where the two boys are literally possessed by a mysterious other being who sometimes takes the "corporeal form" of their father's confessor, the monk Schemoli. They are not haunted, as their father is, by images of crimes committed. Yet their minds are gradually usurped, though the invading evil has not yet taken the form of action. Indeed, action is infinitely preferable to formless anticipation. Orazio's plan is that his nephews should kill their father, in the hopes that, through revenge, he could repossess the castle of his own mind, from which he is now locked out, a wanderer in search of justice and the restoration of his innocence.

His brother, on the other hand, is locked in, as Falkland was, by his own fear of discovery. Without having shed innocent blood himself, he has usurped the Montorio castle, and is egged on by his confessor to imprison Annibal, fearing that this son has guessed his secret. Ippolito, meanwhile, is also locked up, through the machinations of his uncle, by the ever-handy Inquisition. Yet for the two boys physical confinement is almost preferable to the purely mental kind. It is at least a verifiable analogue for the deprivation of subjectivity that leaves them unable to distinguish between external and internal reality, between terrors they imagine and terrors they perceive. At the same time their isolation makes them more subject to external control, not less so, and this sense of being invaded engenders further isolation.

So it is the sundering of the male subject position as a result of its reconstitution as a restricted sphere outside the home that brings death into Maturin's world, and woe to his characters, male and female. Nor can the home, split off from "the world" of action, ever become "a place of peace." Rather it is the matrix of guilt without the hope of its termination or the structures and practices for its absolution. Confession is not a deliberate step toward reintegration into a community, but rather an involuntary lapse against which one must be constantly on guard. "Voluntary spies" are everywhere, their curiosity insatiable and anything but innocent. Hallucinated or observed, they haunt the innocent, flitting and gliding—feminine modes of locomotion, as Eve Sedgewick observes—and blending in with the shadows and the crumbling structures that conceal them imperfectly.[1]

The Montorio family is susceptible to such "hauntings" because they have long been fascinated by "secret studies," and have resorted to "forbidden sources to seek what nature and this world denied them"[2] The great-grandfather of the two brothers had "devoted his entire soul to them" to the degree that "no power could drag him from these studies." He "had invented, by his art, a glass, that could shew him every event and person he wished to see." By these same arts his son discovered a place in the castle "which would be the seat of calamity and destruction to the family." Orazio ordered a monument to himself to be erected on that spot and, after murdering his wife's "revived" husband, arranged his own "burial" there, "hoping by this means to fulfill, and yet to avert the prediction—to defeat, and yet not appear to defy it" (vol. 2, 254–57).

The tree of knowledge has therefore been eaten of, the idea of evil implanted into three successive generations, well before the jealous younger brother plays Iago to Orazio's Othello. We remember that, in Milton's world, evil into the mind of man could come and go "and leave no spot or blame behind." Not so in the Montorio family, intent as they are on secret knowledge. Orazio uses this family skill, supplemented by occult wisdom from the East acquired over the twenty years following his disappearance, to convince his nephews that he is not a mortal but a supernatural being. Thus the Gothic convention of the "supernatural explained" is given the additional twist of being revealed, at the end, as the acts of a human agent who has intentionally simulated the supernatural effects that served as tests for the Radcliffian heroine.

A ghost is, perhaps, even more of an exile than a man who lives beyond a mortal lifespan, since he can be even less present to his fellows. Orazio is an exile both literally and metaphorically. First, he has fled society after discovering secrecy in a sex that is supposed to have no secrets and no past. His life as a "ghost" is both an affirmation and an extension of the antisocial existence he has adopted. Second, as part of this strategy, he claims to be an exile from his own body, and to be inhabiting that of a man who has lived two thousand years in the bodies of others, presumably. Finally, Orazio has allowed the jealousy of his brother to enter and "usurp" his mind. He can only repossess his castle by attaining a higher level of consciousness through his study of the occult, and by giving those powers the task of revenge. "From the moment I conceived this idea," he says, "my reason was not only restored, . . . but my powers were confirmed, condensed, invigorated" (vol. 3, 408).

The erasure Orazio effects between "the images of sleep" and those of waking life is a state that becomes virtually normal for the four haunted protagonists. They are driven literally out of their minds by the thoughts that possess them; their waking lives have the unwilled quality of dreams, while their dreams propel them to act "involuntarily." This adjective appears with noticeably high frequency in the fourteen hundred pages of this highly convoluted novel, bringing home the point that in a state of terror or horror, the will is not only unfree but "stolen," while the imagination, abhorring a vacuum, fills the space with its own introjects. The boundaries of consciousness, of which we have been speaking meta-phorically as "the castle of the mind," become as permeable as Gothic ruin, and the tortuous passageway between "those motions that are hid from man" and the visible world of "objects and agents of life" becomes the principal locus of Maturin's narrative.[3] The locked-in man is doubly imprisoned.

Moreover, once they penetrate the subterranean vaults of our mental castles, thoughts can not be driven out. They lie in wait, "buried alive" outside the reach of "free will."

> The forms that float before us, in our sleeping or waking dreams, or those more substantial ones that mingle in scenes of horror, in the solitude of midnight, in the vaults of the dead, in the chambers of sorcery; these can be banished as they are raised, they can be dispersed by light, by human presence, nay by the effort of a recollected mind. But when they pursue us to the very hold and circle of our shelter, when they sit before us mid our mirth and wine, in the blaze of lights, and the loud and comforting tones of human voices, when they do this and will not be repelled, what shall we think? (vol. 1, 309)

This is a problem not of too much "hardening" by and against the world but of all too little.

Yet the count, whose prison is mental only, ascribes his haunted condition not to external agents nor to his own personal weakness but to "a cursed domestic sensibility of guilt that makes cowards of us [so that] the deed that makes the hero damns the man. I am lost," he continues, "because I am pent up within the walls of a castle" (vol. 3, 320). He connects guilt with a sensibility cultivated in the home, a relationship we have traced in eighteenth-century writings on the new duties of mothers, where socialization by peers, with an accompanying code of honor and shame, is displaced by one administered by the mother and enforced by guilt and forgiveness. In the pure patriarchal order for which Montorio longs, it would be possible for someone like him to go forth and have it out with his enemies for once and for all. But as soon as this code, hegemonic in a culture where the clan takes precedence over the individual couple, has been undermined by maternal control over the children, a secret can neither be kept nor wiped away.

The crux of the Gothic at this point in its development lies in Count Montorio's question to his confessor: "Is it not possible that a man may retain his integrity, and yet cherish some secret he cannot disclose?" (vol. 3, 441). The Catholic answer to this question at that time was the sacrament of confession, backed up by the power of the Inquisition. But the Montorios have Protestant minds in Catholic bodies. "Confession!" cries Ippolito to his inquisitors.

> Of what use were confession to me now? If I should even convince you of my innocence, can you restore me its purity and its praise? . . . He who has once entered your walls, never can regain the estimation of society—can never regain his own confidence and honest pride. . . . No; while he slept in the lethargy of confinement; the vestal fire of his honour, which it was the business of his life to guard, has gone out; and he sees its ashes scattered and trampled on. How are these evils to be anticipated by confession? Confession itself is an engine of mental torture, . . . The thoughts and actions of the purest lives cannot bear this universal scrutiny. (vol. 2, 484–85)

A man must go out if he is to deal with evil that undermines his honor. An inward gaze can discover evil but cannot free a man from the "cursed domestic sensibility" that accompanies it.

The stories of the women in the novel confirm a vision of domestic "virtues" as death-dealing. Death comes to Erminia in part through the suspicion planted in her husband's head by his brother, Orazio being like Milton's Uriel, too innocent to spot evil. But her no-less-innocent habit of visiting, with her still-living first husband, the infant daughter of that secret union gives Orazio the "proof" he was looking for. Most unfortunate of all was "her fatal, fatal wish to spare her husband's feelings [that] prevented her from making the disclosure herself" (vol. 3, 395). For women, virtue requires secrecy concerning the past, however "innocent" it may be. As for men, their desire to enshrine virtue in the home does more than disempower them. It turns them into criminals who "can't go home again." The paradox of the new sensibility is that, to invert the words of Montorio, the deed that damns the man makes the hero.

Clearly what has gone wrong in the Montorio family castle goes beyond the invasion of a domesticated space by forces hostile to the ideals represented by marriage and child-rearing. A second son has set the fatal course of events in motion, but it has been reinforced and made worse by the very "domestic sensibility" that embodies those ideals. Orazio is so obsessed with the idea of female purity that "a dereliction of thought, an imagined desertion would drive me mad" (vol. 3, 355). At the same time, he has so little sense of what women are like that he confesses: "With the purity of a matron, and the delicacy of a woman, I yet expected the blandishments of a harlot, and the ardors of a man" (vol. 3, 340–41). Though not brought up in a monastery, he is not prepared for female "delicacy" in a sexual partner, and suspects Erminia of directing her missing "masculine" passion elsewhere long before his brother gives words to his suspicion.

To be locked in, denied access to the public world where a reputation can be made, not simply lost, where honor can be won and slights to it avenged, has become coded, in Western Europe by the end of the eighteenth century, as the position of the female subject under feudalism. Mobility is a defining condition of (male) bourgeois subjectivity shaping, and being shaped by, the bourgeois revolution. To be deprived of the freedom to move at will is tantamount to being buried alive, the theme that Eve Sedgewick finds at the heart of Gothic darkness. But it is more: it is to lose the signifier of masculinity. Witnessing helplessly the appropriation of their subjectivity, Orazio's victims live out "the subjection of woman" as *feme covert*. To each other they offer a feminine sensibility free of the risks of heterosexuality.

Honor is what holds together a band of brothers united against feminizing inwardness. Even chivalry is dangerous because it leads to an overidealization of women. The strongest ties in Maturin's work, and thus the greatest crimes, transpire between men: between the overly hardened wanderer and the overly softened prisoner. As a young man Orazio loved his brother "with a love 'passing that of women,' " and at the end of the novel this original homosocial paradise is regained by the next generation: Annibal and Ippolito, though murderers, are not held responsible for their crime: an emphasis on responsibility rather than on actions makes them not guilty. In the end they are "distinguished by their silent bravery, their solemn melancholy, their lovely affection for each other, and their reluctance to the society of women" (vol. 3, 493).

The heaviest punishment, moreover, goes to Orazio for turning his two innocent nephews into murderers in the belief that this would inflect the greatest pain upon his brother. But the homegrown serpent this brother transferred to Orazio, and which Orazio thrust back with supernatural force, turns back again. Orazio learns that Annibal and Ippolito are his children. Rescued at the time of their mother's death, they were adopted by the count, whose own two sons died shortly after Orazio's disappearance and who feared that this blow might be a stroke of divine retribution. The discovery of what he has done to his children literally kills Orazio, and he dies imploring their forgiveness. Yet it all began with an excessive belief in female innocence, which made him as powerless to resist his tempter brother as the pre-Richardsonian Eve had been to resist her male seducer.

If the *The Fatal Revenge* demolishes the idea of the castle as locus for Paradise Regained, not only at the literal level of the Radcliffian Gothic but at the metaphoric level ("a paradise within thee, happier far") as well, *Melmoth the Wanderer* continues to explore what happens when men are locked into a fate that deprives them not only of their freedom but of their gendered identity. Using the frame of an enclosing auditor who either reads or listens to six tales in which Melmoth appears, Maturin exploits the open form of the Lewisite Gothic to a degree that surpasses in breadth and complexity all other examples of the genre. This frame auditor, John Melmoth, has come to the deathbed of his uncle, in whose possession are a manuscript recounting the first tale and a portrait of a Melmoth ancestor, dated 1646. Speaking in 1816, the uncle insists that the original of the portrait is still mysteriously alive, and John actually sees him three times at the beginning of the novel and once again at the end.

The interpolated manuscripts, like the novel as a whole, are written from the point of view of an omniscient narrator. The first of these, the one in the uncle's possession, tells of a series of encounters between the protagonist, Stanton, and the original Melmoth. Fascinated by that person's seemingly supernatural knowledge and death-dealing powers, Stanton becomes possessed by Melmoth and in consequence is confined to a madhouse. There Melmoth promises to become for Stanton his exiled partner in his feminized sufferings. "I *never desert my friends in misfortune*," he says. "When they are plunged in the lowest abyss of human calamity, *they are sure to be visited by me*."[4] In fact, however, he does not want to alleviate their sorrows. He will dispel them only if they are willing to take on his, to sell their souls to Satan, as he has done.

While Stanton is in the institution he insists that he, unlike his fellow inmates, is sane. "Doubtless those wretches have some consolation," he says, "but I have none; my sanity is my greatest curse in this abode of horrors." Yet once he is released, observes the omniscient narrator of the frame, "the manuscript told me no more of Melmoth," though Stanton's pursuit of him "was incessant and indefatigable" to the point where "he himself allowed it to be a species of insanity" (43–44). Becoming the pursuer rather than the pursued, he becomes what his pursuers have accused him of being, not a murderer but a madman. As in *The Fatal Revenge*, Maturin is commenting on the process we have been describing metaphorically as usurpation. As long as Stanton is being besieged, he can successfully defend the boundaries of his individuality, just as Caleb Williams can. But once he is "free," he makes the perceptions of his attackers his own.

The next tale frames three others.[5] Taking the convention of the found manuscript used by Walpole and others to authenticate material and protect it from the charge of "romance," Maturin manipulates convoluted plots and gender positions, the most disparaged features of aristocratic romances, which become the medium for his very different message. Here Alonzo, positioned like a Gothic heroine in a convent against her wishes, is denied her happy ending. His mother (backed up, to be sure, by her husband) is the author of his woe, insisting that her son become a monk to free her guilty conscience for having borne him, out of wedlock, to the man of high birth she later married. In the eyes of the law, her second, legitimate son is her husband's true heir. But having made before his birth the same promise to God that almost doomed Agnes in *The Monk*, she wants to go further and inflect on her firstborn the fate traditionally reserved for second sons.

Being legal minors, Agnes and Alonzo have the same status before the law as the *feme covert*. But whereas Agnes's "live burial" below St. Clare's monastery follows the Radcliffian pattern of exile and return, Alonzo can't go home again because it was there that he was stripped of mobility, the gender attribute he demands, at great length, as his right. By the end of the novel he has been sprung from the convent with the help of his brother only to be captured by the Inquisition, saved from there by a fire only to find himself in the hiding place of a persecuted Jew, saved again by the turmoil of violent auto-da-fé to find himself in the underground dwelling of another Jew, Adonijah, to finally make his way across the sea to Ireland, where he finds in John a male auditor for his tale of feminizing confinement.[6]

The "Tale of the Indians," which Alonzo reads to John Melmoth from a manuscript given to him by Adonijah, is Maturin's most direct treatment of the myth of the fall. Immalee, the daughter of a noble Spanish family, was washed up on an island following a storm at sea. Her prelapsarian innocence is shattered when Melmoth the Wanderer appears and becomes her first love object and her first link with the world of other people, or "civilization." Brought back home at the age of seventeen, she is subjected to the usual fate of Gothic heroines when her absent father chooses a husband for her, though she has never seen her father, let alone her future spouse. This father, a good bourgeois, is always away, the manuscript tells us, on business. Melmoth rescues her from this oppressive situation, and they are wedded "in darkness," their hands joined by one that is "as cold as that of the dead." When she gives birth to a child, her father, now returned, surrenders her to the Inquisition. Whether she or Melmoth kills the infant is left uncertain, but she is absolved of the sin of consorting with an agent of the devil when she tells the Inquisitors that she has refused to surrender her soul in return for Melmoth's offered life with him on the island where they met.

Though Maturin never tells us why Melmoth sold his soul for an extended life span, each tale brings us closer to him as a natural, rather than a supernatural, exile. Through the eyes of Aliaga, the profit-motivated father of Immalee, we see the mysterious stranger as a consummate artist, one who "rapidly unfolded the stories of his rich and copiously furnished mind; and by skillfully blending his displays of general knowledge with particular references to the oriental countries where Aliaga had resided, . . . the journey, begun in terror, ended in delight" (338). Aliaga is not a virtuous precapitalist father like Radcliffe's St. Aubert. But just as Immalee's death is not presented as the inevitable consequence of her Clarissa-like flight from home, but rather to show the rigidity of the Inquisition, so the burden of blame in *Melmoth the Wanderer* as a whole does not fall upon individuals as such, but rather upon institutions that try to maintain absolute divisions between good and evil.

This is Melmoth's parting point to Aliaga when he says:

> I tell you, whenever you indulged one brutal passion, one sordid desire, one impure imagination—whenever you uttered one word that wrung the heart, or embittered the spirit of your fellow creature . . . you may have been ten times the agent of the enemy of man than all the wretches who terror, enfeebled nerves, or visionary credulity, has forced into the confession of an incredible compact with the author of evil, and whose confession has consigned them to flames much more substantial than those the imagination of their persecutors pictured them doomed to for an eternity of suffering! (334)

There are no pure heroes or heroines, no spaces closed off from evil, no invaders from without. Against an impossible standard of purity we all become exiles, and thus easy prey for those who would seduce us to a life beyond limits.

Consequently the home "ruled" by a woman held to this standard is as ripe a target for superstition and sadistic practices as a monastery, an asylum, or a prison. For a man, secrecy is the only alternative to surrender to these conditions, and to the unreasonable demand for purity that impels them. So the self is always a haunted self, a contested terrain that must be sought out, pursued into places where few would dare to follow. In this revisioning the instigator of its "fall" is a sympathetic figure whose motives seem quite innocent: curiosity, a thirst for knowledge as an extension of (or a defense against) surveillance, perhaps accompanied by the wish for a companion with whom one might share one's "secret" feelings of alienation. Most important for the line of development that I will complete with Mary Shelley, the Gothic has shifted the focus of the myth of the fall so that the site upon which the contest is played out is not the body of a woman but the mind of a man.

NOTES

1. See Eve Kossofsky Sedgewick, *The Coherence of Gothic Conventions* (1980; rpt. New York: Methuen, 1986), 28. See also this author's immensely suggestive *Between Men: English Literature and Male Homosocial Desire* (New York: Columbia University Press, 1985), esp. chs. 5, 6, 9, and 10.

2. Charles Robert Maturin, *The Fatal Revenge; or, The Family of Montorio*, 3 vols. (New York: Arno Press, 1974), vol. 2, 53. Subsequent references will be to this edition.

3. The confusion of Maturin's characters places this work in the realm of Todorov's "fantastic," which he defines in *The Fantastic: A Structural Approach to a Literary Genre* (Cleveland: Case Western Reserve University Press, 1973) as "that hesitation experienced by a person who knows only the laws of nature, confronting an apparently supernatural event" (25).

4. Charles Robert Maturin, *Melmoth the Wanderer*, with an introduction by William F. Axton (Lincoln: University of Nebraska Press, 1963), 34. Subsequent references will be to this edition.

5. Alonzo tells John Melmoth his own story, which ends with his departure for Ireland with a copy of the "Tale of the Indians." In this tale Don Francisco di Aliaga, the father of the heroine, Isadora (or Immalee, her name on the island where she grew up) hears from an interested stranger two other tales concerning Melmoth, "Tale of Guzman's Family" and "The Lover's Tale."

6. This homosocial ending reinforces a distinction between the Radcliffian heroine condemned to monastic life and Alonzo similarly confined.

The heroine resists the veil because she has fallen in love, and celibacy is as much a death to her as a forced marriage. Alonzo on the other hand resists in principle in order to maintain his right to move about at will and unsupervised, a right he does not share with the heroine. For Sedgewick's interpretation of Melmoth's "unspeakable" request of his interlocutors, see *Between Men*, 94–95.

PART IV

Revoking the Boundaries

No inside is conceivable therefore without the complicity of an outside on which it relies. Complicity mixed with antagonism makes the membrane deploy in order to contain and to secure the constancy of the "internal milieu" against vicissitudes of the *Umwelt*. No outside would be conceivable without an inside fending it off, resisting it, "reacting" to it.

JEAN STAROBINSKI
"The Inside and the Outside"

CHAPTER X

Mary Shelley's Embattled Garden

𝕿HE 1817 PREFACE to *Frankenstein* tells us that the author's "chief concern" in writing the novel had "been limited to avoiding the enervating effects of the novels of the present day and to the exhibition of the amiableness of domestic affection, and the excellence of universal virtue." If Percy Shelley, who wrote this preface, intended his wife's readers to take this statement at its face value, and not as a parody of those declarations of moral intent ritually present in the prefaces of novels by women, he was certainly reading selectively. It is true that the novel's three interconnected narratives are each told by a man to whom domestic affection is not merely amiable but positively sacred. Yet their enthusiasm is surely undercut by the fact that each narrator speaks from the perspective of one who has been denied the experience he reveres so highly, and who therefore cannot transmit it to a future generation.

This is the problem that links the three narratives thematically: a problem of "haves" and "have-nots" with respect to the highly desirable experience of domestic affection. The outer, encircling narrative has Walton writing to his sister Mrs. Saville in distant England about his longing for "the company of a man who could sympathize with me, whose eyes would reply to mine."[1] What comes between him and human sympathy is "a love of the marvellous, a belief in the marvellous, intertwined in all my projects, which hurries me out of the common pathways of men, even to the wild sea and unvisited regions I am about to explore" (21). Not content merely to put his visions on paper as poetry, he must find an actual heaven on earth near the North Pole and benefit all mankind with his discovery. Margaret Saville, who has a husband

and children, cannot know the pain that drives Walton to prefer death to failure.

Out beyond the reach of domestic happiness, Walton meets Victor Frankenstein, who shares his desire to benefit mankind by a spectacular discovery. But Victor must also exile himself from the comforts of home while he is creating his monster, so that, unable to confess what he has done, he cannot warn his endangered family and dearest friend. The monster, whose narrative is at the center of the novel, is in turn placed beyond the reach of domestic affection by a "father" who will not create for him a mate. So the monster determines that Victor will not have "pleasures not for him [the monster] ordained," and kills everyone who might provide them for his withholding parent. Thus Victor, as his position in the narrative structure would indicate, is between two extremes. He is not resigned, as Walton seems to be, to worshipping domestic happiness from a distance, nor does he see it as the only good, as the monster seems to do.

The recurrence of this theme suggests that Mary Shelley was as much concerned with the limitations of domestic affection as she was with trumpeting its praises. She is explicit, moreover, about the source of its limitations. Godwin had hinted, in his two Gothic novels, that innocence was an attribute of questionable value, and that some part of the human spirit could never be entirely subsumed within the domestic parameters of happiness. It is true that Mary Shelley had a complex array of experiences, both as a daughter and as a mother, as a mistress and as a wife, on which to draw in shaping her vision of the family as an institution.[2] But *Frankenstein* is also a highly literary work, with its explicit and implicit references to Milton and other "classics" of Western civilization.[3] Biographical and literary components of the novel come together when we focus on its author, herself the daughter of two Gothic novelists, and her place in the Gothic tradition of her day.

Shelley's use of the writings of her parents makes an interesting pattern out of the reverse side of her closely woven first novel. I will argue that she extended the ideas of her mother with respect to the harmful effects of a rigid separation between social usefulness and female charm. Her relationship to her father's writings, on the other hand, is much more ambivalent. Lee Sterrenberg has argued that Shelley rejected the radical utopianism of Godwin's political writings, citing her use of a figure that appeared routinely in the work of conservative writers hostile to the ideas of the French Revolution, a monster.[4] Yet Godwin gave voice to his pessimistic side in his Gothic novels. The disclosure of a secret in *Caleb Williams* does not bring about the defeat of evil nor even the purgation of the home, as it does in the Radcliffian Gothic. And St. Leon, rebelling against the poverty that is his family's fate, tries to turn his superhuman power to the benefit of mankind but fails. Like Victor, he finds that domestic affection is an ineffective shield against those parts of the psyche that experience denies.

As a literary daughter, then, Shelley can be said to have drawn together in her first novel the "deep subversive impulse" of feminist protest that we found in the Radcliffian tradition and the pervasive pessimism of the Lewisite tradition. The narrators are all outsiders seeking a counterpart. They are driven by a guiding hand in a counterprovidential direction. And finally, the "innocence" in which their early lives were spent is not equal to the seductions of forbidden knowledge by which each becomes, in varying degrees, possessed.

The structure of *Frankenstein*, with its three concentric narratives, imposes upon the linear unfolding of the plot line the very sort of order that Mary Shelley is commenting on in the novel as a whole: one that separates "outer" and "inner," the feminine sphere of domesticity and the masculine sphere of discovery. Moreover, the sequences in which the reader encounters the three narrators give the plot line a circular as well as a linear shape. It begins and ends with Walton, writing to his English sister from the outer periphery of the civilized world, the boundary between the known and the unknown. From there, we move inward to the circle of civilization, to the rural outskirts of Geneva, birthplace of the Protestant ethic. Then, in the physical center of the novel, and accessible only if one traverses many snowy mountains, we come upon the limited Paradise Regained of the De Lacey family. There males and females learn together, role distinctions are minimal, and domestic bliss has ostensibly been recovered, largely through the initiative of Safie, a young woman who comes from a world outside the sphere of Western Protestantism. Nevertheless, we do not end, as so many novels of the period did, with this depiction of domestic affection triumphant in isolation. Rather we move out again, first to civilization and its discontents and finally to Walton, defeated in his attempt to discover, in the land of ice and snow, a paradise beyond the boundaries of the domestic and the familiar.

The circularity of the novel emphasizes another feature of bourgeois family life that is critical in locating, in the text of the novel, Shelley's critique of that institution—the encapsulated consciousness of all the characters who espouse its values. A blindness to the possibilities of other contexts for domestic affection is particularly characteristic of her two "outside" narrators, Walton and Victor, both benevolent men who were exiled from the domestic hearth but never draw from their situations an understanding of the social forces working to drive them deeper and deeper into isolation. A vision that would go beyond the limits of the institution into which they were born is thus not theirs to convey to the reader. But why, then, does Shelley not locate her critique in the consciousness of those who do attain domestic affection, since they achieve this state by transcending, in their actions, the unequal relationships between parents and children, males and females, that bind together the Walton, Frankenstein, Beaufort, and Moritz families?

The answer is that Shelley deliberately kept this family "innocent." That is to say, she kept their consciousness and their actions separate. De Lacey's blindness, combined with the primitive conditions under which the family creates a refuge from the world's injustice, simply makes rigid roles impractical, if not impossible, to maintain. At the same time, Safie asserts her independence from her father in the belief that she will be able, in a Christian country, "to aspire to higher powers of intellect, and an independence of spirit, forbidden to the female followers of Mohomet" (124). She has no idea, in other words, that what she has done would be unthinkable to Elizabeth Lavenza and her virtuous nineteenth-century middle-class counterparts. She and Felix learn from Volney's *Ruins of Empires* "of the division of property, of immense wealth and squalid poverty; of rank, descent, and noble blood" (120). But they do not read *A Vindication of the Rights of Woman*, where Mary Wollstonecraft connects the "pernicious effects" of these divisions with the tyranny of husbands over wives and parents over children in the middle-class home.

This leaves only the monster to articulate the experience of being denied, by a parent, domestic affection as a child, a sibling, a husband, and a parent. But absolute deprivation does not lead to an analysis of what is wrong. Who would listen to the monster and give him the encouragement original thought requires? Instead denial leads to acts of vengeance. The monster is too angry to define for his "father" the forces that led him, the father, to create a monster rather than a lovable child. Yet in his campaign of revenge, the monster goes right to the route of his father's character deformation, and wipes out all who played a part, however unwitting, in fostering, justifying, or replicating it. If we view his violent acts simply as a component of a horror story, the novel can be read as a warning against uncontrolled technology and the ambition that brings it into being. If we see Victor Frankenstein as a representative individual to whom the repressed returns, the novel becomes also a drama of the bourgeois male at war with alienated parts of himself, variously identified. I am suggesting an additional meaning that emerges if we take the violence in the novel to constitute a language of protest whose effect is to expose the "wrongs" done to women and children, friends, and fiancées, in the name of domestic affection. It is a language none of the characters can fully decode because they lack the perspective on the separation of spheres that Mary Shelley had learned principally from her mother's writings.

To grasp the subversiveness of Shelley's critique of the family we need to look more closely at her depiction of the various domestic groupings in the novel. Each of the families in the outer two narratives illustrates a differently flawed model of socialization, ranging from overt tyranny and wrongheaded class pride to an absolute denial of domestic conflict that forces it to go underground or out to sea. None of these arrangements provides the younger generation with adequate defense against powerful forces from the outside world, forces that can neither be controlled nor escaped through the exercise of domestic affection.[5]

Robert Walton's career was nourished and shaped by a sister, on the one hand, and by cultural artifacts of his society on the other.

From his uncle's travel books he learns that his culture confers its highest praise on those who endure great personal hardships to bring "inestimable benefits" to all mankind. This knowledge increases the regret he remembers feeling as a child, he tells his sister, on learning that his father's dying injunction had forbidden his uncle to allow him to embark on a seafaring life. The fact that he received this information before he began to read suggests that his contact with his father, if any, had taken place very early in his life. There is no mention of a mother, only of a sister whose influence upon him is described to her as follows: "A youth passed in solitude, my best years spent under your gentle and feminine fosterage, has so refined the groundwork of my character that I cannot overcome an intense distaste for the usual brutality exercised on board ship" (20). This comment implies an absence, not only of parents but of peers as well. He thus has, while growing up, little to counter the models of superachieving manhood he finds in his uncle's library and these, in fact, prevail over his father's dying injunction.

Walton's brief account of his "best years" parallels in two particulars the more lengthily elaborated early life of Victor. The first involves this dying injunction, which is transmitted, in his account, without any explanation, and which has the same effect on him that Victor's father's cursory dismissal of the work of Paracelsus and Cornelius Agrippa has on the youthful Victor. The other similarity is between the actual brother-sister relationship that has a "refining" effect on Walton and the ersatz sibling bond between Victor and Elizabeth. In Walton's case, whatever sociable impulses he might have developed have given way to a character that is uncomfortable in the presence of men who have not been similarly "fostered" by women like his sister. The effect of this refinement on his feelings for women can only be inferred by their absence (except for Margaret) from his narrative, and perhaps also from the fact that the paradise he dreams of is so bounded by ice and snow and other hazards as to be inaccessible to members of the female bourgeoisie.

Walton's rather meager early family life nevertheless shapes his character along lines beneficial to the advancement of his class. He dreams of making discoveries that will benefit all mankind, but Shelley knew, and we know, that the fruits of those voyages of discovery that served as his models did not enrich all mankind equally. Alienated from the crew whose physical work is necessary to the success of his venture, he is as baffled by their lack of commitment to this "glorious expedition" as factory owners were (and are) by workers unwilling to subordinate their needs to the higher cause of industrial expansion and increased profits. Unlike a factory owner, Walton does not plan to enrich himself at the expense of his seafaring "hands." But he does want them to subsume their wishes (for life, comfort, and the pursuit of domestic affection) to his vision of glory and honor that might substitute for the last of these while falling mainly to him.

Walton is participating in the persistent male fantasy of a "band of brothers" that is at the heart of a "shame culture," a fantasy of unfettered individualism in the wilderness untouched by "civilization." Walton is cut off from his sister by his desire for the male solidarity and control over nature that this fantasy substitutes for membership in a community engaged in reproducing itself.[6] "My life might have been passed in ease and luxury," he tells his sister, "but I preferred glory to every enticement that wealth placed in my path" (17). Like Godwin's Falkland, he believes that "one man's life or death were but a small price to pay for the acquirement of knowledge which [he] sought, for the dominion [he] should acquire and transmit over the elemental foes of our race" (26). Like her father, Shelley is exploring a construction of masculinity in which the pursuit of honor and glory pulls away from companionship and community.

Shelley underscores this concern with the inserted story of the one member of his crew with whom Walton feels some kinship. This man had amassed a sufficient fortune to gain from her father the hand of the woman he loved. But on discovering that her heart belonged to another, he gave his entire fortune to his impoverished rival, thus enabling the woman to achieve both the economic transaction her father wanted and the love match she herself desired. Yet the father's sense of honor put his promise to the prospective groom over his daughter's wishes, and the generous man had to leave the country in order to free his beloved from her promise. Walton does not say that either he or his mariner have given up on love altogether. Nevertheless, it is difficult to imagine a vocation that requires a more drastic separation of home from workplace than that of Arctic explorer, the profession he and his uncommunicative companion have chosen.

In her portrait of Walton, Shelley shows us a benevolent man made incapable of (or perhaps uninterested in) domestic happiness by the very forces that make him an exemplary, self-denying bourgeois male. Since Victor is caught in the same double bind, it is not surprising that similar forces shape his early life, especially those that separate domestic life from work. The Frankensteins have been, Victor recounts, councillors and syndics for many generations, distinguished members of the bourgeoisie of Calvinist Geneva, and respected servants of the state as public officeholders. Victor's father "had passed his younger days perpetually occupied by the affairs of his country . . . nor was it till the decline of life that he became the husband and father of a family." Once he took on this private function, however, he retired from public life entirely. We see, then, in the first paragraph of Victor's narrative, the dichotomy between public service and domestic affection that Walton's career exemplifies in an extreme form and that widens for Victor as his narrative progresses.

The paragraph that follows immediately supplies another instance of a retreat from public life, though not into felicity. Beaufort, a friend of Victor's father, was a merchant who, "from a flourishing state, fell, through numerous mischances, into poverty" (31). Fortunately for him, his motherless daughter follows him into exile, where she makes for him the supreme sacrifice of descending voluntarily into the working class so that her father may be spared a humiliation his male pride could not have endured. Caroline Beaufort's acceptance of this situation says a good deal about her conception of domestic affection. De Lacey in the monster's narrative is blind, and thus actually unable to share the burden of maintaining the family economy. But we are told nothing from which to conclude that Beaufort was unable to work. In the face of misfortune he is passive, a characteristic of other males in the novel, and condones, by that passivity, the exploitation of his daughter.

It is in this nobly submissive attitude that Victor's father finds his future bride, weeping at the coffin of her dead father. This, it would seem, was her finest hour, the shadow of her future idealization and just the kind of scene sentimental nineteenth-century painters loved. Victor's father rescues her from the painful fate of working-class womanhood, bringing her back, after a two-year courtship, by the only route by which women can return, that is, through marriage. Yet Beaufort's response to economic reversal and the success of one friend in finding him serve to comment on the relationship between class and friendship that one exceptional act does not negate. All of Beaufort's other friends have apparently conformed to the usual pattern of bourgeois behavior when one of their number drops over the edge of their formerly shared paradise. Given the turbulence that marked capitalist development in the later eighteenth and early nineteenth centuries, the experience of being "ruined" was an ever-present danger. Yet in the fiction of the same period it is rare to find the victims of that upheaval sustained by friendships made in better days. Class solidarity was not large enough, it would seem, to encompass too much misfortune.

Of course Beaufort's personality has not helped the situation. He was, says Victor, "of a proud and unbending disposition, and could not bear to live in poverty and oblivion in the same country where he had been formerly distinguished for his rank and magnificence" (31). Nevertheless, the oblivion he brought upon himself by moving, but which his fellow merchants would have imposed had he remained where he was, implies that they had similarly proud, unbending dispositions, and viewed a loss of money in the same way he did, that is to say, as a fall from grace. Like Robert Walton, Beaufort has internalized an ideology which, while it causes pain to him and his daughter, advances the interests of his class as a whole by purging it of its failures. Domestic affection may be heavily taxed, but it is the one source of self-esteem left to him once he and his neighbours have collaborated in his emotional "ruin."

At the center of this ideology is the belief that material prosperity and social recognition are conferred on superior merit, and thus the lines that divide the bourgeoisie from the rest of humanity reflect worth, not birth. Nevertheless, the naked hostility to poverty that this view implies, while often expressed in the public sphere without shame, was difficult to reconcile with other Christian teachings. One popular fictional device that obfuscates this ideological contradiction is that of the "noble peasant" and his various fairy-tale counterparts, male and female. Caroline Beaufort's devotion to her father is the glass slipper that allowed her to fit so well into her new role as Victor's father's child bride. For her an important part of this role involved revisiting the fallen world of poverty from which she had been so fortunately rescued. Her son explains: "This, to my mother, was more than a duty; it was a necessity, a passion—remembering what she had suffered and how she had been relieved—for her to act in turn the guardian angel to the afflicted" (34). Like her husband, Caroline rejects the harsher side of an ideology that views poverty as a problem to be solved through hard work on the part of those afflicted, and wishes to apply to her local indigents the remedy that had softened for her father the harsh reality of class divisions. Motherless herself, she attempts to alleviate social injustice by becoming a "good mother" to those for whom no Prince Charming is likely to appear. Yet when she finds one of their number who clearly does not belong where fate has placed her, Caroline's response is to single out this one and give her more than periodic bounty. In fact, she gives Elizabeth everything she herself had: a bourgeois father, a mother who dies young, a Prince Charming, and a view of the female role (though we are not told where Caroline got this) as one of constant, self-sacrificing devotion to others.

To say that domestic affection, extended into the public sphere, is an adequate remedy for the ills of an industrial society would be to fly in the face of an idea that gained immense popularity in the Victorian era, both in England and in this country.[7] But to say that Elizabeth's early death, like her adopted mother's, was a logical outgrowth of the female ideal she sought to embody is a radical statement indeed. Shelley may have thought she was going too far in this direction when she revised her account of Caroline's death from the following: "Elizabeth had caught the scarlet fever; but her illness was not severe, and she quickly recovered. During her confinement, many arguments had been urged to persuade my mother to refrain from attending upon her. She had, at first, yielded to our entreaties; but when she heard that her favorite was recovering, she could no longer debar herself from her society, and entered her chamber long before the danger of infection was past. On the third day my mother sickened."[8] In 1831 Mary revised this passage to say that Elizabeth's illness was severe, that "she was in the greatest danger." Her mother "had, at first, yielded to our entreaties; but when she heard that the life of her favorite was menaced, she could no longer control her anxiety. She attended her sick-bed—her watchful attentions triumphed over the malignity of the distemper—Elizabeth was saved but the consequence of this imprudence were fatal to her preserver. On the third day my mother sickened . . ." (42–43). In the revision Caroline's death is tragic but not gratuitous as well. Her motherly touch would seem to have been crucial, whereas in the first version it kills her without benefiting anyone else.

Yet if the revised Caroline becomes a heroine in death, her daughter's self-effacing behavior throughout the novel is singularly ineffectual in actual crisis situations. Her most dramatic public act is her attempt to save Justine, the young woman the Frankensteins have "adopted" without quite conferring equal status on her in the family. Yet all Elizabeth seems able to do is to display her own goodness, her willingness to trust the accused, saying that she would have given her the miniature of her mother, had Justine but asked for it. Yet feminine sweetness is not what wins court cases. It may captivate male hearts, and even elicit "a murmur of approbation" from those in the courtroom. But making a convincing argument before a judge and a jury (even an all-male one) requires skills that Elizabeth does not possess.

Elizabeth seems unaware of this, however. She hopes that Victor "perhaps will find some means to justify my poor guiltless Justine." Yet Victor has been summoned by his father with a plea not to think in terms of crime and punishment. "Come, Victor," he says, "not brooding thought of vengeance against the assassin, but with feelings of peace and gentleness, that will heal, instead of festering, the wounds of our minds" (73). Both father and daughter have so little idea what they are up against. They see the world in such simple blacks and whites that neither one can conceive of what is, in fact, the truth: that the "evidence" that convicts Justine has been planted. If we look at the description of Justine's apprehension this oversight seems truly incredible. Ernest, Victor's younger brother, tells the story:

> He related that, the morning on which the murder of poor William had been discovered, Justine had been taken ill, and confined to her bed for several days. During this interval, one of the servants, happening to examine the apparel she had worn the night of the murder, had discovered in her pocket the picture of my mother, which had been judged to be the temptation of the murderer. The servant instantly showed it to one of the others, who, without saying a word to any of the family, went to a magistrate; and, upon their deposition, Justine was apprehended. (79)

This act by two servants is certainly one that might reasonably arouse suspicion on the part of their employers, but the Frankensteins appear to view their inability to suspect anyone as one of their greatest virtues. Furthermore, for a knowing murderer to keep such a damning piece of evidence on her person is at least questionable, yet none of the bereaved family thinks even to raise the issue in Justine's defense. Instead, believing in the power (exemplified by Elizabeth's speech) of domestic affection unaided by deductive reasoning, they follow the lead of the elder Frankenstein, who urges his family to "rely on the justice of our laws, and the activity with which I shall prevent the slightest show of partiality." He has missed the fact that they are dealing not with a set of abstract laws but with emotional citizens, rendered vengeful by "fear and hatred of the crime of which they supposed [Justine] guilty."

Yet the passivity of this family in the face of evil in the world goes even beyond this. On hearing of the murder, Elizabeth is not simply devoid of a wish to find out who did it. Her immediate response is that she did it, since she had given little William the miniature to wear that night. And if this is her response, when no finger is pointing at her, how much less able to defend herself against guilt is Justine, whose very confusion is interpreted as a sign of her guilt in the other sense of the word. Both Justine and Elizabeth have learned well the lessons of submissiveness and devotion to others that Caroline Beaufort epitomized for them. Unfortunately their model behavior lowers their resistance to the forces that kill them, just as it did for their model.

Of the education Justine received in the Frankenstein household we know only that it was "superior to that which [her mistress] intended at first," and that Justine thought this second mother of hers to be "the model of all excellence, and endeavoured to imitate her phraseology and manners" (65). Shelley tells us more about Elizabeth's education, particularly in the second edition of the novel, where she expanded two sentences that appear in her husband's handwriting in the manuscript. In the 1818 version, "I delighted [says Victor] in investigating the facts relative to the actual world; she busied herself in following the aerial creations of the poets. The world was to me a secret, which I desired to discover; to her it was vacancy, which she sought to people with imaginations of her own."[9] Here we see the crucial difference in the respective educations of these two people: Victor translates his interest in science into a career aspiration, while Elizabeth translates her interest into a substitute for experience, a way of filling a void created by her lack of contact with the outside world.

In her 1831 revision, Shelley lays even greater stress than in her original version on the domestic harmony that formed the context of the early education of Elizabeth, Victor, and their friend Clerval. She develops the division of the realm of masculine knowledge between Victor and Clerval, connecting (in Clerval's case especially) their studies and their future aspirations:

It was the secrets of heaven and earth that I desired to learn; and whether it was the outward substance of things, or the inner spirit of nature and the mysterious soul of man that occupied me, still my enquiries were directed toward the metaphysical, or, in its highest sense, the physical secrets of the world.

Meanwhile, Clerval occupied himself, so to speak, with the moral relations of things. The busy stage of life, the virtues of heroes, and the actions of men, were his theme, and his hope and his dream was to become one of those whose names are recorded in story, as the gallant and adventurous benefactors of our species. (37)

Elizabeth's literary studies, on the other hand, have been dropped rather than developed. Now she spends her entire time shining "like a shrine-dedicated lamp in our peaceful home." To whom, one may ask, is this shrine dedicated? Both editions remark that Elizabeth and Victor "were strangers to any species of disunion or dispute." But in the first they learn Latin and English together so that they "might read the writings in those languages," while in the second her participation in the studies of the other two is quite different: "She was the living spirit of love to soften and attract: I might have become sullen in my study, rough through the ardour of my nature, but that she was there to subdue me to a semblance of her own gentleness. And Clerval . . . might not have been so perfectly humane, so thoughtful in his generosity—so full of kindness and tenderness amidst his passion for adventurous exploit, had not she unfolded to him the real lovliness of beneficence, and made the doing good the end and aim of his soaring ambition" (38). What Mary Shelley spells out, in these additions, is Elizabeth's role in maintaining the atmosphere of continual sunshine in which Victor claims he spent *his* best years.

One might argue that Elizabeth was not harmed by having her mind filled with the demands and concerns of others exclusively, that she was in fact happy with the "trifling occupations" that took up all her time after Victor and Clerval left their common schoolroom, occupations whose reward was "seeing nothing but happy, kind faces around me" (64). Or one might say that she was being excessively modest, that keeping others happy generally, and softening the "sometimes violent" temper and "vehement passions" (37) of two male students in particular, is no trifling occupation. Yet she was simply performing one of the chief duties of the female sex, displaying that "female excellence" that was best displayed in "the sphere of domestic life," where it manifests itself, as Thomas Gisborne puts it, "in sprightliness and vivacity, in quickness of perception, fertility of invention, in powers adapted to unbend the brow of the learned, to refresh the overlaboured faculties of the wise, and to diffuse throughout the family circle the enlivening and endearing smile of cheerfulness."[10] For tasks like these, a woman needed not so much a mind as a heart. Not all writers on female education opposed intellectual development for women. But as we have seen, it tended to be viewed as harmless by those who did not find it harmful to the very qualities that Gisborne and his sympathizers found essential in a dutiful member of the female sex.[11]

Mary Wollstonecraft, debating on the other side, had very different ideas about the kind of education Elizabeth receives in the second version of *Frankenstein*. For her "the only way to make [women] properly attentive to their domestic duties" was to "open" political and moral subjects to them. "An active mind," she asserts, "embraces the whole circle of its duties and finds time enough for all."[12] Victor praises his adopted sibling for her charms and graces, for which "everyone loved her." But her education has no content, and she does not live long enough for Victor to test Wollstonecraft's assertion that "unless the understanding be cultivated, superficial and monotonous is every grace."[13] What is not evident to Victor is certainly evident to the reader, however. Elizabeth is not a real force in the novel; she is too superficial and monotonous.

The division into roles that takes place in the Frankenstein schoolroom corresponds roughly to the divisions described in Plato's *Republic*. Though Plato argues there that temperament is not gender-based, the citizens of his republic learn in earliest childhood a "myth of the metals" which divides them into groups according to whether intellect, courage, or neither predominates in their makeup. The purpose of the indoctrination is to eliminate friction in the republic. But in Frankenstein it has the opposite effect: Victor, divided from his courageous, moral self as well as from his ability to subdue his own vehement passions, sets in motion a chain of events that will destroy those parts of a potentially whole human psyche that have not been given scope for development within his conflict-free upbringing.

For there was in Victor much that could not find expression without disrupting the tranquility of a happy home. On leaving that home he indulges at first "in the most melancholy reflections." But, he continues, "as I proceeded my spirits and hopes rose. I ardently desired the acquisition of knowledge. I had often, when at home, thought it hard to remain during my youth cooped up in one place, and had longed to enter the world, and take my station among other human beings" (45). Unfortunately for him, these other human beings turn out all to be male, their sisters and daughters being busied with "triflng occupations" within the safety of their domestic circle. Only males, in the world of the novel's second narrator, are seen acting upon their longings to acquire knowledge, to leave a home that coops them up, and to take their place in the world. Thus Victor discovers a flaw in the wall that keeps his hearth untouched by evil from the outside: you cannot take its protective magic with you when you leave.

For Elizabeth's power "to soften and attract" does him little good if he must leave it behind when he goes "to take [his] station among other human beings." He may be devoted to preserving her innocence, and revere her for her self-denying dedication to the happiness of others. But since these qualities cut her off from any active engagement in his life, and thus deprive him of a real companion, her supposed perfection only deepens his guilt for not being passive, and intensifies the isolation he needs to keep it hidden. Unable to express his resentment toward her unreproaching dependency, he creates a dependent "child" who does reproach him for his neglect. Furthermore, by making this child ugly he can justify his neglect by appealing to a prejudice that all the characters in the novel uphold. Resentment toward (and cruelty to) an ugly helpless creature is considered perfectly appropriate human behavior. Indignation is aroused in the novel only by cruelty to beautiful children like Elizabeth and William.

Thus Victor can vent on his monster all the negative emotion that would otherwise have no socially acceptable object, and remain unaware of the transference he has made from his child bride to his child. From his remarks about spending his youth "cooped up in one place," we may surmise that his feelings of resentment, for which the monster becomes an uncontrollable "objective correlative," had their first stirrings while the would-be scientist-hero was still blissfully lodged in the womb of domesticity. But resentment in paradise, for Victor no less than for Satan himself, leads to the expulsion that intensifies resentment. Outside the home, there is nothing to prevent that feeling from growing until it reaches literally murderous proportions. Had Victor not been so furtive about his desire to astound the world, he might have allowed himself time to make a creature his own size, one who mirrored the whole of him, not just the part of himself he cannot bring home. But to do that he would have had to be an integrated person outside the home, and an integrated person within it.

Repeatedly throughout the novel, Shelley gives us examples of the ways in which the bourgeois family creates and perpetuates divided selves in the name of domestic affection, drawing a circle around the home that keeps it in and "disunion and dispute" out. We have noticed already that those whose role is to embody domestic affection cannot go out into the world. "Insiders" cannot leave, or do so at their peril. At the same time Shelley dramatizes, through the experience of Victor's ugly "child," that "outsiders" cannot enter; they are condemned to perpetual exile and deprivation, forbidden even from trying to create a domestic circle of their own. This fate is emphasized by the fate of Justine, who succeeds in imitating to perfection the similarly rescued Caroline Beaufort, but who is abandoned by the Frankensteins at the first suggestion of rebellion. Abandoned first by her own jealous mother, Justine embodies Shelley's most devastating indictment of bourgeois socialization: a second "adopted" family cannot, as Milton put it, "rectify the wrongs of our first parents."

The Frankenstein family failed Justine because their response to her at a time of crisis was passivity. Yet here the distinction between "outsiders" and "insiders" breaks down: the Frankensteins respond to one another, when crisis comes, in the same way, adjuring one another to repress their anger and grief for the sake of maintaining tranquility. The result is that their repressed emotions, especially their anger, are acted upon for them by others. We can see this in the behavior of the jurors at Justine's trial: they are ruled by the spirit of vengeance that the family members themselves refuse to admit into their consciousness. Of course, the monster is the example par excellence of this process of projection, and his victims come from within the family circle as well as outside it. Their only crime is that they participated (voluntarily) in the process of self-division that left Victor incapable of being a loving father, passive in the face of crisis and content to let other people complete him.

The one murder that does not seem to fit into this schema is that of "little William." What we know of him comes only from Elizabeth, who notes two things about him—his beauty and his interest in domestic affection in its traditional form: "When he smiles, two little dimples appear on each cheek, which are rose with health. He has already had one or two little *wives*, but Louisa Biron is his favorite, a pretty little girl of five years of age" (66). Ernest, like Clerval, is drawn to a life of adventure and a career in the foreign service, but does not have Victor's powers of application. But it is on William, preparing to be just like his father, that Victor can visit, through the monster, his resentment against a childhood spent in the kind of domestic role-playing William is doing.[14]

The hothouse atmosphere in which Victor and later William play with their "pretty little" child brides forms a contrast to the mutually supportive, matter-of-fact life of Felix and Agatha De Lacey. Nor is this the only point on which the De Lacey family group contrasts with the other families in the novel. They are the only family that perpetuates itself into the next generation, largely because no one in it is striving for the kind of personal immortality that propels Victor and Walton out of their respective domestic Edens. De Lacey *pere*, like Beaufort and Frankenstein the elder, was once a prosperous member of the bourgeoisie. He was exiled and stripped of his fortune and placed in the social order because his son, motivated by benevolence, impulsively aided in the escape of a Turk who was a victim of French racism and political injustice. But Felix's benevolent impulse precipitates events in "the world" that are beyond his control, events that bring down ruin upon the heads of his whole family.

The De Laceys exhibit a great deal less rigidity, however, when it comes to coping with misfortune than either of the two Genevese families who are called upon to deal with ruin or bereavement. This does not mean they are blissfully happy. The father "often endeavored to encourage his children, as sometimes I found that he called them, to cast off their melancholy" (112) while remaining unaware, because of his blindness, that there is often not enough food for himself and them too. But if the land nurtures them meagerly, even with the help of the monster, it is at least a resource for meeting real needs. The relationship of the De Laceys to nature is thus different from that of Victor, for whom it provides only occasions for the repeated display of sensibility that leads to no action.

Furthermore, their exile from society is entirely involuntary. They did not impose it upon themselves, as Beaufort did, nor do they blame Felix and exile him as a punishment for the fate they must all share. Quite different is the response of Victor's family to his devotion to the welfare of mankind. Returning home after his first encounter with the monster as a speaking creature, he notes: "My haggard and wild appearance awoke intense alarm; but I answered no question, scarcely did I speak. I felt as if I were placed under a ban—as if I had no right to claim their sympathies—as if never more might I enjoy companionship with them" (149). Taken out of context as it is here, one might think this was the monster speaking of his relationship with the De Lacey family. Victor's refusal to be an accepting father to his child, and to give him a companion who would share his sorrows as well as his joys, is a refusal (or perhaps simply an inability) to give his child what his own father did not give him. His exile, as he portrays it in this passage and elsewhere, is largely self-imposed. He answered no question, but questions were asked. Nevertheless, everything we have seen about the Frankenstein family's mode of dealing with disturbing reality emanating from outside their circle indicates that Victor is right to keep quiet, that his revelations might provoke a response that is even more damaging than alarm: they might pretend he had never spoken.[15]

The deficiencies of Victor's family, dramatized in his inability to bring the monster home, to deal with evil in the outside world, or to own the repressed impulses that others are acting out for him, stem ultimately from the concept of domestic affection on which the continuing tranquility of the family depends. The root of this evil is the separation of male and female spheres for purposes of ensuring the purity of the family and the sanctity of the home. The effect of domestic affection on both Victor and Walton is "an invincible repugnance to new countenances" that leads them away from the human community and toward the solitary pursuit of glory. But these pursuits disqualify them from domestic affection. Once the outside world has touched them they cannot reenter the home without destroying its purity. Victor's rejection of the monster, an extension of the "invincible repugnance to new countenances" that is his family heritage, makes it impossible that he could embrace without guilt the enforced innocence of Elizabeth without destroying the purity that is her major attraction in his eyes.

Scholarly interest in the bourgeois family, the target of Mary Shelley's critique of domestic affection, has received a good deal of impetus in the last twenty years from feminists attempting to name and place the origins of "the problem that has no name."[16] It is a problem that arises, in present-day America, when women are immured in the home with nothing but "trifling occupations" to fill their time and no reward beyond the "happy faces" of those who enjoy their unpaid services. Victor might well advise women as well as men entering the postindustrial world of work never to allow "any pursuit whatsoever to interfere with the tranquility of his [or her] domestic affections" (56). But as Victor might have realized had he seen his father attempting to combine the roles of perfect husband and father and that of breadwinner giving his "indefatigable attention to public business" (31), the only kinds of work that do not affect one's domestic tranquility, either by exhausting the body or absorbing the mind, are "trifling occupations."

Shelley seems to be suggesting that, if the family is to be a viable institution for the transmission of domestic affection from one generation to the next, it must redefine that precious commodity in such a way that it can extend to "outsiders," while at the same time proving hardy enough to survive in the world outside the home. It is not surprising that a woman should be making this point. Eradicating the gulf between work and home is more clearly in the interest of women than of men, since it is the latter who profit most from the resultant "unnatural distinctions established in society" against which Mary Wollstonecraft protested (almost two hundred years ago). If we can imagine a novel in which a woman scientist creates a monster who returns to destroy its creator's family, the relevance to woman of the problem that Mary Shelley has imagined becomes more immediately apparent.

The one character who clearly exemplifies such a redefined notion of domestic affection is Safie, the daughter of a Christian Arab who, "born in freedom, spurned the bondage to which she was now reduced" upon her marriage to the Turk, Safie's father. This man had rescued his wife from slavery just as Victor's father had rescued Caroline Beaufort from poverty. But instead of translating her gratitude into lifelong subservience and sporadic charity, this woman "spurned the bondage to which she was now reduced." It was she who taught her daughter "to aspire to higher powers of intellect, and an independence of spirit forbidden to the female followers of Mohomet" (124). Undoubtedly Safie's adoption of her mother's views accounts in some measure for her father's duplicity toward her, encouraging her union with Felix when his purposes were served by doing so at the same time that he "loathed the idea that his daughter should be united to a Christian."

Although she is motherless when she is called upon to put her early training to the test, Safie applies her mother's teachings in a way that is intended to contrast, I believe, with the behavior of the passive Elizabeth, equally influenced by her adopted mother's teachings and example. As a result of the strong impression made by her mother's lessons on her young mind, Safie "sickened at the prospect of again returning to Asia, and being immured within the walls of a harem, allowed only to occupy herself with infantile amusements, ill suited to the temper of her soul, now accustomed to grand ideas and the noble emulation of virtue" (124). In consequence, she not only refuses to wait for the possibility that her lover will miraculously find her, but figures out where Felix is and actively seeks him out, traveling from Italy to Germany with only an attendant for protection. Had Elizabeth been encouraged "to aspire to higher powers of intellect, and an independence of spirit," she might have insisted that Victor make for the monster a companion for his wanderings, one who, like herself, possessed the power to soften and attract. But then she would have had to help him in the making of it, since creatures with this quality are clearly "the other" to Victor. As it was, Victor could not dream of involving Elizabeth in his work on any level. Apparently he preferred a dead wife to a free one.

There remains the death of Victor's father to fill out our analysis of the monster's activity as the revenge of the exile. What is interesting about Alphonse Frankenstein is that he is an absent father for Victor not because he leaves home every day but because he does not. He is so uninterested in matters that do not pertain to domestic tranquility that he does not talk to Victor about his interest in science, an interest he shares with his son in the first version of the novel but not in the second. His decision to postpone family responsibilities until he can give them all of his time means that he relates to his son from a distance once Victor leaves the family nest. Victor, too, is torn away from his child not by the demands of work but by his desire for domesticity, a fact that gives a further ironic twist to the already startling image of a man giving birth and then fleeing his personal responsibility. Within a context of "separate spheres," the revised Victor has two mothers, that is, no role model for male behavior outside the home. Having withdrawn from the world into the home, both his parents devoted all their energies to raising their children in such a way that "we felt that they were not the tyrants to rule over our lot according to their caprice, but the agents and creators of all the many delights which we enjoyed." If they had to discipline their children at all, they undoubtedly concentrated on the wrongdoer's motivation rather than the effects of the deed. But from the description that Shelley gives of the Frankenstein household, parental injunctions seem to have been internalized without even having to be uttered. The very idea of forbidden fruit was thus alien to them.

Perhaps these well-meaning parents, one of whom is young enough to be the child of the other, followed the example of Wollstonecraft's Mrs. Mason, who disciplines her charges by giving and withdrawing "those marks of affection which they particularly delighted to receive."[17] This "gentle way of punishment" creates, as we have seen, a guilt-prone personality. Moreover, when Alphonse departs even slightly from his mode of sympathetic explanation, telling his son that the works of Cornelius Agrippa are "sad trash," Victor is so entirely unprepared for his father's brusqueness that the incident begets "the fatal impulse" that leads him to his "ruin." The influence of peers is not there to offset the power of this constantly surveillant, maternal father because of Victor's "invincible repugnance to new countenances," fostered in his hermetically sealed home. Thus it is Alphonse, more than any other member of Victor's family, who walls off the place of "domestic affection" so thoroughly that not only is the monster shut out but his creator as well.

In each of the three narratives a conflict arises between forbidden knowledge and domestic affection, a conflict so intense that the knower is permanently exiled from the sphere of family life. For

Walton, it is conflict between the manner in which he spent the first fourteen years of his life, namely reading "our Uncle Thomas' books of voyages," and his dying father's injunction that he not live out his childhood dreams. After such knowledge, such intense stimulation, there can be no forgiveness for disobeying his father. For the monster, the knowledge that destroys him comes when Felix attacks him and he learns that domestic happiness wears a cruel face when it turns toward outsiders. For Victor, who has an intuition about the dark side of domestic affection when he refuses to let the monster have it, the denial of conflict that characterized his early years persists right up to his death in the icy regions around Walton's boat. Insisting that he is not "blamable" in undertaking a work "only induced by reason and virtue," he clings, to the last, to his innocence, and it kills him.

This is indeed Godwinian pessimism. Yet the novel does posit an alternative world to that which is stamped by the industrial mode of patriarchy, the separation of spheres. Safie, who traveled far and wide without a proper chaperone in search of a lover her father forbade, holds out a vision of domestic affection that is not endangered by a knowledge of evil in the world. Thus Shelley took the insights of the Lewisite Gothic novel beyond the tentative happy endings of her predecessors. But at the same time, she answered this pessimistic worldview with the optimistic feminism of the mother she never knew.

If we look at *Frankenstein* through the paradigm of opposing systems of value that we have been calling "guilt" and "shame" cultures, we can see that the guilt-imposing home is unable to accommodate whole human beings, but that the flight into a world without women that is counterposed to domestic life is deadly also. The laboratory where the monster is born is homologous both with Walton's imagined kingdom at the North Pole and with the usurped Gothic castle where women are confined or driven out. Both Walton and Victor are compelled by a desire for honor and glory that would elevate them so high above their fellow man that it would wipe out their guilt for standing up to their respective fathers. Given the nature of "home" in a guilt culture, this flight is both necessary and death-dealing, taking on the cloak of "scientific investigation." This is the way the novel is usually read, as a critique of technological hubris, which is why I have focused primarily on Shelley's critique of "domestic affection."

But Shelley reminds us, even as she pulls apart the ideology of separate spheres, that women are even worse off in the world of honor and shame than they are in the home: the intellectual and sexual sides of their nature have as little place in the extradomestic sphere of male domination as they do in the home. We see this when Victor decides not to make his monster a mate on the grounds that "she, who in all probability was to become a thinking and reasoning animal, might refuse to comply with a compact made before her creation." And if she could not be made to be obedient to her husband, what guarantee would Victor have that their children would obey their father and leave the human race alone? Neither a shame culture, which requires absolute obedience from women and makes them objects of exchange, nor a guilt culture that protects women to a degree that disables them from protecting themselves, can bring forth a new Eden in which labor is not backbreaking and enmity between men and women has been transcended. For this we must look to Safie, who actively rebelled against the most repressive of patriarchal cultures, and who becomes, not a "true wife" but an emblem of an egalitarian third possibility.

In *Frankenstein* it is a man, rather than a woman, who brings "Death into the World, and all our woe." Women have become the saviors of a fallen world by reason of their attachment to the home and their greater involvement with children. This is still the case despite the stripping away of their spiritual preeminence by an increasingly secular culture. In fact, it may be that women's role as savior has received greater emphasis as secularization has advanced. The continuing popularity of the concept "Frankenstein," a conflation of the monster and his creator, stems from the fact that Mary Shelley articulated through it the agent of our "fall" into a society in which technology may be out of control. Evil in the form we now fear it most came into the world not through the seduction of a man by a woman, but through a creature abandoned by its maker. The myth that underlies the regaining of paradise through political revolution is the rising up of this creature whose likeness to God has been effaced by human institutions.

NOTES

1. Mary Shelley, *Frankenstein*, ed. M. K. Joseph (New York: Oxford University Press, 1971), 19. Subsequent references will be to this edition.

2. Ellen Moers, "Female Gothic," in *The Endurance of Frankenstein*, ed. George Levine and Uli Knoepflmacher (Berkeley: University of California Press, 1979), 77–87.

3. Harold Bloom, "Afterword" to *Frankenstein* (New York: New American Library, 1965) 212–23; Sandra Gilbert and Susan Gubar, "Horror's Twin: Mary Shelley's Monstrous Eve," *The Madwoman in the Attic: The Woman Writer and the Nineteenth-Century Literary Imagination* (New Haven: Yale University Press, 1979), 213–47.

4. Lee Sterrenburg, "Mary Shelley's Monster: Politics and Psyche in *Frankenstein*," in *The Endurance of Frankenstein*, 143–71.

5. Jane Tompkins's analysis of Charles Brockden Brown's *Wieland* parallels in many points my discussion of the "innocent" Victor and his monster. Gratuitous violence, for Victor as for Wieland and his sister, Clara, rushes in to fill the vacuum created by an absence of structures of authority in his formative years. See *Sensational Designs: The Cultural Work of American Fiction 1790–1860* (New York: Oxford University Press, 1985), 40–61.

6. Judith Wilt, *Ghosts of the Gothic: Austen, Eliot, and Lawrence* (Princeton: Princeton University Press, 1980), explores the Gothic impulse to move away from community.

7. In an important article on George Eliot's eighteenth-century predecessors, Margaret Anne Doody gives a more positive reading of the theme of women taking care of children and of each other in "George Eliot and the Eighteenth Century Novel," *NCF* 35 (1980), 260–91.

8. Mary Shelley, *Frankenstein, or The Modern Prometheus*, ed. James Reiger (Indianapolis: Bobbs-Merrill, 1974), 37.

9. Ibid., 30.

10. Thomas Gisborne, *An Enquiry into the Duties of the Female Sex* (London, 1797), 20–21.

11. Vineta Colby, "The Education of the Heart," in *Yesterday's Women: Domestic Realism in the English Novel* (Princeton: Princeton University Press, 1974), 86–144.

12. Mary Wollstonecraft, *A Vindication of the Rights of Woman*, ed. Carol Poston (New York: W. W. Norton, 1975), 169.

13. Ibid., 170.

14. See U. C. Knoepflmacher, "Thoughts on the Aggression of Daughters," in *The Endurance of Frankenstein*, 88–119.

15. In *Sanity, Madness and the Family* (London: Tavistock Publications, 1964), R. D. Laing and Aaron Esterson discuss this mode of family behavior as a contributor to the experience of schizophrenia.

16. Betty Friedan, *The Feminine Mystique* (New York: Norton, 1963).

17. Mary Wollstonecraft, *Original Stories from Real Life* (London, 1791), 37.

Emily Brontë and
the Technology of Self

ONE MIGHT say that the eclipse of the Gothic novel in the early nineteenth century came about because the project that called it forth was complete: the myth of the fall had been recast so as to express a new set of gender relations and a new bourgeois ideal of true womanhood. But specific local factors are always involved in the death of a genre, the most obvious of which is sheer repetition. The most sustained and drawn-out attack on Catholicism as an institution is to be found in *Melmoth the Wanderer*, whose very encyclopedic quality made it a kind of *summa* of Gothic material engendered by Walpole. Then, too, reviewers from the mid-1790s on pilloried the imitators of Radcliffe and Lewis for their violations of probability and formulaic use of Gothic "machinery," much of which is connected to the Church or justified as a faithful depiction of a superstitious age. The displacement of evil onto a foreign past did not achieve the didactic ends their authors claimed. Rather, their popularity threatened to drive out "the simple, natural, and often instructive novel, founded upon real life."[1]

Underlying this weariness with "yet another haunted castle" is the changing role of Catholicism in English life in the nineteenth century. On the one hand, English tolerance for Catholicism apparently increased in the fifty-eight years between the Gordon Riots of 1780 and the repeal of the Test and Corporations Acts in 1828. The Gordon Riots, "the most violent, and the most savagely repressed of all riots in London's history," were triggered by the passage of a relatively mild measure aimed at removing certain of the additional liabilities imposed on Catholics by William III, whereas the 1828 legislation, though it was only a first step to full civil and religious equality, did allow Catholics to hold public office.[2] In the intervening years, thousands of Catholics fleeing persecution in France had been welcomed in England, which speaks to a diminished sense in England of the threat of "popery," no longer automatically denoting a monolithic political block intent on the destruction of England and everything she stood for.

Concurrent with this diminution of anti-Catholicism as a political issue was the cultural appropriation of a component of medieval life that could be separated from institutional Catholicism, the ideology and practices of chivalry. We have seen how Godwin's Falkland and Mary Shelley's Walton were steeped in the literature of chivalry, and how their reading gave them a model for heroic masculine behavior that had a long and continuous history that predated the separation of spheres. The feudal idea of reciprocal obligations between masters and men extolled the loyalty of the latter and the dauntless courage of the former. It is a discourse about masculinity, one that celebrated its difference from helpless womanhood in need of rescue and protection.[3]

In any event, the body of the Walpolean Gothic was dispersed through English fiction and popular drama in the nineteenth century and beyond. But one novel that preserves many of the characteristic markers of the early Gothic, including its revisionary relationship to *Paradise Lost*, is *Wuthering Heights*.[4] With its succession of father/villains confounded finally by an initiative-taking daughter/heroine, it calls up the resistance to arbitrary authority, with its themes of usurpation, primogeniture, imprisonment, marriage choice, sinister religion and its war against innocence that we have been tracing throughout this book. And though Emily Brontë does not give us "another country" ruled by Catholicism as the source of the destructive forces in her fictional world, the date on the door of Wuthering Heights should not go unnoticed: 1500 was forty-two years before the dissolution of the monasteries in England. The house is thus linked, though less explicitly than Walpole does with his found manuscript dated 1529, to a time when "belief in every kind of prodigy" was rampant.

But if Milton represents one nodal point of my inquiry into the feminist politics of the Gothic genre, inscribing within it the episteme of the "old science" in which enclosure is the highest good, Foucault, with his analysis of power expressed as a probing into privatized spaces, marks an opposite point from which to explore this body of material. Both Wuthering Heights and Thrushcross Grange act upon their "inmates" and produce different kinds of subjectivities, one through direct, specular violence, the other through indirect, invisible discursive practices. Like most of her fellow Gothicists, Emily Brontë dramatizes the interface between these two modes of power by bringing them to bear on the lives of women. Where does women's power come from and how can it be most effectively acquired and deployed? These are the questions underlying my investigation, and no one has answered them with greater clarity than Emily Brontë.

Wuthering Heights can be seen as a double Gothic novel like *The Monk*, with two villain-fathers (three if we count Linton's attempts to confine his lively daughter and control her choice of a husband) and two heroines successively struggling for control of interior spaces. In the success of the younger Catherine, a virtual prisoner when we first see her, we can read the Gothic theme of a "castle" wrested by a woman from the control of the morally flawed but perfectly legal patriarchal inheritance system. The original "crime" for which Mr. Earnshaw sought to make amends by walking the 120 miles to Liverpool and back is appropriately obscure, given that its expiation is not clearly achieved either. But Heathcliff in the beginning has some affinity with Lewis's Agnes de Medina and Maturin's Alonzo di Moncada, both victims of a parental obsession with expiating the failings of one generation through the control of the next. For Alonzo and Agnes, rigid rules contravene "natural" generational succession. In Brontë's novel, the principle behind Mr. Earnshaw's action is never articulated.

Similarly, the cause of the death of the son for whom Heathcliff is named is not spelled out. Perhaps the causes were "natural," but given the paternal negligence and cruelty that occurs at the Heights throughout the novel, one might well wonder. Heathcliff, at any rate, becomes a second son who immediately usurps Hindley's share of paternal affection as well as gaining his own. A second son, we have learned, must have it all. "Slow diligence" does not appeal to him. He is capable of love, as the Gothic second son often is, but his sense of "injured merit" blocks his expression of it and he does not stay to hear what Cathy feels about him, so disturbed is he at what he hears about his rival. The "hot Hell that always in him burns" by which Milton characterized Satan after the fall seems to have been present, in Heathcliff's relationships with his adopted family members, right from the beginning.

A "fall" implies a prior state of harmony, and this is certainly not the case in the Earnshaw family prior to Mr. Earnshaw's death. We have very few clues about life at the Heights before Heathcliff's arrival. We hear nothing of Mrs. Earnshaw between her reaction to Heathcliff's arrival and her death two years later. In particular, we never hear of her expressing anger again after "flying up" over Heathcliff, "asking how he could fashion to bring that gypsy into the house, when they had their own bairns to feed and fend for?"[5] Yet she had already accepted Nelly, the daughter of the woman who nursed her son, as part of the household. About Mr. Earnshaw we know only that he had bought for his children the presents they asked for (a fiddle for Hindley, a whip for Catherine) and had not forgotten Nelly, "though he was rather severe sometimes" (38). In any event, his daughter was eagerly awaiting his arrival, and her mother allowed the children to stay up till eleven, when "in stept the master."

The presents he bought are notable in that they denote a reversal of sex roles which the father, by purchasing the presents, endorses. A fiddle is associated with the female domain, with culture and "inside," while a whip carries associations of domination and the outdoors. Whatever his feelings may have been about his children before he left for Liverpool, it is through Heathcliff that he begins to show favoritism at the expense of both his legitimate children.[6] Thus, if there was an Edenic period in the life of Cathy it was prior to her father's return from Liverpool, when she and her brother slept in the same room and were not divided by this favoritism. Initially united in their opposition to the new addition to the household, refusing "to have it in bed with them, or even in the same room," they give up in the face of their father's superior power, and avenge themselves for his rejection by equally self-destructive courses. The arrival of Heathcliff obliterates the fiddle and the whip, and brings to an end an androgynous childhood that allowed both children to ask their father for what they wanted and expect to get it.

The rivalry between the "true" son and the "usurper" for the attentions of Mr. Earnshaw engenders the novel's plot, though Brontë never tells us directly why the aging father "took to Heathcliff strangely." Might Heathcliff's stoicism have struck the old man as more manly than Hindley's tendency to "blubber aloud" when he does not get what he wants? Crying may have been acceptable male behavior at the time of the sentimental novel, but by the time Emily was writing little boys were supposed to learn that feelings (and particularly tears) were the domain of women. Earnshaw sees his own power declining with age, though the feat of walking sixty miles each way shows that his physical strength is still extraordinary. Obsessive like Lear, Earnshaw rejects his son in favor of a more-uncompromising ego ideal. By the time Hindley is sent away to college, his father has concluded that he will never be a real man. "Hindley was naught, and would never thrive as where he wandered" (42).

The incident in which Heathcliff takes the better of two horses given to him and Hindley by Mr. Earnshaw, and then fights Hindley for his when this better horse becomes lame, shows the child father to the man who ultimately usurps both the Heights and the Grange. Hindley knocks Heathcliff down and runs away after giving over the good horse, whereupon Nelly comments that she "was surprised to witness how coolly the child gathered himself up, and went on with his intention, exchanging saddles and all, . . . I persuaded him easily to let me lay the blame of his bruises on the horse; he minded little what tale was told *since he had what he wanted* " (48, my italics). Even in the so-called Edenic phase of his life, when he and Cathy are "very thick," Heathcliff is busy acquiring property.

Earnshaw's treatment of Cathy after Heathcliff's arrival is as painful to her, and as conducive of destructive defense mechanisms, as Hindley's. Not only does Earnshaw take to Heathcliff "strangely, believing all that he said," he also set him up "far above Cathy, who was too mischievous and wayward for a favourite" (40). She was too mischievous and wayward, that is, for a favorite *daughter*. She does not succumb to male power in the manner of a Fanny Burney (or a Dickens) heroine. Like a true heir of the Gothic tradition, she asserts her superiority over a sexual division of labor that will not let her have a whip. Seeing that control over Heathcliff is now the jealously guarded source of her father's power, she delights in showing him "how the boy would do *her* bidding in anything, and *his* only when it suited his own inclination" (43). As Sandra Gilbert and Susan Gubar have commented, Cathy becomes Brontë's revisionary version of Eve, who resisted her inferior status in the Garden of Eden by eating the apple.

But she cannot have her father's power and his love at the same time.

> "Nay, Cathy," the old man would say, "I cannot love thee; thou'rt worse than thy brother. Go, say thy prayers, child, and ask God's pardon. I doubt thy mother and I must rue the day we ever reared thee!"
>
> That made her cry, at first; and then, being repulsed continually hardened her, and she laughed if I told her to say she was sorry for her faults, and beg to be forgiven. (43)

Forgiveness, the subject of Jabes Branderham's sermon in Lockwood's dream, is alien to Wuthering Heights, as it was in the neighborhood of Haworth, where they had a saying: " 'Keep a stone in thy pocket seven year; turn it, and keep it seven year longer, that it may be ever ready to thine hand when thine enemy draws near.' "[7] Human growth cannot occur under these conditions, which are harsher than those of the Genesis myth. Cathy experiences a fall into an "outer darkness" beyond the reach of her father's love not because of what she has done but because he, a truly Satanic father, cannot forgive her. People who are never forgiven can never forgive, and Heathcliff and his love go to their graves exemplifying this principle.

Being the least-favorite child in the isolated Earnshaw household, Cathy becomes Heathcliff's favorite through her identification with him, to the point that she tells Nelly, at the age of fifteen, that she "is" Heathcliff. Roaming with him on the moors, she can reclaim, through him, that part of herself that was not damaged by her father's fun-loving behavior and favoritism toward his adopted son. Like earlier Gothic heroines she is in rebellion against the injustice of patriarchal control. But now that control is expressed not in the interest of denying a daughter the marriage partner of her choice. Rather, a withdrawal of love has replaced that older form of direct control, just as it has replaced corporal punishment in the middle-class ideology of child-rearing. But her ally in this rebellion is not the brother who was similarly deprived, the one whose father cannot love a boy who wants a fiddle any more than he can love a girl who wants a whip. She allies, in other words, not with the loser but with the winner in the battle for paternal love, with the "poor fatherless child" to whom her father has taken "strangely."

Cathy's rebellion, then, is not simply a rebellion against hierarchy and in favor of egalitarianism. Like the Gothic second son, she has reasons to be aggrieved, but, like him, she cannot tolerate limits. She strives for omnipotence, since the omnipotent need no forgiveness: what they will is Fate. She may be "powerless without her whip," as Gilbert and Gubar maintain. But a whip, for which Heathcliff comes to stand in—the whole standing for the part rather than the other way around—does not confer or take away autonomy. Cathy's whole being is reactive, the very opposite of free. Equality is thus impossible: one either submits or avoids submission by dominating everything that is "other." The place of the patriarch is one of total control, and each member of the second Earnshaw generation tries to appropriate it in his or her own way.

In these efforts, Cathy, being a woman, is the least successful of the three. She begins by bonding with her father's surrogate, exhibiting a strategy of "identification with the oppressor." In this way she tries to circumvent the effects of his rejection, only to be "caught" by Skulker. The indoor world is the arena, for both sexes, of early socialization, of parental love given and withheld. It is where she learns that, because she cannot "always be a good lass," she cannot please her father. The moors make available to Cathy a world untouched by man-made gender divisions. Yet the moors do not really lie outside the patriarchal structure, which inscribes the "good lass" inside and the man outside protecting her (preferably with the aid of servants and dogs) against intruders. In fact, the moor becomes as oppressive as the parlor if one can't go home again.

This is why, when her alliance with Heathcliff is broken by Hindley, Cathy acquiesces to it. Now that Heathcliff is a loser in the struggle to supplant her father, it would degrade her to marry him. Of course she does not give up entirely. Thrushcross Grange is, after all, the novel's locus of feminine power, in contrast to the Heights, where force and violence are enshrined. Linton is the only man who can make her a "queen," give her a garden to "rule," and she plans to use that power in precisely the way that its partisans recommend. Whereas on the moors with Heathcliff she was the leader and he the follower, she now imagines that, married to Edgar, she can use her influence to give Heathcliff the same property qualifications for bourgeois male power that Linton has. But she also hands over to her husband that part of her that *is not* Heathcliff, the part that has been shaped by the wish to gain her father's love not as a son but as a "good lass." She therefore needs both Linton and Heathcliff, one affirming this "feminine" aspect of her while the other is an essential part of its denial.

Yet even the sadism which Wade Thompson finds so overwhelmingly present in *Wuthering Heights*[8] is present in the "outside" world of the moors. Cathy, as befits a female, tries in vain to temper it: "This feather was picked up from the heath, the bird was not shot; we saw its nest in winter, full of little skeletons. Heathcliff set a trap for it, and the old ones dare not come. I made him promise he'd never shoot a lapwing after that, and he didn't" (105). Boys will be boys, one may say. Yet it was Heathcliff's adoptive father who let this boy know that he could do whatever he wanted without fear of punishment, and admired his "hardness" as a sign of masculinity. And Cathy "is" *this* part of him too. Creating the world in her own image, through the agency of the "fatherless child" that she "is," she remembers starving baby birds. She dies simultaneously giving birth and refusing to eat, trying to embody (literally) her vision of a world permeated by parental deprivation. Heathcliff is, of course, the real thing: he really is an orphan and thus a signifier of Cathy's sense of herself, one that is belied by the outward appearance of family membership in which all the characters except Heathcliff are encapsulated.[9]

For Heathcliff the "fall" comes in two phases, one related to class divisions, the other to sexual ones. The first comes when he is forced by Hindley to play the "supermasculine menial" to Hindley's "omnipotent administrator."[10] His sense of class exclusion is then reinforced by his discovery, following Skulker's attack on Catherine, that "she was a young lady and they made a distinction between her treatment and mine" (50). Rejection does not make Heathcliff a monster, but it does make him realize what it means to be an outsider in a world where one is either "out" or "in." What Emily Brontë is telling her readers in the rest of the novel is not that a love that knows no boundaries can triumph over the conditions of the world that create class divisions and sexual "spheres." Rather, she is saying that these conditions, dividing "outsiders" from "insiders," cause irreparable damage—the same pessimistic message we find in *Frankenstein*.

But Emily Brontë, unlike Mary Shelley, does not offer a way of explaining the problem of evil in human nature by making Heathcliff a noble savage rendered monstrous by rejection. Given his size and ugliness, Shelley's monster could never have found a home in the human community. Heathcliff, on the other hand, is not simply Hindley's victim. He is an active collaborator in the usurpation of Hindley's birthright, his father's love. He does this not because he is innately evil, but because such collaboration is the only way he can be loved and fathered. Having been (we assume) abandoned by his own parents, he must steal someone else's. So he usurps the experience of being "taken to" by a parent, and pays dearly for his "crime" at the hands of the "rightful owner" of that experience. Perhaps there is a societal solution to the damage caused by unloving parents, an alternative to the nuclear family that would give a child other sources of love, but the opposite result is achieved by adopting "poor, fatherless" children into patriarchal nuclear families, however well-intentioned.

The wall around the domestic garden, then, can be invaded by evil but cannot incorporate an object of benevolence like Heathcliff. Just as the structure of identity available for Cathy to speak as a subject cannot allow her to *be* Heathcliff and not cancel out the place of the "I," the family within which this "I" was engendered cannot incorporate outsiders except through the ritual exchange of women in marriage. It is a family where not only Cathy, but Heathcliff and Hareton as well, need their father's approving gaze in order to "become someone," just as Radcliffe's Clara La Luc needs her father's assurance that she deserves his praise, or as Wollstonecraft's Mary and Caroline depend for their self esteem on Mrs. Mason's giving, not withholding from them, "those marks of affection which they were particularly delighted to receive."

Brontë's critique of this "technology" of self-production strikes, it seems to me, right at the root. In *The Reproduction of Mothering*, Nancy Chodorow argues that the gendered gaze (coming only from the female) is responsible for the persistence of gender asymmetry in our social arrangements in general.[11] The point that emerges from the Gothic treatment of childhood and child-rearing practices, in the feminine Gothic by way of affirmation, as well as negatively in Lewis, Godwin, Maturin, Mary Shelley, and Emily Brontë, is that this latter condition, male dominance, may have less to do with the sex of the gazer than with the opportunities a culture does or does not provide for the child to constitute him or herself outside of that gaze. For the first Catherine Earnshaw, whose mother is an aporia in Brontë's dense, genealogically structured text, the preconditions for an autonomous subjectivity are not met, and her destiny is a revelation of her compensatory struggle. What she requires is not simply a different set of social arrangments but a paradigm of subjectivity that can be articulated through inclusion as well as exclusion, one in which an "I" can be someone else without negating itself. By designating such experiences of nonmonologic identity as (always already) abnormal, Cathy's relationship to Heathcliff and his to her are kept out of the bourgeois Eden, relegated to the realm of ghosts.

With Cathy's daughter, however, it is a different matter. Her success in redrawing a circle of domesticity around herself and Hareton is initially due to the fact that the original lack in the Earnshaw home (and by implication in the Linton home as well) has been supplied. Heathcliff and Linton may both be deficient as adult men, having divided between them the male domain of intellectual and entrepreneurial ventures. Nevertheless, they both find it in themselves to nurture the next generation. Of Linton's childhood we know only that he and his sister quarreled over trivia, and that his mother's warnings and his father's dogs kept the unruly male world at a distance from him. But Heathcliff's bleak early years did include being loved by a parent, however briefly and (from a literal point of view) illegitimately. Therefore, though he cannot reap its benefits himself, he can love Hareton and be loved by him even as he is outwardly treating the boy the way Hindley treated him, and abusing his own son as well.

If Heathcliff, like old Earnshaw, prefers a stoic adopted child to a blubbering legitimate one, Linton is overprotective to his daughter, perhaps because his own father treated outsiders like Heathcliff as "prey." In this he resembles less a traditionally imprisoning Gothic father than a bookish St. Aubert, anxious to keep his daughter "innocent" of her mother's past. The prevalence of single fathers in Gothic novels is striking. For while death in childbirth was still a common fact in women's lives, the presence of these fathers may bear a relationship to the prevalence of initiative-taking daughters, for whom their fathers (rather than their mothers) function as models.[12] In the younger Cathy, this quality is initially coupled with a contempt for Hareton reminiscent of her mother's insistence that Heathcliff "has no notion of . . . what being in love is" (73). "He's just like a dog, is he not, Ellen?" she asks, and then wonders: "Do you ever dream, Hareton? and if you do, what is it about?"

But this condescension is not a betrayal of a prior intimacy, nor is it directed at someone she insists is more herself than she is. She is not expressing an opinion, but asking a question whose answer she does not know because of the sheltered life she has led. Unlike her mother, Cathy lives with an explicit prohibition. As in Eden, only one is needed to set the fall in motion. But when she and her father differ in their goals for her, her solution is to disobey, not to become someone else. When she comes downstairs after a fortnight of seclusion following Linton's death and two weeks alone with her dying husband, she declares that she has been "starved for a month and more." But she is angry at the way the household has treated a helpless Linton, not because her desire for omnipotence has been thwarted. Her wish to eat contrasts with her mother's anorexia: food is not a symbol for something else.

Hareton, too, deals with obstacles in a realistic rather than a symbolic level. Orphaned and immiserated, as Heathcliff was, he acknowledges his disparity with Cathy, and so is able to overcome it by learning from her rather than by the incorporation that is Heathcliff's defense against his loss. He is rebuffed by Cathy when he touches her for the first time, but gradually she is drawn away from the self-absorption, and its concomitant scorn for others, with which her mother defended herself against an original sense of being unforgivable. Thus Hareton is able to express his fear of rejection to her. "Nay, you'll be ashamed of me every day of your life. And the more, the more you know me, and I cannot bide it" (249). This admission might or might not have helped the adolescent Heathcliff. But in choosing symbolic action over words Heathcliff was expressing his commonality with the elder Cathy, his lack of faith in language, and his crucial difference from the younger generation.

When this younger generation leaves the Heights, "with wandering steps and slow," they enter the imperfect world of bourgeois society, the world that first appeared to us guarded by a predatory dog and where children were quarreling over inanities behind the panes of glass and the velvet curtains. It is the world that produced the controlling but deluded Isabella and her well-meaning but weak brother, and served as a metaphorical coffin to a high-spirited woman deprived of her father's love. But whereas this deprivation bred in Cathy an unwillingness to acknowledge the possibility that she could make mistakes, her daughter sheds her egocentricity to the point where she can ask Hareton to forgive her. The signifier of her autonomy beyond a constitutive parental gaze is her gift to Hareton of the ability to read, a gift not simply of the spoken *parole* but the *langue* whose emergence depends on the durability of writing. Standing in for the constituting parental gaze, the printed page makes the reader's horizon coterminous with that of her or his culture.

The Gothic genre, as my title suggests, is a discourse about the home, about women's inscription into that space and men's relationship to the home thus defined. Men usurp the home from other men, but the real usurpation seems to be the power of women that they have erased, or which women have surrendered as the price of integration into a culture that "placed" them in the home. Men who attempt to engender life, or to prolong or control it "unnaturally," are the ones who bring "evil into the world, and all our woe." But Ambrosio and Melmoth meet death at the foot of high precipices, St. Leon is reabsorbed into his son's family, Falkland collapses into Caleb's embrace, and Shelley's monster is "borne away by the waves and lost in darkness and distance." The Gothic novel's greatest popularity coincided with the beginnings of the feminist movement, whose founding insight is that men and women are *made* as well as born. By rigorously interrogating the separation of "home" from "world," the early Gothic novel enshrines the optimism engendered by that insight.

But the title of this book also suggests that power is the central issue of these novels. I want to draw together the threads of our discussion by focusing on the struggle for control over and within the domestic sphere that my title implies. I began by locating in the feminine Gothic a "deep subversive impulse" to undermine the constitution of the home as a "place of peace" into which evil never came, a garden in which the promise of the first Eden might be fulfilled if the wife succeeded in her task of "watchman . . . to blow the trumpet and warn the people, which if he [*sic*] neglect to do, their blood shall be required of the watchman's hand."[13] The power inscribed in this metaphor lies not in force but in surveillance. It is through her vigilance that the woman not only keeps evil out of the home but arms "the minds of the rising race" committed to her charge with the shield of faith and the sword of the Spirit.

The situation of the feminine Gothic heroine calls into question this positioning of the female in two ways. It offers a counterdiscourse to the one on female innocence upon which is based the woman's custodial relationship to "the minds of the rising race." Evil has entered the castle and usurped it, imperiling the virtue, and perhaps even the survival, of the "watchman" herself. It then questions the wisdom of a woman's remaining within the ostensibly impregnable walls of such a place whose "voluntary spies" are not necessarily on her side. Some of these spies may be servants but almost invariably the leader to whom they report is a member of the very institution constituted to protect her, the family. When this usurper appropriates her power of surveillance, the home becomes a site of resistance, a mirror of those institutions of confinement that became symbols in the eighteenth century of a new architechtonics of power exerted discursively and invisibly rather than through spectacle and force.

Yet the Gothic discourse on the home is not univocal. Though fallen, indeed because fallen, the home is the site upon which, literally, the Gothic "subversive impulse" is articulated as resistance and put into circulation by the notorious Minerva Press. The power of surveillance expressed in the true wife's duty to penetrate the surface of her children's innocent play in order to discover the hidden fault, the lie, the secret sin that is brought from the private into the public realm through questioning, confession, and appropriate punishment and forgiveness, is deployed also in the writing of novels in which this process is displaced onto a "superstitious age." If the Gothic novel participates in the production of a self that can be isolated from others in an attempt to bring about a confession of a crime, it also articulates a self that can resist when the accusation is misplaced.

Of the Gothicists we have discussed, only Maturin is unequivocal in his critique of all institutions that deal with madness, criminality, insubordination in children, all challenges to authority perceived as arbitrary, through regulation of the body, through work, isolation, enforced self-examination, and other forms of what Foucault calls "the gentle way of punishment." In the feminine Gothic the family is both a point of departure and a point of return, a site upon which is produced both the villain father and the resistance that overcomes him. Or, as Milton put it in the *Aereopagitica:* "It was from out the rind of one apple tasted, that the knowledge of good and evil, as two twins cleaving together, lept forth into the world." As we get further away from a defeat of the villain, the feminine paradigm is replaced by the masculine, or, in the case of Lewis, the two are unfolded in tandem.

On the surface, the feminine Gothic would seem to resolve the problem of evil inside the home as an always already condition, a sign of our fallen state. The heroine marries and creates a happy home, while the hero of the masculine Gothic dies or roams the face of the earth eternally. But the ritual is still being repeated in drugstore Gothics, in horror movies and television miniseries, which may suggest that the home can never be purified once and for all, that it is inextricably connected to "the world," whose violence and danger must be faced, and wrestled to the ground, again and again. The question then is, who will do this? In drugstore Gothics, as in their eighteenth- and early nineteenth-century counterparts, it is the heroine who purifies the castle. That is to say, it is a female subject, individual and inviolable, not owned by anyone.

Thus it is the discourse of the individual, inviolable self that has made available to women possibilities for action outside the code of female passivity and sublime helplessness. Brontë's second Cathy embodies these possibilities with their attendant limits, as her mother's life dramatized the amputations entailed in the construction of that bounded identity. For it is these practices, this "technology of the self," that engender the individual female subject, the new Eve who, by her resistance, defines male power and thus makes it available for contestation.[14] Though not every Gothic novel that I have discussed ends with a woman in possession of a previously contested castle, the others can still serve to remind us that, within the structures of separate spheres now losing their hegemony in the industrialized nations, we cannot incorporate the possibilities that these very structures have enabled us to imagine.

NOTES

1. *Analytical Review* 23 (Jan. 1795), 55.

2. George Rude, *Hanoverian London* (Berkeley: University of California Press, 1971), 224.

3. See Mark Girouard, *The Return to Camelot: Chivalry and the English Gentleman* (New Haven: Yale University Press, 1981).

4. For another interpretation of this relationship, see Sandra Gilbert and Susan Gubar, *The Madwoman in the Attic: The Woman Writer and the Nineteenth-Century Literary Imagination* (New Haven: Yale University Press, 1979), 248–308.

5. Emily Brontë, *Wuthering Heights*, ed. William M. Sale, Jr., 2d ed. (New York: Norton, 1971), 308. Subsequent references to the novel will be to this edition.

6. Mary Burgan makes a similar point about the Earnshaw family using the work of Erik Erikson in " 'Some Fit Parentage': Identity and the Cycle of Generations in *Wuthering Heights*," *Philological Quarterly* 61 (1982), 395–413.

7. Elizabeth Gaskell, *The Life of Charlotte Brontë* (Harmondsworth: Penguin, 1975), 61.

8. See Wade Thompson, "Infanticide and Sadism in *Wuthering Heights*," *PMLA* 76 (1963), 69–74.

9. See Leo Bersani, *A Future for Astyanax* (1976; rpt., New York: Columbia University Press, 1984), 197–223.

10. Eldridge Cleaver, *Soul on Ice* (New York: McGraw Hill, 1968), 162.

11. Nancy Chodorow, *The Reproduction of Mothering: Psychoanalysis and the Sociology of Gender* (Berkeley: University of California Press, 1978). For a discussion of the maternal gaze and its role in the development of female autonomy, see Jessica Benjamin, "Master and Slave: The Fantasy of Erotic Domination," in *Powers of Desire: The Politics of Sexuality*, ed. Ann Snitow, Christine Stansell, and Sharon Thompson (New York: Monthly Review Press, 1983), 280–99.

12. Carolyn Heilbrun, *Reinventing Womanhood* (New York: Norton, 1980), discusses achieving women and their fathers.

13. Hannah More, *Strictures on Female Education*, "Of Influence," in *The Works of Hannah More*, 11 vols. (London: T. Cadell, 1830), vol. 5, 41.

14. This is Foucault's term for describing the project underlying his *History of Sexuality*. See Hubert Dreyfus and Paul Rabinow, *Michel Foucault: Beyond Structuralism and Hermeneutics*, 2d ed. (Chicago: University of Chicago Press, 1983), 175 and passim.

INDEX

A Note on the Author

KATE FERGUSON ELLIS received her Ph.D. from Columbia University and is Associate Professor of English at Rutgers University. She is a coeditor of *Caught Looking: Feminism, Pornography and Censorship* and a founding member of the Feminist Anti-Censorship Task Force. She lives in New York, where she is currently working on a novel about the sixties.